VICTORIA EMBANKMENT
FOR THE
WEST END & CITY
VIA KINGSWAY · WESTMINSTER · BLACKFRIARS

LONDONS TRAMWAYS

SOUTHWARK BRIDGE
THE NEW TRAMWAY CONNECTION WITH THE CITY

HIGHGATE
BY SERVICES
7 11 AND 15

LONDON'S TRAMWAYS

FOR THE CITY
SERVICES · 6 · 10 · 34 · 46 · 52 · 60
VIA SOUTHWARK BRIDGE
ALSO EMBANKMENT SERVICES
TO BLACKFRIARS

LONDON'S TRAMWAYS

TRAVEL BY TRAM FOR
COVER AND COMFORT.
DESIGNED AT THE L.C.C. CENTRAL SCHOOL OF ARTS AND CRAFTS.

London County Council Tramways.

Publicity Sub Section L C C Tramways

LONDON'S TRAMWAYS

VICTORIA EMBANKMENT
400 CARS AN HOUR
AT HIGH TIDE

LCC ELECTRIC TRAMWAYS

Robert J. Harley

Capital Transport

ISBN 185414 256 9

Published by Capital Transport Publishing
38 Long Elmes, Harrow Weald, Middlesex

Printed by CS Graphics, Singapore

Designed by Tim Demuth

I dedicate this book to the memory of my grandparents, Patricia and Alfred Little.

Contents

Title page picture **A** scene at the Lewisham Obelisk in Loampit Vale with Class C/2 Car 216, left and Class C/1 Car 240 on the right, taken in February 1906.
Perkins & Sons, Lee

Left **Standard E/1 Car 798** hugs the kerb on the eastbound track over Westminster Bridge on one sunny day in the early 1930s. Note how most of the traffic wisely kept clear of the tramlines.

Introduction and Acknowledgements

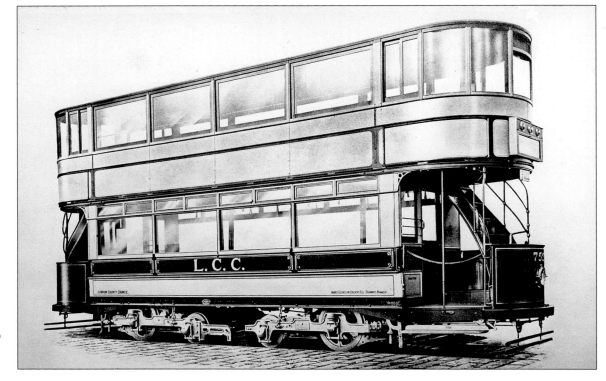

Right **The standard LCC E/1 Class tramcar is pictured in its prime. This type of vehicle was a very familiar sight to Londoners. It gave an impression of solid reliability – a vehicle that would get you to your destination through all weathers.**

Below **Big Ben towers over the Houses of Parliament, as LCC Car 320 crosses Westminster Bridge in the first decade of the twentieth century.**

MAYBE IT'S because I'm a Londoner that I wanted to chronicle the heyday of the London County Council Tramways. Many learned volumes have been written on the social history of the capital and almost all of them have paid only lip service to the role of street tramways in the development of the urban landscape. I suspect that aspects of this era have eluded past historians, or have received scant mention, because the humble tramcar was banished from the West End and the City of London. *Out of sight, out of mind* seems to have been the prevailing philosophy. Also, dare one suggest that the tram was the *bête noire* of fashionable circles? It had its roots in working class society, far from the affluent exclusivity of upper class London. The tram, rocking and swaying on its tracks, was part of the music of London – a moving icon shifting the masses along a rich variety of animated streets, a reliable and cheap friend to all those who had to make the pennies stretch to the family budget.

The LCC Tramways network was the largest municipal system in Great Britain. For three decades, the familiar brown and primrose electric trams served the needs of Londoners. Advocates of the tramways described the well lit cars as *gondolas*

of the people. Rather less romantically, bitter opponents feared that the *tramway evil* could block the streets of the City of London and provoke another Great Fire! Friend and foe alike agreed that the crowd shifting capacities of lines of tramcars along the Victoria Embankment could not be equalled by other forms of transport. Sadly,

the reign of the Council Tramways was too short, and the efficient network deserved a better fate than that which awaited it, on 1st July 1933, at the hands of the London Passenger Transport Board. But memories linger of riding for miles and miles along the highways and byways of the greatest city in the world – all for a shilling a day!

277   LONDON. — *Westminster Bridge.* — LL.

In assembling the text and photos for this volume, I am very indebted to John Wills, John Gent, B .J. 'Curly' Cross, John Price, Richard Elliott, The Right Hon Tony Benn MP, Ted Oakley, John Gillham, Robert Perkins, Adam Gordon, Dr Gerald Druce, Terry Russell and Alan Watkins. My profound thanks go to Dave Jones of the LCC Tramways Trust for his indefatigable efforts in locating source material, and to both him and John Perkins for their conscientious checking of the manuscript. Rosy Thacker of the John Price Memorial Library at the National Tramway Museum deserves special mention for her work in supplying copies of important documents. I tender my apologies to anyone omitted through oversight on my part. The provenance of some photographs is unknown and therefore I have not been able to give a credit to the individual concerned.

I am grateful to Professor George W. Hilton for permission to include an extract from his book THE CABLE CAR IN AMERICA. My thanks also go to the executors of the estate of Richard Church, Laurence Pollinger Ltd, for allowing publication of passages from THE GOLDEN SOVEREIGN.

Readers unfamiliar with London place names are reminded of the following pronunciations: Greenwich and Woolwich are well known, being spoken as *Grin-idge* and *Wool-idge* respectively. Southwark is pronounced *Suth-ark*, and Holborn as *Ho-bun*. Deptford is vocalised as *Det-ford*, Marylebone as *Marry-le-bone*, Streatham as *Stret-em* and Chiswick as *Chis-ick*.

Younger readers will have to visualise a world very different from that which exists in the first decade of the twenty-first century. In order to aid their understanding, I have included metric equivalents where appropriate. Trade and commerce in Great Britain and the Square Mile of the City of London was founded on the Pound Sterling, which in pre-decimal currency days was divided into twenty shillings. Each shilling was made up of twelve pence.

Last but not least, I would like to thank my wife Janet and my children Matthew, Abigail and Rachel for their love and support whilst I was writing this book.

Top **Trams at the Elephant and Castle convey the working population of South London in an endless spectacle of activity. Transporting volumes of people was all in a day's work for the Council tramcars.**

Left **'Rus in Urbe' – some LCC lines, like Service 44, escaped the town and headed through open country. Car 1436, working on the double trolley Eltham route, is pictured in Academy Road, Woolwich Common.** J.B.Gent Collection

Below **At the corner of Mitcham Lane and Southcroft Road D Class Car 342 takes the wet and miserable winter weather in its stride. The score marks in the roadway indicate that several derailments have already occurred on this bend.** LCC

CHAPTER ONE
Horse Tramway Legacy

THE PHRASE *street life in Victorian London* conjures up for many people images of the hustle and bustle of one of the world's most important and populous cities. Somewhere in the semi conscious mind of native and visitor alike there lie scenes of fog haunted streets traversed by hansom cabs, one of which may be carrying a shadowy passenger for an important consultation at 221B Baker Street. Pictures of stately thoroughfares lined by elegant shops, government and office buildings contrast starkly with the drama of narrow streets, which echo to the calls of market sellers. At night, crowds of theatregoers add to the broad canvas of metropolitan life.

This overly romantic scenario rather masks the fact that wealth and poverty lived cheek-by-jowl. Outside the fashionable areas of Westminster and the West End one could find a seething world of industry – the docks, so vital for the trade and commerce of a world empire, and the countless small businesses established to cater for an ever-growing population. The villas of the middle classes had already established a pattern of streets in the burgeoning suburbs. Tenements for those of lesser financial means were tucked away in some of the most squalid areas of what was the world's richest city. Towering above all, quite literally in this era, was St Paul's Cathedral – a landmark of the City of London.

This whirlpool of humanity was governed, at a local level, by the London County Council, which had been created by the Local Government Act of 1888. The Council assumed formal control of the metropolitan area on 1st April 1889. It consisted of 126 councillors who were elected every three years. Another tier of administration rested in the twenty-one aldermen elected by councillors to serve for six years. Political control of the newly elected assembly was in the hands of the Progressives, a left of centre coalition of Liberals, Socialists and Trade Unionists. The opposition party members were known as Moderates, and their support mirrored that of the Conservative Party nationally. Both groupings recognised the need for change in the capital's transport infrastructure, especially in light of projected trends for the coming twentieth century. However, the position of the county council *vis-à-vis* the promotion and ownership of street tramways was always a bone of contention. Naturally, the Progressives favoured municipal ownership hand in hand with a comprehensive policy of track reconstruction and the provision of new routes. Another tenet of their philosophy concerned the provision of new housing for the working classes; housing estates were planned to be adjacent to tramway routes. In short, the Progressives viewed the tramways as an instrument of social

Car 25 of the Southwark & Deptford Tramways Company is depicted in the depot yard. This general design of four wheel double decker was familiar to Londoners, either in its knifeboard seating form as illustrated here, or in the later garden seat style. This particular tram was delivered in 1880 and passed, together with all the other SDTC assets, to the LCC on 7th July 1904. *LCCTT*

reform, an instrument furthermore, which would enhance the fight against poverty and slum housing. Many of the Progressives regarded the reform of London as a moral crusade. The Moderates, on the other hand, were not at all sure of the benefits of *municipal trading*, as it was referred to in capitalist circles. They supported a more *laissez faire* approach, which championed the rights of private companies to run public transport. They cited the success of the British Electric Traction group to bolster their argument that the LCC should not expend ratepayers' money on tramways.

A second tier of local government involved the twenty-eight metropolitan boroughs, which were created by the 1899 London Government Act. These new authorities were generally amenable to the expansion of the LCC tramways system; many boroughs shared the LCC's vision of a municipally driven future. On the other side of the coin, four metropolitan boroughs – Kensington, St Marylebone, Chelsea and the City of Westminster – proved implacable opponents of any tramway scheme, which would have seen rails placed on their hallowed streets. Only a peripheral tramway presence was permitted in the City of Westminster; the heart of the capital – the West End – was to remain territory served exclusively by buses and underground railways.

The metropolitan boroughs also gained from the tramways by means of local rating income on buildings and track laid in the public highway. In terms of the Tramways Act of 1870, where a private operator was concerned, the annual rental sum charged by the local authority was considered to include a contribution to the rates. A judgement in 1904 regularised this arrangement and the LCC was regarded in law as the hypothetical tenant of each metropolitan borough through which the Council tramways ran. A percentage figure was worked out by the interested parties and the system worked until the end of tramways in London. Of course, competing buses contributed nothing to the upkeep of the roads.

One final flaw in the tramway set up was the hole in the centre of the County – the City of London. The idea of County Council tramcars plying their trade past St Paul's Cathedral or outside the Bank of England was anathema to the wealthy burghers of the Square Mile. At every twist and turn of the tramway debate, the City and their local allies in the anti-tramcar cartel used their veto (as enshrined in the 1870 Tramways Act) very effectively to block progress. Thus, the construction of cross-London tramways remained a pipe dream, and save for the Kingsway Subway, the LCC were thwarted in their designs – such was the background to the early tramway era in London.

Away from the bastions of privilege and short sighted vested interest, the supporters of street tramways could point to a number of successful horse tramway companies which had established routes along most of the major highways leading

from the centre of town. The first horsecar lines (later to be acquired by the LCC) had been pioneered by the North Metropolitan in 1870. In the same year the Metropolitan Street Tramways and Pimlico, Peckham & Greenwich companies commenced operations south of the River. The network was densest in South London and on roads serving the East End and northeast suburbs. The heart of the metropolis was left untouched; most lines ended at the boundaries of hostile local authorities, like the City of London, or they terminated within sight of the River Thames. Tracks were not permitted over the Thames bridges, therefore many folk were obliged to get off and walk in order to complete their journeys. The option of continuing by bus was ruled out by the extra expense of the higher omnibus fares. These were in sharp contrast to the cheap workmen's fares, which offered a lifeline to regular tram users, who relied on a frequent service of cars to reach their places of employment.

In 1889, when the LCC assumed control of the capital's affairs, there were fifteen registered tramway companies working in London. Some, like the North London, the North Metropolitan, the West Metropolitan, the Harrow Road & Paddington and the Croydon & Norwood, had a part or all of their trackage outside the county boundary and therefore could not be purchased in their entirety by the LCC. However, most of the lines fell into the ambit of the Council, which then prepared plans for the compulsory purchase.

The crucial wording of Section 43 of the Tramways Act 1870 reads as follows:

Where the promoters of a tramway in any district are not the local authority; the local authority if, by resolution passed at a special meeting of the members constituting such local authority, they so decide, may within six months after the expiration of a period of twenty-one years from the time such promoters were empowered to construct such tramway, and within six months after the expiration of every subsequent period of

seven years . . . with the approval of the Board of Trade, by notice in writing require such promoters to sell to them their undertaking . . .

In simple terms, tramway routes constructed in the County of London could be purchased 21 years after the date on which authority was given for their construction.

The reaction of the companies was predictable. Company secretaries were active in their correspondence with the LCC. Fears were expressed over levels of compensation; added payments for the goodwill of a going concern were solicited. Suspicions were also entertained that the local authority might just press for the various undertakings to be sold at scrap metal prices. In short, a period of uncertainty was followed by what could only be described as a time of asset inflation on behalf of the companies. Suddenly, ramshackle rolling stock, long retired from active service, returned to the fleet list, which was submitted to the council's valuers. Dilapidated outbuildings, grain stores and stables miraculously acquired higher property values, some of which were based on pious hopes that these sites would provide suitable depot locations in costly electrification plans. The stark truth about the expense involved in installing electric trams, was that such a project was completely beyond the financial capabilities of most of the metropolitan horse tramway companies. Realistically, only the County Council had the wherewithal to instigate and complete such a vast civil engineering scheme.

In South London the LCC began its activities by looking at the London Tramways Company lines in Kennington Park Road, New Kent Road, St George's Road and London Road. These routes had been authorised in 1873 and could be acquired by the council in 1894. On 18th January 1895, the LCC gave the necessary notice of compulsory purchase. The matter went to arbitration, and on 6th January 1897, the value of the undertaking was settled at £22,872.

The acquisition of the remaining company lines was also under consideration. The practical solution to maintaining an intact system was solved by the council proceeding to buy the whole network at a cost of £850,000. At this stage, by means of the London County Tramways Act of 1896, the council had been granted the right to run the tramways with its own cars, instead of being tied to a leasing arrangement, whereby the local authority acquired the tracks and buildings, but the cars were supplied from the former companies.

HIGH STREET, CAMDEN TOWN.

Competing modes of public transport are observed in High Street, Camden Town. The horsecar in the centre of the picture belongs to the London Street Tramways Company, and is probably working the Holloway to Euston Road service.

In the summer of 1900, the South London lines between St George's Circus and Waterloo were acquired, and this was followed on 21st November 1902 by the transfer of routes serving the Borough, Battersea and Wandsworth. Further horsecar lines in Deptford, Greenwich, Camberwell and Lewisham were later brought into the fold. All these companies used standard gauge tracks. A cheerful exception was the rather idiosyncratic organisation, known as the Woolwich & South East London Tramways Company, which had opted for the narrow gauge (3ft 6ins). This fact did not prevent the WSELTC being absorbed into the LCC monolith.

North of the Thames matters took the same general course. On 27th October 1891, the council served notice on the London Street Tramways Company in respect of their lines in Euston, Hampstead and Kentish Town. This action stirred up a hornets' nest, causing many months to be lost in negotiation and litigation until a final purchase figure was imposed on the warring parties. The North Metropolitan Company lines within the County of London were later acquired, which only left a couple of small undertakings, such as the Highgate Hill Cable Tramway and the Harrow Road & Paddington Tramways, to be added to the Council's realm. Having mentioned the Highgate Hill operation, it must also be recorded that Kennington and Streatham line of the London Tramways Company was the only other London tramway to be worked by cable traction.

Attention was given to passenger requirements and the new owners set about rationalising the fare structures of the former companies. Penny stages were lengthened and the practice of charging double on Sundays and Bank Holidays was abandoned. As regards workmen, it is worth quoting from the official council account:

The Council also gave consideration to the advisability of extending the practice of running workmen's cars on the Council's lines in the early morning. As a result the Council decided that, on and after 1st

January 1901, the services of workmen's cars, which had previously ceased at 6.30 a.m, should be continued until 8 o'clock, and that the fares to be charged should be, for any distance beyond those covered by the existing ha'penny fares, one penny for a single journey and 2d for a return . . .

A noteworthy fact in connection with workmen's fares occurs in a 1903 survey, which revealed that the number of regular tram passengers to central London, up to 8.30am on one particular weekday, was 55,582.

From the same council source we find out that new employees could also expect enhanced working conditions:

The question of the relations to be established between the Council and its tramway employees naturally engaged considerable attention during the period immediately subsequent to the transfer, and, as a result of careful consideration, the Council made some very important alterations in the conditions of the service of the staff. It was regarded as essential that the wages paid by the Council should be equivalent to the best rates paid for similar work in other parts of the County of London, and, further, that

The lunchtime exodus by workers at the Royal Arsenal Gate, Beresford Square, Woolwich threatens to engulf a narrow gauge horse tram, which formerly belonged to the Woolwich & South East London Company. The conversion of the WSETC line was to prove long and costly;

piecemeal reconstruction by the LCC meant that through electric services had to wait until 5th April 1914. In the foreground the three boys and the girl who have no shoes strike a jarring note of reality – deprivation and poverty were never far away. J.B.Gent Collection

the Council's rule with regard to one day's rest in seven should apply to tramways employees . . . these changes involved a cost to the Council of about £13,300 a year. Concessions were also made with regard to the allowance of clothing made to various classes of the employees.

A further change of great importance was also decided upon by the Council, viz:– the institution of an average 10 hours' day (or 60 hours' week) for employees of all grades in its tramway service. This change, which came into operation on 1st May 1900, cost the Council, it is estimated, about £10,120 a year.

In company days the general rate of pay for a horse tram driver was in the region of five shillings per day; a conductor could expect to receive around four shillings and sixpence. Duty times could range from early in the morning to midnight. Some companies instituted a system of fines for their employees. Minor offences, such as missing a fare, or holding up the service by helping an old person off the tram and safely to the kerb, were punished. There was no provision made for meal breaks, sick pay, holidays or pensions, although it is worth recording that the North Metropolitan Company did establish a provident society for their employees. Against a deduction of sixpence a week, an employee

LCC horse tram Car 911 was converted to cable traction to serve on the section of route from Kennington to Streatham. Here in Brixton Road we note the Bon Marché and Quin & Axtens

department stores. Both commercial establishments were pioneers in their field and were a sure sign of the growing prosperity of the area. J.B.Gent Collection

could receive two shillings and sixpence sick pay per day, and his family would receive £15 in the event of his death.

Conductor James Jenner of the London Tramways Company records in an interview conducted in December 1940 some facts concerning the demands of the job:

In those days we conductors were paid by the mile. I used to keep an account of everything. During 1895, I worked 307 days, travelled 19,375 miles (31,181km), took £968. 3s. 6d. and earned in wages £79. 0s. 10d. Electric (LCC) trams made an enormous difference: in 1907 my takings were £1,420, wages £94.

The Metropolitan Police under the Metropolitan Public Carriage Act of 1869 licensed tram crews and the vehicles on which they worked. Each tram had to be inspected annually and a numbered metal plate (the Metropolitan Stage Carriage Plate, or MSC Plate) was affixed on the lower bulkhead of the vehicle. Drivers and conductors were also required to display a badge. After 1907, the licensing system for drivers included separate badges for Animal Power and Mechanical Power. In practice the powers vested in the Metropolitan Commissioner of Police meant that he had an important say in the functioning of London's trams, buses and cabs.

It is doubtful whether Scotland Yard applied the same standards of roadworthiness to all rolling stock, because the LCC inherited a rather motley collection of vehicles. At one end of the scale were the insurance write-offs, which included some heavily built cars dating from the 1870s; by the time of Council acquisition it could honestly be said that rot and rust had pretty much rendered these trams unserviceable. Vehicle design favoured a general standard of a four wheel, double deck car drawn by two horses. Passenger seating in the lower saloon was by means of two facing longitudinal benches; on the top deck, or *outside* as it was popularly known, intending customers could expect transverse, *garden* seats arranged in pairs either side of a central gangway. This arrangement had become more fashionable in the 1880s, having replaced the earlier, back-to-back *knifeboard* type seating. Single deck trams featured in some of the ex-company fleets; for example, the American carbuilder, John Stephenson of New York, had supplied to the London Tramways Company some one man operated vehicles for working lightly loaded routes.

Company liveries were retained on the cars transferred to the Council; gradually the large gold letters L. C. C. appeared on the waist panels of each tram. As regards a unified colour scheme for the new fleet, the Council seemed to have experimented. Some cars were painted a pleasing shade of off-white, whilst others were turned out in what was to become the standard livery of midland lake red and primrose. It must be assumed that the attractive white livery was not carried over to the electric fleet

(except for certain cars used on very special occasions) because of problems in maintaining a pristine appearance. Atmospheric pollution was high during the tramway era, and any light coloured vehicles would soon have suffered from the grime and street detritus common on thoroughfares subject to high volumes of horse drawn traffic.

Advertisements continued to be a handy source of extra revenue, although the habit of some companies in filling almost every available space with commercial material was looked on askance by the council. As one official document states:

It was felt that window advertisements were a source of annoyance and inconvenience to persons riding inside the cars, since they were unable, by reason of these advertisements, to see clearly the names of streets or the numbers of houses. On the expiration of existing contracts, therefore, they were not renewed.

The man appointed to manage this new municipal enterprise was Alfred Baker. He was granted a salary of one thousand pounds per annum. In all there were fourteen senior male staff to oversee the tramway workers. The fifteenth member of the team was Miss E. Penman, who was employed as Superintendent of Women Checkers and Conductors; she had a salary of four hundred pounds per annum, plus an allowance for her heating and lighting expenses. The whole team was tasked with the efficient operation of a horse tramway

DEPTFORD & TOOLEY STREET VIA LOWER RD ROTHERHITHE reads the indicator board on the approaching two horse tramcar. The scene is in Evelyn Street opposite the LCC Deptford Fire Station. This building and similar fire stations around the capital represented another important public service run by the Council. This postcard view was sent on 19th May 1909 – some two years before this route was converted to electric traction.
J.B.Gent Collection

network that had to be transformed into a capital wide transit system powered by electricity. There would be many problems to be solved, however, the experience of other major metropolitan centres in the world, where electric trams were commonplace, would be of particular assistance to the policy makers of the LCC Highways Committee. They could not afford to delay, and the annual statistics for passengers carried by the tramways confirmed a growing trend. In 1897, the number of passengers carried was quoted at 297,577,240; in 1900 this total had risen to 340,203,066.

The turn of the new twentieth century would see frantic activity to establish the LCC tramways system on an equal footing with the best networks in the rest of the world. The horsecar era had to be phased out as soon as possible. However, as we shall see, there would be many delays on the road to complete electrification, and it was to take the LCC over a decade to consign equine traction to the history books.

In the days when England was *the* power in world cricket, the game had a massive following at grassroots level. Here just beyond the boundary rope these two London horsecars serve out an honourable and useful retirement as a cricket pavilion and makeshift grandstand. The wonderful array of Edwardian sporting fashions completes a memorable scene.

CHAPTER TWO
Spark of Progress

THE VICTORIAN era was powered by the steam engine – the twentieth century was set on a different, more dynamic course. A spark of progress offered by the nascent electric revolution was about to transform the lives of millions. In the local transport arena, the dominance of the steam railway suburban trains and the street based horse bus services was about to be challenged by the electric tramcar.

In historical terms London was rather slow off the mark in adopting the new and superior mode of transport offered by electric tramways. Outside observers remarked rather caustically that the

The need for electric traction is obvious in this view of Walworth Road with its seemingly endless line of horse trams. Conduit slot rails attached to short yokes await the attention of permanent way workers who will finish the concrete foundations and fit the current collecting T rails.
LCCTT

citizens of the Kentish seaport of Dover had had the benefit of a fine municipally run system opened in September 1897, whilst many continental and American cities had far outstripped London in the provision of modern rapid transit. In the popular press there was much agitation for the elected representatives on the LCC Highways Committee to set the ball rolling and come up with a scheme worthy of the capital city. However, caution was the watchword of the LCC, and the Council was determined that it was not going to be hurried into decisions it might regret later. In the spirit of this measured approach, the Vice-Chairman of the Highways Committee, J. Allen Baker, produced a report in October 1898. It was entitled TRAMWAY TRACTION, and its remit was:

Report on some forms of mechanical tramway traction that have been tried and more or less successfully worked in various towns and cities in England, on the continent of Europe, and in America.

The indefatigable Mr Baker himself had actually undertaken the study tour at his own expense. He was accompanied by his friend and colleague, John McDougall (Chairman of the LCC Asylums Committee), who was on a fact finding mission to evaluate American institutions for the treatment of the insane.

The illustrated report dwelt on the different forms of mechanical traction then being tried in urban environments. After examining the benefits and drawbacks of steam, gas, compressed air and cable haulage, the author alighted on the promise of electric traction:

I think there can be no doubt that in solving the problem of haulage of our tramways, we must look to some form of electric traction . . . It has been proved in scores of cities in America, and on the continent as well as in this country, that the cost of operating by horse traction is from 50 to 100 per cent greater than by the electric system, while the latter has been proved to be more economical than any other form of mechanical haulage.

A chart accompanies this statement and J. Allen Baker recorded that in 1897 there were in America 14,263 miles (22,954km) of electric tramway, which were worked by a staggering total of 39,748 trams – no wonder he was impressed by the state of progress in the New World. The problem was, how to translate these benefits in public transport to the streets of London, where entrenched attitudes would have to be won over to the idea of trams receiving power via overhead wires. Mr Baker wasn't at all sure that this method of current collection would go down well with the voters back home. Therefore, he inclined to look favourably at alternatives:

In estimating the value of the trolley for London, I fully realise that as the pioneer system in popularising electric traction it has a strong claim to a first place; and were there not a rival system, which (though more costly to install) has been

proved to work with equal economy and to be free from the objections and dangers of the trolley, I should unhesitatingly say that the advantages of the trolley, compared to our present horse system, so far outweigh its objections that even London might adopt it. I am of the opinion, however, that the solution of our traction problem lies in the electric conduit.

The conduit system in its present form is no doubt largely the result of the objections that have been consistently urged in many municipalities against the overhead wires. Some of the earlier installations may be regarded as only a qualified success, but with the more recent improvements, particularly those that have been carried out during the last two years in America, but little is left to be desired from an electrical and operating point of view.

The *objections and dangers* of the overhead trolley system can neatly be summarised as the desire of many town dwellers to avoid the blue vault of heaven being festooned with electric cables, which might – subject to the rigours of climate – snap and descend to earth to electrocute the unwary. Such a scenario was a hot debating point in council chambers at the beginning of the twentieth century. Aside from the rhetoric, it is worth pointing out that all the other electrified tramways in London eventually adopted the overhead trolley system, as did the overwhelming majority of tramways worldwide.

The impressive performance of conduit equipped lines in New York and Washington DC no doubt swayed Mr Baker into thinking that the way forward for London was obvious. The smooth working of electric trams along New York's Lenox Avenue, plus the impressive spectacle of a tram every 10 to 15 seconds along Broadway was the clinching factor. The report's author also managed to examine the construction techniques on a further 55 miles (88.5km) of conduit track in New York City.

In summing up his experiences, J. Allen Baker gives a clear message to his fellow decision makers on the LCC:

It therefore becomes simply a consideration of the difference in first cost between the street construction of the conduit as versus the overhead – a matter perhaps of £1,000 to £2,000 per mile of track for the cheaper form of conduit, and £2,000 to £4,000 for a heavier construction similar to that of New York and Washington – and the question whether for so comparatively small a sum any portion of our great city should have anything but the best obtainable. Provincial cities with their wider and less busy streets and comparatively small populations, may find it to their interest to adopt the cheaper overhead construction, and tramway companies will naturally always prefer the cheaper form where they obtain municipal sanction to install it. But London, with its endless

population, its unprecedentedly busy streets and congested traffic, need not hesitate to adopt the system that will give the greatest satisfaction to the public and the local authorities through whose districts the lines may pass; and of all the systems before us for consideration, the one in my judgement best suited to the requirements of London is the electric conduit.

Of course, with hindsight, many of these conclusions seem flawed. To maintain that provincial cities should have different treatment to the capital in the provision of tramways can be challenged. However to be fair, at the time this report was written many of the future networks surrounding cities such as Glasgow, Manchester and Birmingham were still very much in the embryonic stage. A more serious criticism concerns the wishful thinking over the adoption of a cheaper form of conduit. This siren song to win over those on the Council, who wanted to be economical with ratepayers' cash, seems based on the triumph of hope over experience. Almost every single conduit system other than the heavily engineered ones (and therefore the most expensive) had failed in urban conditions. The overhead wire method of current collection was quite simply the best and most efficient way of powering tramcars. In many continental and American cities the alleged unsightly impact of the overhead was minimised by attaching span wires to buildings by means of rosettes, thus doing away with the need for traction standards situated on the pavement. Although the TRAMWAY TRACTION report contained pictures of this method of overhead suspension in Dresden and Milan, the opportunity was not followed up for a closer inspection.

The aesthetic qualities of streets sans overhead wires also appealed to the author of the report, and it probably seemed reasonable at the time to expect all the London metropolitan boroughs covering the more select quarters of the metropolis to fall in with these conclusions. As we now know, the prospect of electric tramways, with or without the conduit, was anathema to the local authorities of the West End and City of London areas. This potential sop of no overhead wires to the wealthier parts of the capital backfired on the Council, when representatives of the less affluent boroughs also demanded they receive the same treatment. Thus, the opportunity was lost in cutting the construction bill, and many thoroughfares, which could quite easily have had overhead wires, were saddled with the huge expense of the conduit.

Such were the bones of contention contained in the report; however, there was one farsighted, almost visionary, section of the account of urban transport in America. The Boylston Street Subway in Boston came under particular scrutiny. Here in this populous New England city, tram services had been diverted below the surface of congested streets, and this method of dealing with traffic jams (or *blockades*)

There were precious few mechanical aids in those days to alleviate the manual toil of those excavating the roadway. Work has ceased for a moment to let the photographer record the scene as short conduit yokes are placed in a trench. Temporary horsecar tracks are on the other side of the rope.

appealed to J. Allen Baker. He writes, quoting the American STREET RAILWAY JOURNAL:

The subway is well lighted throughout the route. It is cool in summer and warm in winter . . . and the saving of time is indeed remarkable. Under the old conditions it would normally take at least thirteen minutes to go from the present subway entrance on Boylston Street to Park Street. Now the time is but three minutes, including a stop at Boylston Street Station. There are no blockades and everything is working in the most satisfactory manner.

This idea of a sub-surface tramway caught the imagination and it seemed to offer at least a partial solution to the thorny problem of through routes across London. Ironically, the Boston Subway, which was in many ways the inspiration for the later Kingsway Subway in London, was equipped for overhead trolley operation!

The report eventually found itself on the desks of the members of the LCC Highways Committee. In many respects J. Allen Baker was typical of the enlightened, informed Victorian reformer who sought to balance the equation of private profit versus social

gain. The judgement of history may be harsh on him for championing the very expensive conduit system, but in the context of contemporary political pressures, it is not surprising that he reached the conclusions printed in the report. In the following months after his return from the study tour, the Council unwittingly compounded the conduit mistake by appointing a former professor of engineering at University College, London as its electrical engineering consultant. In fact, Dr Alexander Kennedy was effectively given carte blanche in the construction and design of the Council's new conduit tramways.

The employment of Dr Kennedy appeared on the surface to be a sound one,

but it soon became clear that the LCC had spent the (at that time) princely sum of £500 per annum on a consultant with only a sketchy knowledge of electric tramways. He seems to have suffered from a surfeit of self-belief, not in itself a bad thing, but in practice this character trait tended to affect his opinions, especially when it came to costing construction projects. On the positive side, he did in fact retrace the steps of J. Allen Baker and he made his own journey to the United States. His findings were generally in line with those of the TRAMWAY TRACTION report and this influenced the Council to adopt the conduit system, with the added prospect of sub-surface tramways under the centre of London.

The intricacies of conduit pointwork construction are laid bare in this view of part of Balham High Road. We can assume that this particular piece of ironmongery was carefully laid out in the manufacturer's yard first, before being reassembled on site.

As the expert, Dr Kennedy erred in his judgement over the design of the London conduit. Although he was undoubtedly informed by the engineers in New York and Washington as to the benefits of an integral long yoke pattern to support both running rails and conduit, he patently thought that short unsupported yokes were the way forward for London. Also, he toyed with the idea of a surface contact method of current collection, which he felt could effect savings on streets subject to lesser tramway traffic. Again, he was barking up the wrong tree, and the Westinghouse surface contact system, which he favoured, looked good on paper, but failed to live up to expectations in the experimental stage. Interestingly, the distribution of traction power via surface contact did come back to haunt the Council in 1908 (qv) – the baleful influence of Dr Kennedy obviously lingered on in the minds of some councillors.

In June 1900, members of the Highways Committee visited the International Tramways & Light Railways Exhibition, which took place at the Agricultural Hall in Islington. An exhibit by Westinghouse of a bogie, double deck, open top tram on a demonstration length of conduit track caught their attention. In an act of untypical haste, they bought the whole shebang – lock, stock and barrel – and had it re-erected in the confines of Camberwell Depot. The purchase price of £1,075 even included the services of the Westinghouse tram driver! At this point, some of the wiser heads on the Committee felt that it was about time the Council appointed a salaried electric engineer. Their choice fell on John Hall Rider who took up his post in March 1901. Mr Rider had previously been the chief engineer for electric tramways and lighting to Plymouth Corporation.

It was probably thought that this new appointee would have some influence on the redoubtable Dr Kennedy, but before any noticeable change in policy could be detected, the Council received a nasty surprise.

In the prestigious journal the TRAMWAY AND RAILWAY WORLD for 7th March 1901, there appeared an article entitled *The Proposed Electric Conduit System of the London County Council*. The author, whose name did not feature at the beginning of the piece, was obviously no respecter of reputations. He proceeded to castigate members of the Highways Committee, and he reserved a special place in his firing line for Dr Kennedy. He obviously had in mind an attack on the *Emperor's New Clothes* mystique which had grown up around the good doctor. A mystique, furthermore, which threatened to put a severe dent in the Council's finances.

The following quotes are taken from the article in question:

. . . Dr Kennedy was asked to act as expert adviser with respect to the equipment and certain parts of the Council's tramways . . . it appears that more than a year has been spent in devising a form of conduit and in securing tenders for boilers. As far as we can ascertain no detailed plans for a power station and its equipment have yet been presented to the Council, which is still apparently in the experimental stage, with small prospect of emerging therefrom for some time to come.

The exact amount of progress that has been made could be noted by anyone familiar with present practice in electric traction at the exhibition given by the Council last month . . . Members of the Metropolitan Borough Councils and other interested persons attended at the Council's tramway depot at Camberwell on the afternoon of 14th February, to inspect 'a specimen electrical car and a short length of line, with the view of indicating clearly the details of the conduit system of electrical traction devised by Dr A. B. W. Kennedy, and provisionally adopted by the Council.' From what was seen and heard on the occasion, it was only too evident that the Council had reached a critical stage of its work, and that unless certain errors are speedily corrected they may not only entail waste of money, but seriously detract from the success which the public have a right to expect after the prolonged delay in the adoption of electric traction.

As some explanation in regard to the exhibit at Camberwell, and its relation to contemporary development in conduit tramway construction, may at the present juncture be useful, and may possibly be the means of correcting certain erroneous impressions which were evidently carried away by many visitors, we propose to discuss the matter at some length.

One of the principal exhibits at the Tramways & Light Railways Exhibition was a length of conduit tramway with a luxurious car in actual operation on it. This car and the track equipment were bought at the close of the exhibition by the LCC from the exhibitors, the British Westinghouse Electric and Manufacturing Company, and were installed in the open air at the tramways depot in Camberwell. The conduit was put down and entirely closed in, as it would be in normal street practice. The only visible part of the construction which differs from the two ordinary track rails of the tramway, is the surface slot of the conduit, about three quarters of an inch wide (19mm), running down the centre of the track. Upon this line the car has been in actual operation for some months past, and it was this Westinghouse line which was shown in operation at the inspection on 14th February.

Considering the wording of the illustrated pamphlet issued by the Council in connection with affair, it can easily be understood where the mistaken ideas of the visitors had their origin. The only plant in operation was that originally shown at the Tramways Exhibition, and the design, the engine, the dynamo, and the installed conduit were of Westinghouse origin, while the body of the car was built by George F. Milnes & Company of Birkenhead, and was mounted on Brill trucks.

The conduit which the LCC propose to adopt was shown by a very short length of skeleton track resting on the surface of the ground. It was not in operation, had no connection with any electrical circuit, and was not, and never has been actually worked. Whether it is better than the one

At a suitable distance from the upheaval of road works and track laying, the new fleet is being assembled in Clapham Depot.

which was shown in operation is a question that anyone, who knows anything whatever of electric conduit traction, will be able to answer. It ought, however, to be mentioned for the benefit of those who may have had no experience in electric conduit practice, that there are certain points in its construction which were abandoned years ago, because in practice they proved to be more or less faulty . . .

The author then continued in similar vein to list his main concerns, which centred on the design and strength of the conduit yokes, the inadequacy of the drainage system and the insulating materials. He also had grave doubts as to the general strength and cost of the whole construction. That the LCC was in deep water was further borne out by a critical selection of diagrams which bolstered the author's argument that the LCC's plans, under Dr Kennedy were neither well thought out nor particularly practical. One specific design fault was the three quarter inch gap in the conduit slot rail, which the author predicted (rightly as it turned out) would be subject to contraction, thus

jamming the plough current collectors of passing tramcars.

As a parting shot the writer of the article could barely contain his stark disapproval at the turn of events, which had led to so many delays:

From a remark made by Mr Benn, chairman of the Highways Committee, at the inspection, the completion of the first line cannot be expected for two years. Making due allowance for unforeseen delays, this may be taken to mean that the first car will not run until about midsummer of 1903. Until that time the public must content itself with glowing anticipations of good things to come. The time when the entire system south of the Thames will be converted to electric traction would appear to be so remote that the present inhabitants of London can take little interest in it, unless an important change is effected in the procedure of the Council. It is clearly necessary that the Highways Committee should be relieved of a part of its work, and that a Tramways Committee should be constituted, and should give its whole attention to the work of supplying London with a modern tramway system at the earliest possible day . . .

We do say that a delay of two years in the construction of sixteen miles (25.7km) of track is wholly unnecessary. If the work were entrusted under a suitable guarantee to a responsible firm of contractors, it could be completed in half

the time proposed, while the conversion of the whole system could be effected within three years at the outside. Is it, we would earnestly ask the Council, still too late to adopt the businesslike policy of getting competitive designs from firms of experience, and contracting with one or more of them to complete the work at the earliest moment possible? Why need London wait for such facilities as other modern cities already enjoy?

If, however, the Council must follow its own dilatory methods, the least that it can do is to see that no system is put down that is in any way experimental. When so many well tried designs are in existence to serve as guides, there is not the slightest necessity to attempt more or less precarious experiments, the possible failure of which may entail a waste of enormous sums of money, and deprive the public of the full benefit which a well designed and successful system of local transport must confer on them.

So much for the exclusive consultancy offered by Dr Kennedy! The latter's reaction to this article is unrecorded, but in what many would regard as a hallowed tradition of the British Establishment, after doing a less-than-perfect job, Dr Kennedy was given a knighthood! In his new guise as Sir Alexander Blackie William Kennedy, he was elected President of The Institution of Civil Engineers in 1906. His inaugural address to the learned members dwelt on his personal philosophy born out of his

Newly laid conduit track had a fascination for the public, as here at the Elephant and Castle. This view dates from July 1903. What provision, if any, was made for other users of the highway during the construction work is not apparent. The predominately horse drawn traffic would often use side roads and unmade pavements to circumvent the track laying. J.B.Gent Collection

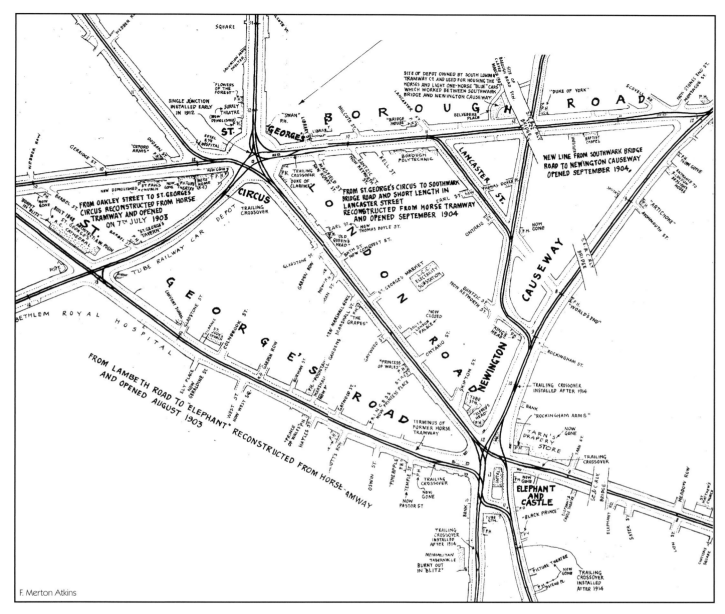

F. Merton Atkins

St Georges Circus –
Elephant and Castle 1912.

experience. No mention was made of tramways or the London County Council – perhaps, in the end, least said was soonest mended!

However, we are getting ahead of our story; Dr Kennedy was still in a position of influence when work started in earnest on the South London conversion. The Council got the go ahead from the Board of Trade in April 1901 for the reconstruction of the following sections:

• Westminster Bridge terminus (i.e. the south bank of the Thames) to Tooting, Totterdown Street via Kennington Road, Clapham and Balham.
• Blackfriars, Stamford Street to Kennington Road via St George's Circus and the Elephant and Castle.
• Waterloo Station to St George's Circus.

The opening up of the carriageway and the removal of redundant horsecar tracks began at Tooting at Easter 1902. All in all, about eight and a half miles (13.6km) of

new double track on the conduit system were being constructed.

The tone of the TRAMWAY AND RAILWAY WORLD article of 11th September 1902 is in marked contrast to the previous account of missed opportunities and bungling. We can only assume that a different author was only too happy to swallow the party line from the LCC. Consequently, the write up has a mildly reverential tone, as the achievements of this great construction project are described in detail. No mention here about the potential instability of the slot rail and the short yokes, instead the reader is treated to a glowing account of the progress. We are informed that construction work of a single line of conduit track is proceeding at a rate of 700 feet (213.3 metres) per day, and that everything is on schedule for the grand opening. The process of replacing the horse tram service started with the opening up of the roadway so that the old rails could be jacked up and

removed. The next stage involved the breaking up of paving and concrete before a trench could be dug ready to receive the conduit yokes. Slot rails were then bolted to the yokes, with the whole assembly being supported by transverse timbers and wooden shuttering in readiness for the pouring of concrete. The two running rails were then secured by means of tie bars to the slot rails. The road surface was then made up either by means of granite setts or hardwood blocks. Special work such as the complicated junctions at the Elephant and Castle, and St George's Circus was manufactured off site. The Johnstown (USA) Works of the Lorain Steel Company forged and laid out the junctions and crossings in a large warehouse before dismantling them for shipping via New York. On arrival at the

15

docks in London the rails and castings were transferred to barges, which were then unloaded at the nearest practical location on the south bank to the tramway construction works. Cartage from the River to the Elephant was by means of large floats drawn by traction engines. Over 150 different plans and diagrams, many of them full size were deposited with the Lorain Steel Company so that all the special work on the Tooting route would be accurate.

J. G. White & Company carried out the general contracting work and W. Scott Ltd of Leeds supplied the rails. The job of supervising the laying of feeder cables and electrical connections to substations at Clapham, Brixton Road and the Elephant Castle was delegated to J. H. Rider, who liaised with Alfred Baker, the Tramways Manager. A temporary power generating facility was erected at Loughborough Junction, because work on the new power station at Greenwich had fallen behind schedule. Construction at the Greenwich site was given top priority in view of the conversion of the New Cross and Greenwich routes, and the cable tramway between Kennington and Streatham. These new sections, totalling some 19 miles (30.5km) of track, were authorised in 1902, but it was decided that, after cable traction ceased on the Streatham line, horse trams would work the route. Thus the necessary electrification would be delayed until sufficient horses (made redundant by the Tooting conversion) became available.

Slowly and steadily, the main highway leading from Tooting to London was transformed into *an avenue of steel*. The appearance, on 7th April 1903, of the first A

Class tramcar on trial heightened public interest. The training of 250 motormen commenced in earnest, with the section of track between Tooting and Clapham being used as the proving ground. Drivers normally boarded an electric at midnight after the horse trams had retired to the depot. An inspector would then supervise each trainee motorman. Also on the tram was a young man whose job was to keep a log of the journeys. Although there were no recorded major incidents, it is known that the white painted inaugural car intended for the royal party was slightly damaged on a trial run and was hastily repaired before the opening ceremony (other sources maintain that a different tram was substituted for the damaged car).

The official Board of Trade inspection took place on 8th May, and all seemed ready for the big event, the royal opening, which was scheduled for Friday 15th May. However, the fates weren't quite with the Council and a dispute blew up which could have wrecked the pomp and circumstance planned for the opening day. It seems Alfred Baker had to act very swiftly to head off an attempt by the Metropolitan Commissioner of Police to deny licences to the new electric trams. Here the Council were at fault, in that the upper deck guardrails needed to be raised by 6 inches (152mm) to satisfy Col. H. A. Yorke, the Board of Trade inspector. Of course, the spirit of Col. Yorke's judgement was that this remedial work should be carried out over the next few weeks, and should not detract from any arrangements made by the Council. Unfortunately, Scotland Yard took a more legalistic view of the matter, and the affair of the missing six inches threatened to scupper the whole ceremonial inauguration of the tramways. Alfred Baker attempted to see the Commissioner of Police on 13th May to bring to his attention the unreasonableness of the demands that new handrails be fitted within seven days. The commissioner

refused to see him! Rescue came at almost the last moment, when Mr Baker persuaded the Board of Trade to grant a stay of six weeks so that the work could be carried out. The police were then placated and the licences were issued.

The great day duly arrived. At around half past three on the afternoon of Friday, 15th May 1903, the Prince and Princess of Wales and their two sons joined local dignitaries at a large marquee close to St Thomas's Hospital, near the eastern end of Westminster Bridge. The usual speeches were made, and a flavour of the day's proceedings can be gleaned from the following account, which appeared in the May edition of THE ELECTRICAL REVIEW:

Mr J. W. Benn, Chairman of the Highways Committee, made a statement relating to the Council's action in connection with the London tramways. Out of 100 miles (161km) of route, the Council had acquired 88 (141.6km); the lines on the north of the Thames had been leased to a company, but the Council decided to work 24 miles (38.6km) on the south side as a municipal service, with cheaper fares than any other tramway in London, and had carried 50 million passengers last year at halfpenny fares. The conditions of service of the employees had been improved, and during four years a net profit of £70,000 had been made, while £89,000 had been paid off capital account, and £30,000 put to reserve. Mr Benn regretted that, owing to the wise action of Parliament, the Council could not meet their Royal Highnesses, with electric cars, on the other side of the bridge.

That was a great meeting of tramway shareholders, all the Metropolitan Boroughs being represented; but the board of directors was free of cost to the undertaking. The LCC, as tramways authority, had allocated £293,000 in aid of the rates. The conduit system was costly, but was free from the drawbacks of overhead wires, poles etc., and had received the approval of the Board of Trade; however, the Council was not bigoted in favour of the conduit. It hoped, in the course of a few years, to bless London with a system of electric traction, which should command the admiration of the world, solve the great housing problem, and confer other benefits upon the people . . .

THE ELECTRICAL REVIEW then continues to describe the speech given by the Prince of Wales and the subsequent official inaugural journey on the electric tramways, which was performed on Car 86 of Class A.

His Royal Highness expressed the pleasure of the Princess and himself in identifying themselves with the new scheme; they and their two sons would not begin by defrauding the Council, so they had brought four halfpennies to pay for their tickets. Londoners hardly realised the immensity of their capital; the means of conveyance were not a luxury, but a

Before passenger services commenced various LCC employees were 'volunteered' to act as guinea pigs in an experiment to determine the best arrangement for a queuing system. This contraption being tried out at Marius Road depot thankfully failed the quality control stage!

Below All along the route patriotic crowds gathered to cheer the royal guests on their way. Whether the onlookers realised what effect this new, reliable and cheap form of transport would have on their lives and employment prospects, is uncertain. However, the promise of the up to date benefits of electric traction would encourage crowds to patronise the tramcars over the next few weeks, and the passenger figures soared as a result.

Right The Great Day has arrived! The ceremonial opening car is positioned on Westminster Bridge Road and is about to convey the Price of Wales past the guard of honour assembled by members of the LCC Fire Brigade. The rest of the official party, seated on trams in the conventional LCC livery, are waiting for their vehicles to reverse and follow the Royal Tramcar.

THE PRINCE'S CAR STARTING.

H.R.H The Prince of Wales opening the South London Electric Tramway, May 15th, 1903.

necessity, not only in the Tooting district, but also all over London. Not only would the tramways provide these facilities, but they would also bring the benefits of light and fresh air within reach of the working classes. London should be a model to all the cities of the Empire, but it was behind the times; it was to be hoped that such great undertakings as that would make up the leeway.

The Royal party then proceeded to board a beautifully decorated car, which was painted white, with festoons of evergreens round the outside, and fitted up as a saloon inside; in this they rode through dense crowds to Tooting, where the Prince and Princess inspected some of the Council's working class cottages. Afterwards their Royal Highnesses returned to Westminster in the same car, and took leave of the Council at the terminus.

The proceedings passed off practically without a hitch, and the tramways staff, from the highest to the lowest official, is to be congratulated on the success of the first day's working. The cars were freely – almost too freely – patronised by the

public in the evening, and were very popular over the weekend, in spite of the weather.

It would be too much to expect that a brand new underground conduit system could be started absolutely without mishaps, nor was this the case; but with only one exception the accidents were of small consequence. The exception, on Saturday last, was of an unexpected nature: a pointsman in the roadway at the Elephant and Castle – a most complicated junction – was in the act of moving the points for a car when he was knocked over by a van; the plough ran into the half open points, and had to be cut away, occasioning a stoppage of two hours. Seventy-two cars were running on

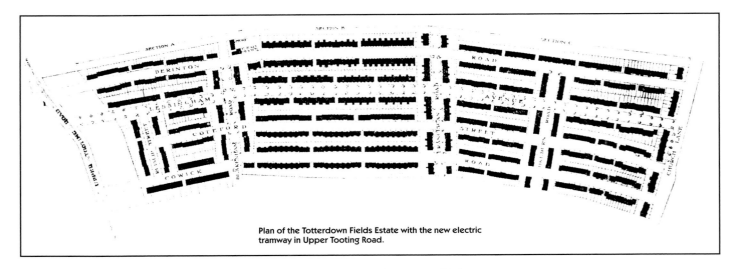

Plan of the Totterdown Fields Estate with the new electric tramway in Upper Tooting Road.

Monday, and the number is being gradually increased; a four minute service is given during the busy hours, and the Tooting cars are on the line from 4.53 a.m. to 1 a.m.

In this account of the opening celebrations there are a number of points, which need further explanation. The Prince and Princess were invited to inspect cottages built for those displaced by slum clearance. The rehousing of those who were living in appalling inner city conditions was high on the Council's agenda, and the provision of efficient and reliable transport for the working population of London was an absolute necessity. It has to be remembered that the elected officials of the LCC perceived the electrification of the tramways as part of a grander scheme to enhance the quality of life in the metropolis. Hence the construction of the new Totterdown Fields Estate, Tooting, which was firmly tied to the improvement in tramway services. Between June and December 1903 the Council built 260 cottages on the estate. By 1911 there were 1,129 dwellings on the site. A contemporary LCC account refers to the development:

The cottages are designed to afford as much variety as possible, and to provide the requisite accommodation for small and large families at varying rents.

It was further stated in the 1908 LCC Tramways Guide that *cottages containing three, four or five rooms with good gardens* were to be had at rents from six shillings to thirteen shillings per week.

Obviously, possessing a roof over one's head in suburban Tooting made little sense if a workman could not afford to travel to his place of employment in the inner city – inexpensive transport had to be provided. Here the Council came up trumps and cheap workmen's fares, which had been a feature of the horse trams, were extended to the electric fleet. *Two Journey* (return) tickets were issued to artisans and labourers who took special workmen's trams on weekdays. One penny fare entitled the workman to travel the whole route in the morning before 8am. The return journey, also costing a penny, could be undertaken at any time on the day the ticket was purchased.

From the opening of the Tooting line to the end of 1903, a total of 309,598 electric car miles (498,143km) was run at workmen's fares. In the financial year 1911–12 this had increased to an impressive 5,339,899 electric car miles (8,591,897km). On one day in 1912 the Council's assessors noted that there were around 1,689 workmen's trams covering the equivalent of 17,928 miles (28,846km)! Although the suburban steam railways also operated a similar service, the train fare was usually double that of the tramcar. As for the bus, the return fare could be anything up to four times the tram fare – obviously, the omnibus companies were not interested in soliciting this type of customer!

In Mr Benn's speech he remarked with regret that Parliamentary powers had not been granted for trams to cross Westminster Bridge. It had been the intention to meet the royal party in the shadow of the Houses of Parliament, but the forces of reaction had effectively stalled any further tramway progress on the west bank of the Thames. Eventually, the LCC did get their tracks across both Westminster and Blackfriars bridges, and along the Victoria Embankment, but it was a hard battle.

After the pomp and ceremony of the opening, this shot of Car 91 shows a more work-a-day environment. The conductor cuts a dashing figure as he poses by the lattice gates of the motorman's platform. The driver himself looks a little less confident. Note that he is still wearing his leather apron from horse tram days. This would give him some protection from the South London rain.

As a final aside to the report of the opening day, the unfortunate contretemps at the Elephant and Castle was the first of a series of mishaps. Here the LCC were slow to learn, and they persisted in stationing pointsmen in the public highway adjacent to the tram tracks. With the inevitable increase in road traffic many of these brave souls, whose job was to direct trams on to the correct route, suffered accidents and near misses. The situation was eventually remedied and the point changing apparatus was moved to the pavement, although the operators were denied any protection against the elements. Canvas huts for pointsmen had to wait for the London Transport era.

Thus, the LCC electric tramways got off to a regal start. However, it did not take long for the prophecies of the writer of the first TRAMWAY AND RAILWAY WORLD article to come true. The incidence of jammed ploughs and track settlement, which caused power conduction problems, mounted to a degree that wiser counsels soon prevailed. The slot in the top of the conduit was widened to one inch (25mm) and long yokes, which fastened the running rails and the conduit in one rigid assembly, were introduced – eventually, the preferred method of construction involved alternating long and short yokes. The anonymous writer in the first critical article had also expressed reservations about the depth of the conduit channel and its lack of drainage when the rains came down. Results on the streets bore out this opinion; furthermore, the conduit also became a repository of all the detritus that was put there by street sweepers. The resultant mixture, which can only be termed *a rose grower's delight*, gradually piled up and interrupted the free flow of the tram service. The LCC then had to instruct local councils not to use the conduit as a convenient receptacle for road sweepings.

In the summer of 1903 new electric routes were added to the original London to Tooting axis. On 25th June, the section between Kennington Church and Camberwell Green was opened to traffic. This was followed on 7th July by Westminster Bridge Road to St George's Circus, thus closing the gap between the three original termini. The line from Vauxhall Cross to Kennington Church was inaugurated on 2nd August. All these new services experienced teething troubles and the depot staff at Clapham had to learn quickly how to maintain a fleet of electric cars. The car shed at Clapham had suffered delays in its construction, and although the final capacity of the building was some 164 trams, only 48 could be accommodated on the inauguration of the Tooting route. An interesting description of the building appeared in the TRAMWAY AND RAILWAY WORLD:

The Clapham car shed is situated close to the Plough, Clapham, not far from the northeast corner of Clapham Common. It has two entrances or exits, one directly into the High Street, Clapham, and the other via Clapham Park Road. The conduit is diverted to the side of the car pits, so that full access may be obtained under the body of each car. Two traversers are in use for working the cars from the various tracks, as the layout of the shed, coupled with the enormous cost of special work for the conduit system,

Above **Awaiting the call to passenger service, cars 22, 3, 37 and 4 line up outside the (temporary) depot at Balham. In front of the trams is the transfer pit.**

Right **Under cover in Clapham Depot Car 5 basks in splendid isolation save for the dapper, bowler hatted gent holding his pipe. Behind the car is the traverser – a useful device, which would shift cars sideways from track to track.**
D. Jones Collection

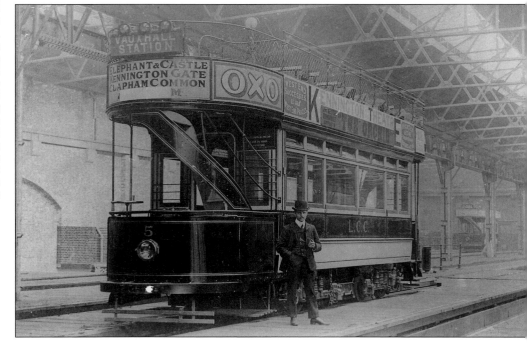

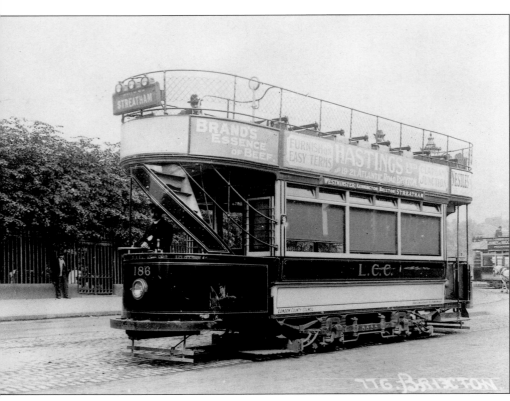

prohibited the use of points and crossings. The shed was erected in two portions, one by the Works Department of the Council, and the other by Kirk and Randall.

Adjoining this shed are a temporary paint shop, a small workshop, and a plough repair shop. The workshop is only of a temporary nature, as it is intended ultimately to do all the repairs at a central depot.

The substation adjoins the car shed, but has a separate entrance from the Clapham Park Road. At the present time it contains only a low tension distribution switchboard, which is fed by direct current from the Council's temporary power station at Loughborough Junction. When the Greenwich generating station is completed, this substation will be equipped similarly to the other substations.

Because Clapham Depot was not fully operational, a temporary solution was

Left **Class B Car 186** is seen at Kennington whilst working from Streatham to Westminster Bridge. The two passengers on the top deck and the drawn blinds at the lower saloon windows suggest this might be a test run before the inauguration of public service.

Below **Kennington 1912**.

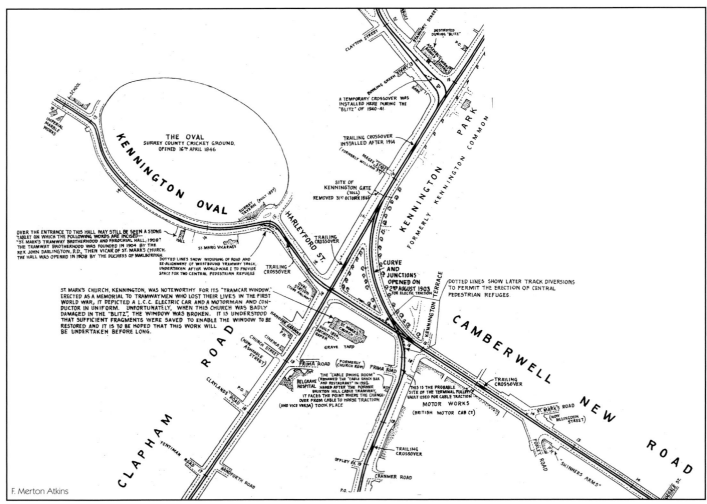

F. Merton Atkins

found in the conversion of the Marius Road, Tooting facility into a running depot. For just over a year it housed electric trams until Clapham was ready to receive the fleet, then around 1905 there was a proposal to build a permanent depot holding 200 cars on the site. However, neither this scheme nor another plan to convert the buildings to an ice rink reached fruition. Latterly the site was used for storage, and a section at the side of the depot became a repository where old horse trams could be dismantled.

In the months of August and September 1903 attention turned to the main Brixton Road south of Kennington. Mechanical traction in the form of cable hauled tramcars had been employed on this route as far as Streatham Village. The opportunity seemed to present itself for combining the benefits of mechanical operation by hitching conduit trams to the cable at the Kennington end of the route.

This *ideal* solution was to prove another costly mistake. Both J. Allen Baker and Dr Kennedy should have observed from their visits to America that transport experts on the other side of the Atlantic had already dismissed the notion of mixing cable and conduit. Although the idea was tempting, American experience had also demonstrated that it was impractical to adapt cable fittings to conduit use. In George W. Hilton's standard work THE CABLE CAR IN AMERICA, he sums up the situation:

Even for companies, which electrified with underground pick-up, cable conduit was unsatisfactory. An electric conduit required an access hatch over every insulator supporting the underground electric rails, but normal practice was to have insulators at triple or more the 32-foot frequency of the access hatches over carrying pulleys. Cable conduit was about twice as deep as electric lines required. Consequently, even though cable conduit was used for the electrifications in New York and Washington, it was subsequently replaced with heavier but shallower conduit specifically designed for the purpose.

In New York the conversion process from cable to conduit lasted from 1899 to 1901, and in Washington DC full electrification was achieved by 1898. The information concerning this transition from cable to conduit was readily available to the visiting parties from the LCC.

Top right **Several ladies have just climbed the stairs of Car 132 as it passes along Brixton Road. Brixton, then as now, is a good place to do your shopping.**
J.B. Gent Collection

Centre right **Car 255 has stopped at the northern end of Walworth Road, Elephant and Castle. The rails curving to the left** form a link with other tram routes using Newington Butts.

Right **On the other side of the famous tramway junction at the Elephant a brace of Class C trams is depicted in Newington Causeway. Car 267 is making its way to Tower Bridge, whilst sister Car 295 is heading in the Peckham direction.**

Top **High Street, Peckham** in the Edwardian sunshine – Car 285 has just passed the entrance to Martin's Road. The points in the foreground lead to a connecting track to Rye Lane Depot and Workshops. Even on this busy day there is no other form of mechanical transport to challenge the supremacy of the LCC tramcar.
B.J.Cross Collection

Above Looking in the opposite direction to the previous view, C Class Car 239 stops for passengers before continuing its journey to Blackfriars Bridge. In these early views places served by the route are painted on the top deck canopy end. This system was soon given up as the network expanded. Basically, it was too inflexible and did not allow easy transfer of cars between services.

Right **Peckham Rye Lane Depot 1912.**

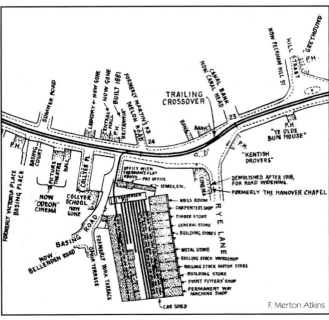

On 2nd August 1903, a service of 4-wheel, open-top B Class cars commenced from Streatham to Westminster. At the northern end of Brixton Road, Kennington there was a change pit where conduit ploughs were lifted from the conduit and stowed between the truck and lower saloon floorboards of each B Class car. The tram was then attached by a gripper to the underground cable, which then hauled the vehicle in the direction of Streatham. Only a few B class cars appear to have operated alongside the existing cable trams.

The service was abysmal. And the strain on the cable system was further aggravated on 11th September when trams started working from Streatham to Blackfriars Bridge. The weight of each B class tram was simply too much for the cable machinery. An unladen B class car weighed in at seven tons, whereas a cable car topped the scales at only two and a half tons. After frequent breakdowns, the whole project was abandoned on 14th October, and the old lighter cable cars were reinstated until 5th April 1904, when the line was closed for reconstruction on the conduit system.

Again, there is a suspicion here that the advice given by the experts was defective. It is likely that, since Dr Kennedy was still on the scene, he concurred with the ill fated scheme for the Streatham to Kennington line. Almost certainly he was asked for his opinions at this critical phase of the Council's electrification programme. His part time consultancy fee, as charged to the Council, eventually totalled £2,500. This was at a time when the most an LCC tram driver, working a sixty hour week, could earn was £93 12s per annum.

All this excitement was obviously too much for Alfred Baker, who decided to leave the employ of the LCC. He was appointed Manager of Birmingham Corporation Tramways and was instrumental in persuading his new tramways committee *not* to adopt the conduit system in the centre of Birmingham! His replacement as Chief Officer to the LCC Tramways was Aubrey Llewellyn Coventry Fell, who took up the reins of the job on 7th December 1903.

Meanwhile, as the map on page 25 will show, there was a full schedule planned for 1904. The conversion of the horse tramway routes south of the Thames was going ahead with some alacrity. As well as the on-street works, a large depot, specifically designed for electric traction, was rising on the Fairlawn site by New Cross Road. Situated near the important tramway junction at New Cross Gate, where lines from the Old Kent Road, Queen's Road and New Cross Road converged, the depot would eventually hold over 300 trams. It was also equipped with workshop facilities, an electrical substation and a plough repair shop. The whole edifice was the subject of an extensive illustrated article, which was printed in the TRAMWAY AND RAILWAY WORLD for 9th August 1906. The entrance tracks from New Cross Road climbed a slight slope. These lines were equipped with catch points to prevent any errant trams rolling back into the highway. On either side of the central traverser pit there were 34 stabling roads, which would accommodate the growing fleet needed for the new services. At times of great activity, a tram would use one of the traversers every thirty seconds. The staff numbered 95 men.

Former horsecar depots at Rye Lane, Peckham; Leo Street, Old Kent Road and Bowles Road, Old Kent Road were upgraded to provide short term storage for electric trams and other equipment. Hoskins Street, Greenwich was also on the list for partial conversion to electric traction, but examination of the Highways Committee minutes indicates that this option was not taken up. A single conduit approach track was provided for access to these depots, but cars were shunted around inside by means of a cable attached to a small troller, or pulley device, which took power from two overhead wires. None of the aforementioned locations would figure in the LCC's final plans for housing the expanding fleet; the Bowles Road and Hoskins Street sites were disposed of in 1906 and 1905 respectively. Leo Street was vacated by the tramways department, but retained as a storage depot. Rye Lane fulfilled a similar function and was later used as a motor garage for some of the Council's ancillary vehicles.

On 17th January 1904 another major trunk route was opened from the Elephant and Castle to Trafalgar Road, Greenwich. The tracks ran via New Kent Road, Bricklayers Arms, Old Kent Road, New Cross and Deptford, before terminating end on to the narrow gauge rails belonging to the Woolwich & South East London horse trams. Passenger traffic on this route lived up to expectations, with not only regular commuters, but also trippers who came to view the architectural splendours of the Royal Naval College and the famous Royal Observatory. For those not so culturally minded, there was the attraction of Greenwich Beach, where many folk who were too poor to visit the real seaside, had the opportunity to bring the kids for a paddle and a penny ice cream. Some parents with large families sometimes spread their offspring around on both decks of the car. There was then a greater chance of the conductor missing a child, and that particular fare could be saved! Needless to say, LCC tram inspectors had cottoned on to this one and on several occasions forgetful parents and their children were removed from Sunday evening trams at New Cross Gate to be given a lecture on their civic responsibilities. Apocryphal stories abound of luckless families being told of draconian punishments being meted out by the company owned tramways. Fare dodgers on the London United, they were informed, could expect at least one month's hard labour punishment. However, the LCC ran tramways for the people of London, and as such, it was shameful to defraud one's fellow citizens. After this official warning

Greenwich terminus in 1904. Note the change of track gauge from electric to horse traction.
F. Merton Atkins

the family was usually ushered out; parents and children all then faced an invigorating walk back home.

A week after the opening of the Greenwich section, the connecting line from New Cross to the Elephant via Peckham and Camberwell Green received its first passengers. These tracks also formed a natural traffic route and provided a conduit connection between Rye Lane and New Cross depots. On 20th July 1904, the usual travellers on this line were greeted with the sight of newly top covered Car 310 – the first in the fleet to provide protection from the weather for upper deck passengers. The idea was to catch on, and earnings per car mile would rise accordingly, as the prospect of sitting outside in the cold and rain lost its charm.

An interesting aside to this work was published in October 1946, in the form of a letter from Mr F. Cook, London Transport Rolling Stock Engineer. He recalled an amusing incident from the first decade of the twentieth century, when he was sent out

At the junction of Royal Hill and London Street, Greenwich, Car 155 goes about its business. This postcard view was sent on 21st August 1905, when the electric tram service was barely eighteen months old. Greenwich presents an interesting mixture of fashion styles reflecting the differences in prosperity of its inhabitants.
B.J. Cross Collection

on a tram to check clearances. He used to stand on the open top deck and sometimes had to scramble up on to the bridge itself:

When we LCC people proposed to run top roof covered trams, I used to go out at night after the service had stopped and measure up bridge heights. I climbed on to the side of Clapham Road Bridge, took the measurements, and then – My driver, the late Motorman Instructor Howard, had driven away and left me in a precarious position. Luckily he missed me, came back and helped me down from my frail perch.

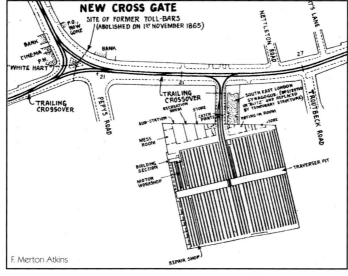

Above **The photographer
was obviously mightily
impressed with his
assignment and he has
climbed on to a top deck
to get a better vantage
point. All around him lies
the vast expanse of New
Cross Depot – one of the
largest such facilities in
Europe. The fleet is in a
state of transition, as not
all cars have yet received
top covers. The
maintenance pits between
the rails were not fenced
off and it was assumed
that any depot worker
falling down on the job
lacked the necessary
attention and common
sense!**
D. Jones Collection

Right **New Cross Depot
1912.**

NEW CROSS GATE
SITE OF FORMER TOLL-BARS
(ABOLISHED ON 1ST NOVEMBER 1865)

F. Merton Atkins

Many LCC crews would not think twice
about clambering out of a stationary
tramcar to effect repairs on the roof. As long
as they took care, the danger of falling off
was minimised. However, in Mr Cook's case,
it seems that it was a genuine case of forget-
fulness on the part of the driver. It is
interesting to note Mr Cook's devotion to
duty, because it was he who supervised the
fitting of top covers to the LCC fleet. He was
obviously a man who had to check everything personally, even down to the last inch.

On the ill starred Kennington to
Streatham section the cable cars had been
withdrawn. Unlike other conversions it was

not deemed feasible to maintain a service of
horse trams, operating on temporary rails
adjacent to the new trackwork needed for
electrification. In fact, the horse trams in
the district had been having a rather torrid
time of it. Running a mixed horse and
electric service on some sections of the
newly electrified route north of Kennington
had provoked public complaints, mainly on
account of the slow horse cars holding up
the progress of the more speedy electrics.
Again, those making the decisions in the
LCC Tramways Department seem to have
miscalculated.

On 21st May, much to the relief of the

Council and the local residents, the route
was opened between Kennington and
Brixton Station. Electric trams were now in
direct competition with suburban steam
railways, and the street based vehicles could
offer a cheaper ride and more frequent
services. The line was further extended nine
days later, when Water Lane, Brixton was
reached. Finally, on 19th June, the section
was opened up through to the southern
terminus outside Streatham Library.

The Kennington to Streatham line was
the first complete route to have modified
conduit fixtures and fittings as designed by
Mr Maurice Fitzmaurice, Chief Engineer to
the LCC. He was ably assisted by Mr J. H.
Rider. It can be assumed from this information that Dr Kennedy's original designs had
been altered in the light of experience and
traffic requirements. The contractors, J. G.
White & Co, priced the contract at £13,000
per mile. The length of the route was just
less than four miles and conversion was
completed in eleven weeks, which was three
weeks *under* the deadline. The latest design
of conduit slot rail points was used and a
new substation was commissioned at
Streatham. Each substation had a theoretical capacity to supply current for 150 trams
in active service.

On 1st August 1904, various important
short connections were brought into use
throughout inner South London. Tracks
were opened from St George's Circus to
Newington Causeway, from Newington
Causeway to the southern approach to
Southwark Bridge, from the Elephant to St
George's Church, from Hop Exchange

(Borough Market) to Southwark Bridge Road and from Southwark Bridge Road to Bricklayers Arms. This tightly knit arrangement of interconnecting lines was to prove most useful when traffic conditions or delays forced diversions of tram services.

The LCC had been working on a new southern approach road to Tower Bridge. Demolition of property had made 535 people homeless and they had to be rehoused by the Council. A brand new double track tramway was laid on Tower Bridge Road and was opened to traffic on 12th September 1904. It is worth recording that construction work in association with the erection of the Greenwich Power Station had also caused problems for local inhabitants. No fewer than 214 people were transferred to a new estate at Hughes Fields, Deptford. The expansion of the Greenwich site also involved the eventual demolition of the Hoskins Street horse tram depot.

During the twenty-four months beginning in January 1903 electric traction had gained an important foothold in South London. The success of the Council Tramways, in spite of some embarrassing setbacks, had attracted the notice of politicians and public alike. Figures issued by the Council suggested that passenger growth, encouraged by electric traction on the Tooting to Bridges route, had reached an

impressive 41 per cent more than the 1901 horse tram figures for the same route.

It became increasingly obvious to those who had to plan for the future that mechanised road transport was here to stay. Cognisance needed to be taken of the changing patterns of housing and the lengthening of the average journey to work – clearly, old *horse drawn* attitudes had to

be adapted to the demands of the new twentieth century. A serious investigation into the state of London's traffic was called for. The Royal Commission on the Means of Locomotion and Transport in London was set up in 1903 and published its findings in 1905. Was this a new dawn for the LCC Tramways? We shall see in the next chapter.

Above **Just outside the enormous depot, life went on as normal. Cyclists are out for a ride, mothers push babies along the pavement and youngsters gaze wide eyed at the procession of trams occupying the centre of New Cross Road. Car 163 is outbound to Woolwich Road; open top Car 75 is London bound on the Southwark Bridge service.**

Right **The Council issued a sketch map on a regular basis to many engineering journals. This map was published in December 1904.**

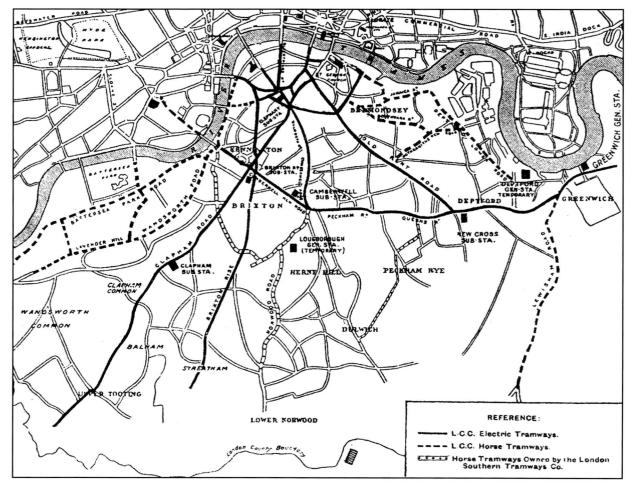

REFERENCE:
L.C.C. Electric Tramways.
L.C.C. Horse Tramways.
Horse Tramways Owned by the London Southern Tramways Co.

CHAPTER THREE

London Traffic – 1905

LONDON HAS been a centre of trade and commerce for centuries. Much of the street pattern of the inner city can be traced back to Roman and Anglo-Saxon times. After the Great Fire of 1666 the opportunity was missed to endow the capital city with broad thoroughfares and spacious squares. Although a certain amount of demolition and property clearance had occurred during the nineteenth century, especially in connection with railway building schemes, many streets were simply too narrow to cope with the increase in traffic. Into this melee stepped the Royal Commission on London Traffic. Its remit was to get to grips with the problems and to make practical suggestions for a range of solutions. The Commission was empowered to summon witnesses and to undertake visits both home and abroad to evaluate best practice in the transport and town planning fields.

The activities of Charles Tyson Yerkes had also caused widespread concern. He was an American-born traction tycoon, who is said to have inspired Theodore Dreiser to write his fictional trilogy: *The Financier, The Titan* and *The Stoic*. Yerkes's business methods were anything but fiction, and his manipulation of London public transport companies was ruffling more than a few feathers in government circles. His link up with banker Edgar Speyer enabled him to form the new Underground Electric Railways Company of London. His famous phrase 'it is the straphangers who pay the dividends' refers to the philosophy of packing people into the tubes. Unfortunately his investors came off rather badly because the expected profits failed to materialise. Yerkes passed away in 1905, largely unmourned, but his cut and thrust methods had left a lasting impact on the committee of the Royal Commission.

The challenge to the free passage of goods and people along London's streets was made more acute by the introduction of mechanised vehicles. Dire predictions were uttered that a great mass of automobiles, motorised buses, steam lorries and electric tramcars would strangle the very arteries of the chief city of the British Empire. It was clearly a time for words then action to create an environment, where citizens could flourish and the trade of the nation would be unimpeded.

New Cross Gate in 1905 already showed the characteristics of a congestion hot spot. One lone horse bus looks out of place on a highway dominated by LCC trams. On the far left a pointsman, poised for action, stands in the carriageway. Such a scene as this, could not fail to impress those charged with sorting out London's traffic problems. The electric tramcar was obviously here to stay.
J.B. Gent Collection

With hindsight, the debate about traffic congestion has been a perennial one, and a lasting solution has eluded every generation for the past two hundred years. The 1905 report made a number of imaginative suggestions, which would not only have enhanced the LCC tramways system, but would also have equipped London with a couple of grand avenues planned to alleviate the worst of the bottlenecks caused by through traffic. That very little of substance was actually achieved after the publication of the Commission's findings was entirely regrettable, but in many ways not surprising. It was a question of *so bright the vision*, and the powers that be simply would not, or could not, find the money to carry out visionary projects. Some Metropolitan Boroughs allied themselves with the City of London to maintain the status quo, and would only permit relatively minor street improvements to be completed. These forces of reaction were of course totally hostile to tramways and, as we shall see, they used their veto very effectively to block further encroachments by LCC trams.

The facts and figures relating to the Royal Commission were impressive. Eight volumes were published encompassing many thousands of words, opinions and conclusions. Maps, diagrams, plans and indices completed the magnum opus. This vast amount of paperwork probably deserves several learned tomes of comment, but for the purposes of this book, only the salient points of the recommendations with specific reference to electric tramways will be covered.

The preamble of the Commission reads as follows:

To report as to the measures which we deem most effectual for the improvement of the same by the development and inter-connexion of Railways and Tramways on, or below, the surface; by increasing the facilities for other forms of mechanical locomotion; by better provision for the organisation and regulation of vehicular and pedestrian traffic, or otherwise.

To report as to the desirability of establishing some authority or tribunal to which all schemes of Railway or Tramway construction of a local character should be referred, and the powers which it would be advisable to confer upon such a body.

After stating the aims and objectives, the final report, as published in volume one, outlined some of the evolving problems concerning: increase of street congestion, overcrowding of transport facilities, rehousing of slum dwellers, provision of affordable transport, the acquisition of land for improvements and the antagonism between the LCC and private promoters. All of which brings us to the first section, which focused on tramways. In the introduction entitled *History of the Construction of Street Tramways in London*, the committee set out some of the main arguments surrounding the extension of tramways in the capital. Briefly stated, it regarded the building of new lines to be hampered by the inflexible attitude of the LCC to company owned tramways, which manifested itself in the former's reluctance to enter into through running agreements. Another stumbling block was the persistent veto of the Corporation of the City of London to any tramway encroachment on its territory. The narrowness of some streets in London was also cited as a significant obstacle to the establishment of double track tramways.

The Report then altered its line of enquiry to examine the various plans for new through highways, which were likely to ease congestion in and around the central area. It tackled many of the sensitive areas, such as amenity values of property blighted by new roads. The accumulated cost of new highway projects also loomed large in the Commission's thoughts, but eventually they settled on a scheme involving twenty road improvements associated with new thoroughfares. The most significant recommendation concerned the construction of two grand avenues. Route A would stretch from Hyde Park to Gardiners Corner, Aldgate, and it would intersect with Route B half way along the existing Grays Inn Road. Route B would commence at Holloway and finish at the Elephant and Castle. Each avenue was to be 140 feet (42.6 metres) wide, and was to feature four lines of tramway on the surface, with four lines of

CROSS SECTION

CROSS SECTION

Above **The main avenue as envisaged by the Royal Commission includes four conduit tram tracks. The inner pair are designated for use by express, limited stop trams. The outer two tracks are for local trams with frequent stops.**

Above right **The trams on the First Class Arterial Street would still have to compete with a four track underground railway running just beneath them. Has the artist put the motor car in on purpose as a portent of the chaos to come?**

railway a few feet below the surface. Electricity was envisaged as the motive power for both tramways and railways. These new civil engineering works were costed at £30million, but this expense was to be offset by the considerable passenger revenues, which would be generated.

The thirteen members of the Royal Commission heard evidence from a number of people directly concerned with tramway matters as they related to the metropolis and elsewhere in the country. Those called in front of the Commission included: C. R. Bellamy, Manager of Liverpool Corporation Tramways; J. W. Benn, Chairman of the LCC Highways Committee; J. Devonshire, Managing Director of the Metropolitan Electric Tramways Ltd; J. M. McElroy, General Manager of Manchester Corporation Tramways; J. Clifton Robinson, Managing Direct of the London United Electric Tramways Ltd and C. T. Yerkes, Chairman of the Underground Electric Railways Company of London Ltd. Also invited to appear were influential members of the metropolitan boroughs and the Corporation of the City of London. Officials from those outer London boroughs, which had commenced municipal tramway operation, were asked to testify. Prominent among the professional experts were civil engineers, electrical engineers and highway surveyors.

The final recommendations concerning tramways were contained in chapter six of volume one, which ran to some fourteen

pages. Two large maps, one of the centre of London showing proposed tramway routes, and the other a full survey of lines throughout Greater London, were appended to the recommendations. The main findings centred on the fact that tramway development in London lagged behind other provincial and foreign cities. Although the number of inhabitants per route mile of tramway was 8,937 in Manchester, in London the total rose to 33,661, thereby implying, as was only too obvious to the outside observer, that there were large tramless tracts of the capital.

There was, according to the Commission, *a want of through communication by tramway* and this state of affairs had hindered tramway development in London. The nature of this problem is plainly stated:
. . . *Great districts in the centre of London, including the City, the West End, and the chief places of public resort, are entirely unprovided with tramway service. The different lines approach those districts and then break off abruptly in the middle of the street.*
As *a result, all the cars are obliged to discharge their passengers at dead end terminals. At the six principal terminals (Westminster Bridge, Shepherds Bush,*

Blackfriars Bridge, Aldgate, Moorgate and Euston Road), nearly a quarter of a million passengers alight from, or join, the cars every day in the streets. Apart from the great inconvenience caused to all or most of the passengers, the result is a great congestion, both of tramcars, and of ordinary vehicular and pedestrian traffic, at these terminal points; and the same congestion, though in a lesser degree, occurs at the other terminals in London.
The Advisory Board of Engineers estimate that the carrying power of a tramway system may be diminished by about one half by reason of the cross shunting (reversing at terminals and getting the cars in correct order – author) at dead end terminals. In the absence of delay from this cause, 150 cars, or upwards, per hour, may be run on a single track, even in busy thoroughfares; but at Westminster, for example, where a number of cars from different lines converge at the Lambeth end of Westminster Bridge, the necessity for cross shunting creates so great a delay, that all the lines taken together cannot run more than 72 cars per hour in one direction, and that only under pressure.

Camberwell Green is depicted in the early years of electric tram operation. The top deck of a C Class car has just slipped into the picture. Cars 249 and 171 are on the Church Street tracks, south of the Green. It was from here that the author, Richard Church, used to commute to central London.
J.B.Gent Collection

Blackfriars Road by
Southwark Street was a
classic example of what
the Royal Commission
members wished to avoid.
In brief, it was a tram
terminus well short of its
traffic objective. In this
case, the Corporation of
the City of London had
objected to trams running
across Blackfriars Bridge.
Lines of homeward bound
City workers effectively
block part of the
carriageway as they wait
under the supervisory eye
of an LCC inspector.

This was really the nub of the argument and the *idée fixe* throughout the whole report. Put simply, the Commission concluded that the fragmented nature of central London tramways constituted a serious obstacle to the movement of passengers across the metropolis.

The *Advantages and Cost of Street Tramways* were then examined in a number of paragraphs. The members of the Commission were favourably impressed by the cheap fares offered by LCC trams, which confirmed to the travelling public the usefulness of a convenient and popular transport facility. This affordable system of fares was very competitive with those offered by suburban steam railways. Indeed, it is stated in the Report, that the convenience and accessibility of street tramways gave them the edge over railways. The only reasonable alternative to the tramcar was the horse bus and its new motorised successor. Here the threat to the tram's supremacy was only significant if motor buses could provide a reliable and efficient service.

The Commission concluded:

But we think that, on routes suitable for tramways, where there is a large traffic, tramways will continue to be the most efficient and the cheapest means of street conveyance, and we cannot recommend the postponement of tramway extension in London on the ground of any visible prospect of the supersession of tramways by motor omnibuses.

The cost of tramways compared with the cost of underground railways is then considered in the report. This is stated as between £250,000 to £300,000 per mile for tube railways, as opposed to £39,512 for a double line of overhead wire equipped tramway, and £52,602 for conduit construction. Obviously, there was a clear advantage for street tramways, but the tramway costs did not include estimates for property demolition, necessary if narrow streets were to be widened to accommodate double track. The proper width for thoroughfares carrying tramways was stated as an ideal 48 feet (14.6 metres) between kerbs, although the LCC seemed to be happy with a minimum of 33 feet (10 metres). This lower measurement was only acceptable for short distances or in the case of a suburban road with less traffic. On the basis of these figures, it was concluded that most of the main thoroughfares in central London could accommodate a double track tramway.

The Advisory Board of Engineers to the Commission consisted of a number of civil engineering experts and planning consul-

tants. The new tramways recommended by the Board, some on street and some sub-surface similar to the Kingsway Subway, are listed as follows – they make interesting reading in the light of subsequent developments, which are indicated in heavy print. The proposed lines are designated as Routes 1 to 23:

Route 1. Across Hammersmith Bridge.
– A surface tramway to connect the authorised tramways of the LCC, at the north of the bridge, with those at the south of the bridge. *Never constructed.*

Route 2. Hammersmith to Knightsbridge.
– A surface tramway, starting by a junction with the London United Tramways and the LCC authorised tramway in Hammersmith Broadway, and passing along Hammersmith Road, Kensington Road and High Road, Knightsbridge, and terminating by a junction with Routes 3 and 4 in Knightsbridge at the northern end of Sloane Street. *Never constructed.*

Route 3. Knightsbridge to Aldgate.
– A subway continuation of Routes 2 and 4, starting in Knightsbridge at the northern end of Sloane Street, and passing under Hyde Park Corner, Piccadilly, Coventry Street, King William Street, Strand, Fleet Street, Ludgate Hill, Cheapside, Cornhill, Leadenhall Street, to Aldgate, and terminating by a junction with the LCC tramways in Aldgate High Street. *Never constructed.*

Route 4. Fulham and Brompton Roads.
– A surface tramway, starting by a junction with the LCC authorised tramway, at the junction of Fulham Palace Road and High Street, Fulham, and passing along Fulham Road and Brompton Road, and terminating by a junction with Routes 2 and 3 in Knightsbridge at the northern end of Sloane Street. *Never constructed.*

Route 5. Grosvenor Place and Hyde Park.
– A surface tramway, starting by the junction with the LCC tramways at their

terminus in Vauxhall Bridge Road, and passing along Victoria Street to Grosvenor Gardens, and thence in subway, under Grosvenor Gardens, Grosvenor Place and the eastern side of Hyde Park, and terminating by a junction with Routes 6 and 9 at the southern end of the Edgware Road. *Never constructed.*

Route 6. Edgware Road and Maida Vale.
– A surface tramway, starting by a junction with Route 5, near the Marble Arch and passing along Edgware Road, Maida Vale and High Road, Kilburn, and terminating by a junction with the existing light railways of the Middlesex County Council (Metropolitan Electric Tramways) at Cricklewood. *Never constructed.*

Route 7. Harrow Road.
– A surface tramway, starting by a junction with the Harrow Road and Paddington Tramways at their eastern terminus in Harrow Road, and passing along Harrow Road, Westbourne Terrace and Bishops Road, and terminating by junctions with Routes 6 and 22 in the Edgware Road. *Constructed, but worked by the Metropolitan Electric Tramways. Westbourne Terrace and Bishops Road section never constructed.*

Route 8. Cambridge Avenue.
– A surface tramway, starting by a junction with the Harrow Road and Paddington Tramways at their terminus in Cambridge Road, and passing along Cambridge Avenue and terminating by a junction with Route 6 in the Edgware Road. *Never constructed.*

Route 9. Uxbridge and Bayswater Roads.
– A surface tramway, staring by a junction with the London United Tramways at their terminus at Shepherds Bush, and passing along Holland Park Avenue, High Street, Notting Hill Gate and Bayswater Road, and terminating by junctions with Route 5 at the Marble Arch. *Never constructed.*

Route 10. Westminster Bridge and Victoria Embankment. – A surface tramway, starting by junctions with the LCC tramways in Westminster Bridge Road and Stangate at their termini, and passing over Westminster Bridge and terminating by junctions with the LCC authorised subway at Waterloo Bridge, and Route 11. *Constructed by the LCC.*

Route 11. Waterloo Bridge and Blackfriars Bridge. – A surface tramway, starting by a junction with Route 10 at Waterloo Bridge, and passing along the Victoria Embankment and terminating by junctions with Routes 12 and 13 at Blackfriars Bridge. *Constructed by the LCC.*

Route 12. Queen Victoria Street and Southwark Bridge. – A surface tramway, starting by a junction with Route 11 at Blackfriars Bridge northern approach, and passing along Queen Victoria Street, Cannon Street, Queen Street and over Southwark Bridge, and terminating by a junction with the LCC tramways at their terminus in Southwark Bridge Road. *Constructed by the LCC: Southwark Bridge to Queen Street Place only.*

Route 13. New Bridge Street and Farringdon Street. – A surface tramway, starting by a junction with the LCC tramways at their terminus in Blackfriars Bridge Road, passing over the suggested viaduct from the centre of Blackfriars Bridge to Farringdon Street, then along Farringdon Road and terminating by a junction with the LCC tramways in Clerkenwell Road. *Constructed by the LCC: Blackfriars Bridge. Farringdon Road from Clerkenwell Road to Cowcross Street only.*

Route 14. Holborn and Charterhouse Street. – A surface tramway, starting by a junction with the LCC tramways at their terminus at the southern end of Grays Inn Road, passing along Holborn and Charterhouse Street, and terminating by a junction with Route 13 in Farringdon Road. *Never constructed.*

Route 15. York Road, Stamford Street and Southwark Street. – A surface tramway, starting by a junction with the LCC tramways in Westminster Bridge Road, and passing along York Road, Stamford Street and Southwark Street, terminating by a junction with the LCC

Map of the tramway proposals (shown in red) advocated by the members of the Royal Commission. The broken lines indicate subway routes. The routes numbered 24 and 25 shown in red outline were the two new cross-London avenues A and B (see pp 27 and 28). Routes shown in blue and black were existing tramways.

tramways in Southwark Bridge Road, also with a branch down Waterloo Road to join up that terminus. *Constructed by the LCC: Southwark Street to Hop Exchange only.*

Route 16. Tower Subway.
– A subway tramway, starting by a junction with the LCC tramways at their terminus in Leman Street, and passing under the River Thames at a point east of St Katherine's Docks, and terminating by a junction with the LCC tramways at the southern approach to the Tower Bridge. *Never constructed.*

Route 17. Tottenham Court Road and Whitehall. – A surface tramway, starting by a junction with the LCC tramways at their terminus at the southern end of the Hampstead Road, passing along Tottenham Court Road, Charing Cross Road, Trafalgar Square (east side), Charing Cross, Whitehall, Parliament Street and Bridge Street, and terminating by a junction with Route 10 at the western end of Westminster Bridge. *Never constructed.*

Route 18. Moorgate, Liverpool Street and Norton Folgate. – A surface tramway, starting by a junction with the LCC tramways at their terminus at South Place, passing along Finsbury Pavement, Finsbury Circus, Liverpool Street and Bishopsgate Street Without, and terminating by a junction with the LCC tramways at their terminus in Norton Folgate. *Constructed by the LCC: Norton Folgate to Bishopsgate, Middlesex Street only.*

Route 19. Aldersgate Street to Post Office. – A subway tramway, starting by a junction with the LCC tramways at their terminus near Charterhouse Square, passing under Aldersgate Street and St Martins le Grand, and terminating near the General Post Office. *Never constructed.*

Route 20. Kings Road, Chelsea and Buckingham Palace Road. – A surface tramway, starting by a junction with the LCC authorised tramway in High Street, Fulham, at the northern approach to Putney Bridge, and passing along New Kings Road, Kings Road, Chelsea, Sloane Square, Lower Sloane Street, Pimlico Road and Buckingham Palace Road, and terminating by a junction with route 5 at the western end of Victoria Street at Grosvenor Gardens. *Never constructed.*

Route 21. Victoria Street, Westminster. – A surface tramway, starting by a junction with route 5 at the northern end of Vauxhall Bridge Road, and passing along Victoria Street, Broad Sanctuary and Parliament Square, and terminating by a junction with Route 17 at Parliament Street. *Never constructed.*

Route 22. Marylebone and Euston Roads. – A surface tramway, starting by a junction with Route 7 at the Edgware Road opposite the Harrow Road, and passing along the suggested new street

and the Marylebone Road and Euston Road, and terminating by a junction with the LCC tramways in the Euston Road, at Kings Cross Station. *Never constructed.*

Route 23. Finchley Road.
– A surface tramway, starting by a junction with Route 22 at Upper Baker Street, and passing along Upper Baker Street, Park Road, Wellington Road and Finchley Road, and terminating by a junction with Middlesex County Council authorised light railways (Metropolitan Electric Tramways) at Childs Hill. *Never constructed.*

After describing these proposals, the Commission insisted that the advantages of the new lines were obvious. Unfortunately, this tramway wish list and the plans for the two cross London super avenues had the effect of galvanising the opposition. We can only wonder what course London traffic management may have taken had these suggestions been acted upon. As it was, only a disappointingly small mileage was ever placed in active service and the bright vision for the future soon faded.

The next part of the Report dealt with concerns over the lack of through running between London's tramway operators. The conclusion was reached that this impasse needed to be sorted out quickly for the convenience of all concerned. Through booking, cheap fares and interconnecting services were recommended, so that passengers could avoid the hold ups occasioned by having to change cars at boundary points.

The topic of through running naturally led the Committee on to the subject of company v municipal operation, and how the two seeming opposed worldviews could co-operate in the interests of public service.

We have been told by witnesses that . . . the various tramway systems within Greater London ought to be worked by one and the same authority, and that for this and other reasons it is inexpedient for the LCC to operate their own tramways.

So far as the question involves considerations of municipal trading, we

Artificial gaps in the transport system caused by local authority boundaries were also of concern to the traffic planners. Here at Finsbury Park, electric trams belonging to the MET can go no further as they risk trespassing on LCC territory. The connecting horsecar looks out of date, but through passengers from Edmonton to Euston Road will have to put up with the delays for a while longer. On the left of the picture is the two track horse tram depot.

do not think it is within our province to express an opinion. We think it reasonable that some profit should be derived from the tramways for the benefit of the municipality, but it does not follow that the best way of securing the largest profit will be that the municipality, even if it finds the money for construction, should undertake the task of operating. In other countries, it is not unusual for municipalities to construct, purchase or otherwise acquire the tramways, but in such cases the actual working is generally left to operating companies, with provision for proper rates and general control.

It is claimed that such methods yield better financial results to municipalities, and avoid difficulties which might arise from municipal authorities carrying on a business of this kind on a large scale . . . If the tramways are operated by the municipalities concerned, we think that they should be worked on sound financial principles, with ample provision for depreciation and repayment of capital or discharge of debt. It also appears to us that any profit from tramways received by a municipality should, preferentially, be applied to necessary tramway developments and to street improvements . . .

The matter is one of such importance that, having regard to the conflicting views that have been laid before us, we strongly recommend that the whole question of the expediency of the working of large tramway systems by municipalities be specially investigated.

More hustle and bustle at New Cross Gate. The Tillings horse bus will soon be put out of business on its New Cross to Lewisham Station run. On 30th January 1906, electric traction will sweep it aside!
J.B.Gent Collection

The tone of these paragraphs was not lost on the LCC. Suspicions were always entertained by some members of the Council, that the Royal Commission maintained a bias towards company operators, and that this bias was reinforced by the evidence given by witnesses and experts. What was clear to the Council was the duty of elected officials to see that any profits accruing from the tramways were ploughed back into the general relief of the rates. Surpluses could also be used to upgrade the system and keep pace with contemporary developments in electric traction.

Modern readers will not be surprised that the public v private debate has its roots in history, as demonstrated by this Report, and still has echoes which reach to the present day. The 1905 Commission was not disposed to recommend that the LCC be granted total control of the Greater London tramways. Nor were the Commission members of a mind to see such a municipal body, as the LCC, dominate the proposed London Traffic Board.

The closing debate in the tramway recommendations was on the local authority power of veto, which had been used frequently to stifle tramway development. The situation as then existed was described by the Royal Commission:

. . . *The London County Council, when promoting a tramway scheme, must get the consent of any Metropolitan Borough Council which may be concerned as road authority, or, in case of a through route, of two thirds of the road authorities. On the other hand, the LCC can use the same check as the local authority in order to defeat any other promoters who seek to construct tramways within their area, either under the Tramway Act 1870, or by method of Private Bill.*

This right of veto, as enshrined in the 1870 Act, was known as STANDING ORDER 22. Needless to say, witnesses called from those local authorities, which were opposed to the extension of tramways throughout central London, were most vociferous in their support of Standing Order 22. The conclusions reached by the Commission were as follows:

There is no doubt that tramway development has been seriously checked by the operation of these vetoes, and, although it is not suggested that any unworthy use has been made of them in London, it is clear that the veto is sometimes exercised without due regard to the importance of establishing through tramway communication.

We have come to the conclusion that the best course is to abolish the veto in all cases, but to provide that, in Greater London, the county councils and the Corporation of the City of London shall have a preferential right to construct any tramways in their districts . . .

It was obvious in the evidence to the Commission that the right of veto was being abused in some quarters, notably in the City of London. However, any overtly critical reference to this obstructive behaviour was absent in the findings of the Commission.

Chapter nine of the Report deals with the establishment of the proposed London Traffic Board, which would act as one unified, regulatory body for railways, tramways, tubes and buses in the metropolitan area. The general consensus of opinion seemed to be that a statutory board ought to be set up with specific powers and duties – a board, furthermore, which would avoid interfering with the functions of the existing local authorities. This new organisation would also be charged with the responsibility for highway planning, traffic regulation and construction of houses on green field sites within the boundaries of Greater London.

Appointees to the Board should not have any conflicting business interests, not should they be active in local politics. An exception to this rule would be the appointment of one member by the LCC, and one member by the City of London. Above all, the Board should maintain a conciliatory

and friendly attitude to all the interested parties, both public and private.

The aforementioned plans were very worthy of consideration, but they were in advance of their time. In 1905 the privately owned transport undertakings were still thinking of making increased profits from the travelling public. On the other hand, London's municipal tramways were in the throes of expanding, and – in many cases – interconnecting their networks. The promise of municipal trams paying back considerable sums of money for the relief of the rates was a very real one. Therefore, there was insufficient impetus for all the operators to sit round the table and hammer out a coherent policy, which could lead to the formation of a joint board.

As we now know, transport co-ordination in the capital came with the formation of the London Passenger Transport Board in July 1933. Circumstances then were different – traffic congestion and private car ownership had increased, trams were not making the profits they used to, and the expanding population demanded a new approach to commuting from home to office. Also in 1933, the political will existed to effect changes; this was not the case in the first decade of the twentieth century.

There were two members of the Commission who felt that they could not support the final report. Sir Joseph C. Dimsdale and Sir George C. T. Bartley were adamant that the power of veto over tramways should not be abolished. Readers of this book may judge the validity of Sir J. C. Dimsdale's arguments for themselves:

It seems, therefore, manifest that the right of veto upon the construction of tramways in the City should be preserved, so that aggravation of existing evils from that cause may be capable of prevention by the City authorities. The streets of the City from their narrowness and irregularity being obviously unsuited for tramways to be placed in them, the carrying capacity of the roadways would be diminished, and the risk of accident both to persons and vehicles would be increased if they were allowed.

It is only necessary to call attention to the terrible calamity that might result if a breakdown, or other dislocation of tramway traffic, occurred in the City at the time of a fire there, so as to prevent the necessary and rapid action of the Fire Brigade and their engines: in such a case another Great Fire of London might ensue.

The last paragraph of the eminent knight's report is pure theatre. As for the rest of his opinions, they can all be challenged. Provincial tramway systems serving towns and cities all seemed to overcome *the intractable and unique problems*, which the City of London might face. Further on, in this addendum to the official report, Sir Joseph's ire was directed at the notion of ratepayers footing the bill for *relieving the overcrowding of the poor class of workpeople in the Metropolis*.

In truth, the City establishment epitomised a form of reactionary politics, which was prevalent in 1905. Further proof of this trend was confirmed by the second minority report presented by Sir George Bartley. He argued that the streets of the City were totally unsuitable for tramcars. He also objected to the sub-surface tramway schemes, one of which would *kill many of the older trees in Hyde Park*. The proposed surface lines fared no better in his estimation. They *would provoke immense opposition: they would injure . . . the property in many districts*. In short, property values would be hit.

The housing problem of those in society not fortunate enough to be concerned with property values, received very short shrift:
It seems to me as not reasonable or politic for the rates to supplement either the tramways or the housing.

As a final nail in the tramway coffin, Sir George was of the opinion that:
The Report seems to suggest that motor

omnibuses will not take the place of tramways as a means of popular locomotion. This may be so, but the evidence does not appear to be conclusive either way, though tending rather in favour of motor omnibuses than the reverse.

On this matter, he was spot on, and over the next few decades the motor bus would eventually reign supreme as a short term solution to London's traffic problems.

To end this chapter, it is worth quoting those witnesses to the Royal Commission who were directly involved in the promotion of the London County Council Tramways. The following people all contributed to the LCC's submission: J. W. Benn, S. G. Burgess, W. H. Dickinson, C. M. G. Fitzmaurice, G. L. Gomme, E. Harper, H. E. Hayward, W. E. Riley, and The Earl Russell. Their evidence, which can only be summarised here, gives a unique insight into the early years of electric tram operation by the LCC.

Mr J. W. Benn had been member of the LCC since 1889, and had served as Chairman of the Highways Committee of the Council for five years, when he was called before the Royal Commission. He stated that it was Council policy only to apply for powers to build double track tramways and that his committee was not inclined to consent to company proposals to construct lines within the County of London. He remarked on the failure of the LCC to get a Light Railways Order in 1900 to cover lines from Clapham Common to Kingston Vale, from Deptford to Woolwich and from New Cross to Eltham. It seems the Light Railway Commissioners considered the LCC's submission to be an abuse of the Light Railways Act of 1896. The Act was passed to facilitate rural and interurban communication, and it was considered by the Commissioners that purely urban or suburban schemes concerning one or two local authorities did not fall into the ambit of the Act.

Mr Benn promised a complete system of through running cars over an enlarged network. He quoted many facts and figures in his testimony: The cost per mile of single track on the overhead system was £6,446 to £7,496 depending on the number of traction standards used. Conduit single track worked out at around £13,087 per mile, however, this figure did not allow for special work such as bridge reconstruction. On the new Greenwich line an extra £554 per mile was added by this bridge work.

He cited the low fares offered by the Council's trams, a workman's journey of almost six miles 1,400 yards (10.9km) – Streatham to the Lord Wellington, Old Kent Road – was charged at one penny. The council had earned a net profit of £72,910 on its tramways south of the Thames in the period 1st January 1899 to March 1903. Electric tramcars, he stated, could replace many horse drawn trams and omnibuses, and this would remove much of the filth and dirt on London's highways.

The Housing Manager of the London County Council, Mr Samuel G. Burgess was adamant in his support of moving folk from overcrowded areas out to the new suburbs. In this respect, he felt that the electrification of the tramways would play a significant role in supplying *a cheap and rapid means of locomotion* for those working people who had to be rehoused.

Alderman W. H. Dickinson's main concern was the extension of suburban and tube railway services. On tramway matters, he did say that the LCC would welcome the abolition of the Metropolitan Boroughs' power of veto over new routes. He went on to remark that, in road widening schemes necessary for double track, the LCC paid one third of the cost, the rest being shared equally between the LCC Highways Department and the local Metropolitan Borough.

The Chief Engineer of the LCC, Mr C. M. G. Fitzmaurice, was one of the star witnesses in terms of his knowledge, which was acquired from on site experience. He presented the Commission with an in depth description of road and highway engineering as applied to day-to-day conditions in the metropolis. He informed the members of the Committee that the new fifty-foot (15.2 metres) wide roadway on Vauxhall Bridge had been designed to take conduit tram tracks. Further, that the sub-surface tramway beneath Kingsway was budgeted at £247,000, and that the cost of this tramway subway was much less than a deep level tube railway. On the topic of new highways, the LCC, he stated, had their own plans for a north-south thoroughfare from Holborn to Crystal Palace. For this project, three designs of road had been considered.

16197   ELECTRIC TRAM TERMINUS.
BLACKFRIARS ROAD. LONDON S. E.

A three track terminal layout and a tram shelter went some way to alleviate the rush hour problems in Blackfriars Road. Buses of course were not affected by the intransigence of the City authorities, nor did they pay rates to the respective metropolitan boroughs.

Type A was 160 feet (48.7 metres) wide with a double track tramway on the surface and a subway tramway for single deck trams underneath. Type B was 100 feet (30.4 metres) wide with motor traffic on the surface and tramway traffic underneath the roadway. Four tracks were proposed, two for slow, local traffic, and two express tracks for through trams. Type C was similar to Type A, but single deck trams were to be carried in deep level tubes instead of a sub-surface alignment.

Mr Fitzmaurice also gave insights into other Council plans. He said that powers had been obtained in 1902 to construct a tramway across Putney Bridge and that this tramway would eventually become part of a north-south through route. The LCC and the LUT had also tried to promote a Bill to cross Hammersmith Bridge, but without success. The construction of a tramway subway connecting the new lines at Hammersmith Broadway with those at Bishopsgate had also been the subject of a feasibility survey. The Chief Engineer remarked that this project would be almost a million pounds cheaper than a deep level tube railway. He implied that a shallow, sub-surface tramway could carry as many passengers as a tube railway. He also maintained that there was work enough for both motor buses and electric tramcars. Each form of transport would find its niche in serving the public.

Mr George Laurence Gomme was Clerk to the London County Council, and his evidence related mostly to the intricacies of obtaining Parliamentary powers for various railway and highway improvements. On the subject of tramways, he proved a champion of the right of the LCC to plan and execute large schemes without the interference of the Metropolitan Boroughs. He cited the construction of the new Kingsway plus the tramway subway as an example where

the local authorities were not asked to contribute funds.

Twice the Commission interviewed the Statistical Officer to the Council, Mr Edgar Harper. From an overview of his evidence, one suspects that his encyclopaedic knowledge of facts and figures was probably too much for his inquisitors to take in at one go! He presented a wide ranging summary of the LCC's activities, and he was particularly supportive of the Council's housing policy. He stated that a working man could be expected to spend one to one and a half hours a day in travelling to and from work, at a cost of one shilling per week. Furthermore, the LCC was particularly concerned to rehouse those workmen (and their families), whose wages did not exceed thirty shillings per week. For these folk, the tramway was a vital element in their lives.

The number of buses on the road also interested Mr Harper and he calculated that in 1903 the length of streets traversed by buses was 242 miles (389km). Bus fares, he noted, were higher than tram fares. In 1902, a total of 350,180,257 passengers carried by tramways in Greater London paid on average 1.03d per head; two omnibus companies in the same year carried 279,466,557 passengers at an average of 1.39d per head. He further stated that most bus services were slow and started too late in the morning to be of much use to working people. Horse and motor buses also damaged the road surface and could run on any street without sanction from any authority.

Mr Harry Haward was Comptroller of the London County Council, and, as such, he had responsibility for overseeing the financial affairs of the local authority. We learn from his evidence that up to 31st March 1903, the LCC had expended £3,650,000 on tramways and £750,000 on

power supply. A further outlay was in prospect for the future; this would amount to £200,000 for the purchase of horse tramway companies and £2,720,000 for conversion of the remaining tramways to electric traction. This latter sum did not include the costs of conversion of the narrow gauge WSELT line from Greenwich to Plumstead. It also assumed that about half the new lines would be electrified on the overhead trolley system. Finally, new lines (i.e. not horse tram conversions) were budgeted at £1,077,000 – this sum included the requisite street widening costs. Augmented power supply facilities would add a further £2,000,000 to the end bill.

The Comptroller predicted a rosy future for the LCC tramways, based on the fact that the new electric trams were yielding a profit of 6d per car mile. On the existing mileage, he calculated, this would eventually add, per annum, an amount of £668,000 to the Council's coffers. Tramway debt would thus be diminished; provision had been made for a capital expenditure fund for further investments in rolling stock and repairs to the system.

Mr W. E. Riley, Architect to the LCC, discussed the layout of the streets of London and the chief congestion spots of the capital. He was principally concerned about the design and construction of broad avenues, which would bring traffic relief to many central areas. He also championed sub-surface tramways that could alleviate the contemporary nonsense of a ring of isolated tramway termini around the heart of the capital.

The testimony of The Right Hon. The Earl Russell added an aristocratic endorsement to the Council Tramways. The Earl had served on the LCC since 1895, and was active in promoting electric tramways. At one time he was Chairman of the Highways Committee, and he had been in several scraps with J. W. Benn and J. Allen Baker over the policy adopted towards the North Metropolitan Tramways Company. Earl Russell wanted to extend the operating company's lease; Benn and the other progressives opposed this policy. During his interview with the Royal Commission the Earl's sense of *noblesse oblige* was in marked contrast to the whining of the servants of mammon ensconced in the City. He confined himself to remarks on the nature of street widths and the advisability of providing fixed stopping places for both buses and trams. The present situation, he opined, was chaotic and led to traffic congestion.

The Elephant & Castle was an important tramway junction. It was also high on the list of potential traffic congestion black spots. At the bottom of the picture a four wheel, open top Class B car heads for Newington Causeway. Coming in the opposite direction is Class C Car 264, southbound for Streatham. On the far left, a D Class bogie car emerges from London Road on its journey to Blackwall Tunnel; it is following a top covered B Class tram.

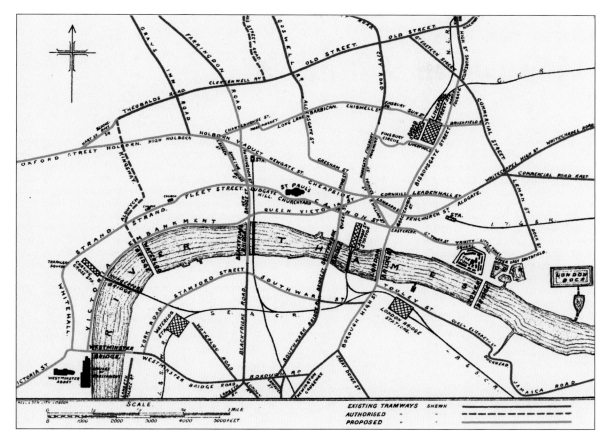

EXISTING TRAMWAYS SHEWN ————————
AUTHORISED " " - - - - - - - -
PROPOSED " " - · - · - · - · -

This map was appended to the testimony of Stephen Sellon. It presents an interesting contrast to the findings of the Commission. No doubt the City Fathers were apoplectic on seeing their precious square mile crisscrossed by tram routes!

We leave the final words to Stephen Sellon, Chief Engineer to the British Electric Traction Company. He had had some experience in dealing with the LCC and other local authorities. His testimony painted the LCC in a less favourable light than the previous witnesses would have wished:

The British Electric Traction Company are the lessees of the electric tramways owned by Croydon Corporation, and in 1902, promoted a Bill for powers to construct tramways outside districts with the Croydon lines, and also to join up the Mitcham Light Railways, which have been transferred to the Company by the Croydon Rural District Council . . .

This proposition included a line from the northern end of the Mitcham line to the Tooting terminus of the South London Tramways owned and worked by the County Council.

The Company approached the Council with a view to obtaining their consent as the local authority, and, in order to facilitate the construction of this line, offered to transfer the portion within the Council's area to them, the Council then to grant a lease of the line to the Company. The Council, however, showed great disinclination to enter into negotiations and withheld their consent . . .

Mr Sellon was fighting his corner, as would be expected from a leading light in the BET. His points have some validity; they demonstrate the complex relationship in the argument of municipal enterprise

versus private profit. Co-operation not confrontation was his message. Although one must also take into account that it was frustrating for Croydon trams, or any other metropolitan tramway company, not to reach their natural traffic objectives. It would be naive to expect that Mr Sellon was acting out of purely altruistic motives. Company owned trams that reached important urban areas via LCC rails would naturally enhance their earning potential.

He summed up his opinion regarding the role of tramways in the metropolis and the formation of a new unitary transport board for London:

I believe the only way of dealing with the street traffic in London is by tramways on the surface and in shallow subways. The particular points where tramways should either rise to the surface or fall underground is a question of detail proper for settlement by such a Commission as I suggest (Mr Sellon had suggested previously the setting up of a Tribunal with powers to deal with all urban and suburban traffic – author).

I am of the opinion that along any street the electric tramcar is a great assistance in relieving congestion, provided that the tramways are under unified management, and have sufficient extent to avoid termini in crowded places.

Many of the streets in London are congested by reason of no proper regulation of classes of traffic.

Others are limited in their effective area by the genius who puts up centre poles for

lighting or places a cabstand in the middle of an important thoroughfare (Victoria Street) . . .

In fact I am of the opinion that a single working authority for the whole of the London Tramways will afford the only satisfactory solution . . .

The witness continued his lengthy testimony be referring to other transport modes in London – the buses and underground railways – and drawing unfavourable comparisons between their performance and the potential of an integrated tram system with through routes across central London. He submitted a plan of proposed cross-London links and added several detailed street plans showing the effect of parking problems on the flow of traffic. There was much here for the Royal Commission to consider.

Thus the LCC and other witnesses left the arena and the members of the Royal Commission withdrew to formulate the conclusions, which have already been cited in this chapter. Cynics might allude to the fact that London's road to traffic hell was paved with well intentioned reports, and that the 1905 document made a few ripples in the metropolitan pond, but then sank without trace. The Royal Commission on London Traffic, with its futuristic vision of broad avenues, express tramways, sub-surface tramways, cottage estates and cheap fares for all, was consigned to the archives. Perhaps, one day, some of the ideas will be resurrected, and Londoners will receive the transport system they deserve!

CHAPTER FOUR
Vision of the Future

AS WE HAVE noted, the proposals of the Royal Commission in respect of the expansion of the London County Council Tramways were largely obstructed by vested interests. However, the Council already had one prestige project underway when the Royal Commission convened. An Act of Parliament in 1902 had granted powers for the first section of the Kingsway Subway. The projected sub-surface tramway was to pass through an area of great social deprivation. The Clare Market, Strand Improvement Scheme of 1895 was initiated by the LCC to eradicate an overpopulated and disease ridden part of central London. The mortality rate of this inner city slum was two and a half times the metropolitan average. Clearly, something had to be done. The work of property demolition got under way, and no less than 3,700 people had to be rehoused by the LCC. In 1899 the Council planners altered their tack somewhat, when they envisaged a new thoroughfare from Holborn to the Strand. This street, named Kingsway, was included in a revised Clare Market scheme.

The idea of tramway subways had been planted firmly in the mind of J. Allen Baker during his American visit of 1898. In Boston, Massachusetts, he had observed the success of the Tremont Street Subway, which had opened on 1st September 1897. Councillor Baker was mightily impressed by this new rapid transit facility, which in places featured four parallel underground tracks. The subway also boasted six stations to which access was gained by stairways from the streets above. A second Council delegation to the United States in 1901 confirmed that the Boston subway had contributed substantially to the freedom of movement in the city. The obvious benefit of such an underground tramway was the avoidance of traffic congestion on the surface. All round, the service was speeded up, and passenger numbers rose.

Since Kingsway cut across central London, the new highway plus subterranean tramway seemed a logical solution to the problem of connecting the two halves of the LCC tram system. The Council also reasoned that objectors to a surface tramway would be placated if the through route did not impinge on their line of vision! All well and good – however, there was one fly in the ointment. The proposed southern

terminal of the subway adjacent to Waterloo Bridge and the Victoria Embankment still had no rail connection to the tramways in South London. Parliament, in its wisdom, had resolutely refused to grant track construction powers over Westminster Bridge and along the Embankment.

Construction of subway commenced before land clearance of all the slum dwellings. The *cut and cover* method was employed. This technique was well known to Londoners of a previous generation who had witnessed the building of the Metropolitan and District underground railways. The major difference in the Kingsway project being that existing main thoroughfares were unaffected by the work, and road traffic was not disrupted. The Chief Engineer on site was, not unnaturally, Mr Maurice Fitzmaurice. He and Mr Rider followed up their success on the Streatham route by designing and testing the conduit

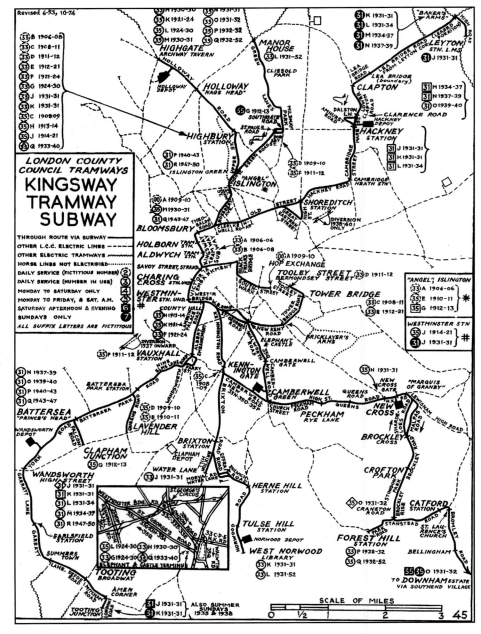

This map by J.C.Gillham details the history of tram services using the Kingsway Subway.

enduring monument to one of the most farsighted transport innovations in London. Tourists today can still inspect the remains preserved with conduit tracks in situ.

Underground Tramway, London

fittings needed for the running tunnels. Single deck operation was envisaged, although it was clear that standard double deck cars would be used either side of the subway. It has been suggested that the Council was unwilling to go to the greater expense of expanding the facilities to cope with standard cars, and this theme was taken up in an article, which appeared on 9th June 1904.

The tramways will be laid down for the conduit system, of course; what is not so easy to understand is that the headway given is 3ft 6ins (1.07 metres) short of that necessary for a double deck car; so that when connection

is made, through cars will all have to be single deck ones, and, until that connection is made, passengers will have to change cars at Theobalds Road, unless all the electric cars running to that spot are single deck cars. The extra cost of this additional depth would have been enormous it is true, but pity 'tis all the same.

Wicked tongues might suggest that the Council have not the courage of their convictions, and that, considering the enormous additional cost of the conduit system over almost all their lines, the cost of the extra lowering would have been but a small proportion to the total expenditure.

The probable reasons for the adoption of single deck operation were centred on the access slope to the northern portal – the gradient from Theobalds Road, at 1 in 10

L.C.C. TRAM SUBWAY, KINGSWAY, LONDON.

Above The northern ramp to the subway was a favourite for postcard photographers. The metal pole on the roof of Car 569 strikes the lever of the signal lamp, which will remain at danger until this car has cleared Holborn Station. The whole impression is one of the utmost modernity. Londoners were very proud of their new sub-surface rapid transit system.
J.B. Gent Collection

Right We are looking along Southampton Row in a northwesterly direction. The car coming from Theobalds Road on the right will shortly descend into the subway. On the way down it will pass the ascending tram, which is en route to Highbury Station.
J.B. Gent Collection

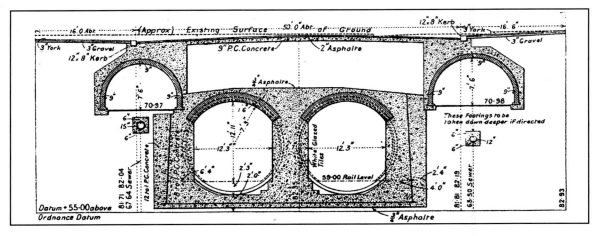

Section of double tunnel at the northern entrance of iron tubes under Holborn.

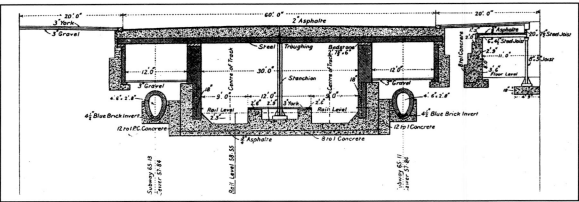

Section through Queen Street (Holborn) Station.

(10%), was considered too steep for double deck trams. There were also several pipes and sewers which imposed height restrictions on the completed subway. Finally, the Highways Committee was certainly influenced by American best practice, whereby frequent services supplied by single deck cars seemed to avoid the loading and unloading delays associated with passengers having to negotiate staircases on double deck tramcars.

A gentle downhill gradient governed the journey from the northernmost station, originally christened Queen Street Station, to the proposed southern exit by Victoria Embankment. For many of the technical details it is worth quoting a contemporary technical article written in 1904 by Robert H. Smith, Professor Emeritus of Engineering at the University of Birmingham. The LCC Chief Engineer, Mr Maurice Fitzmaurice, aided Professor Smith in his article.

The London County Council is now completing an extremely important shallow subway tramline under the new street to be called King's Way . . .
The new street on the surface is 100 feet (30.4 metres) wide, 60 feet (18.2 metres) of carriageway, and 20 feet (6.1 metres) of pavement on either side.
Starting from the north end at Vernon Place, the two tramlines descend from the street level by a sharp incline of 1 in 10 (10%) gradient and 345 feet (105.1 metres) in length, the first 170 feet (51.8 metres) being in the open. The next

75 feet (22.8 metres) is covered masonry work, and this is succeeded by 250 feet (76.2 metres) length of duplex tube tunnel . . .
The first steep incline is followed by 200 feet (60.9 metres) of 1 in 200 (0.5%) downgrade, and this again by 120 feet (36.5 metres) of steep 1 in 10 (10%) upgrade. This dip is necessary to take the subway under High Holborn and under the large sewers and other pipes that run east and west along the line of Holborn. The rails are here 31 feet (9.4 metres) below the road surface in Holborn. At Gate Street, at the end of the 1 in 10 (10%) upgrade, the depth below the surface in King's Way is 17 feet (5.1 metres), and this depth is maintained until the dip to pass under the Strand is reached. The down gradient along the King's Way is 1 in 105 (0.9%). The dip under the Strand is commenced at the north end of Aldwych, the great new crescent on the Strand, which is one of the fine features of the clearance of slum property. The dip is at 1 in 20 (5%) gradient through 490 feet (149.3 metres) length, and 1 in 108 (0.9%) through 210 feet (64 metres) length in passing under the Strand. An almost level stretch of 450 feet (137.1 metres) brings the tramway to the Embankment at the same level as the roadway. From this terminus stairs lead up to the higher level of Lancaster Place and Waterloo Bridge. In passing under the Strand the rails are 34 feet (10.3

metres) below the road surface. The total length is a little over 3,500 feet (1.07km).
At intervals are built underground station platforms. Access to each of these is obtained by a wide and easy staircase, descending from an island pavement in the middle of the King's Way. Underground entrances from the side pavements are unfortunately impossible, because of the pipe subways.
The subway is 20 feet (6.1 metres) wide by 13 feet (3.9 metres) deep. The walls are throughout faced with white glazed tiles. The floor and foundation bed are of concrete, 4 feet 3 inches (1.3 metres) thick, with two layers of asphalt laid in it. The concrete walls are 5 feet (1.5 metres) thick in their lower part and 3 feet 6 inches (1.07 metres) in their upper halves, alongside of which are built two semicircular arched subways for pipes. These are each 12 feet (3.6 metres) wide by 7 feet 6 inches (2.2 metres) deep, and under each is laid a new sewer of large size. The roof of the subway is made of trough girders. The troughing is 12 inches (305 mm) deep, of 32 inch (813 mm) pitch, and of half inch (13 mm) thick steel plate. On the top of each wall is a heavy coping of York stone, and on this are bedded the ends of the trough girders in cement concrete with two thicknesses of tarred roofing felt interposed. The troughs are filled with concrete to a small depth above the metal, and over this are laid two successive

layers of asphalt, each about one inch (25 mm) thick. Over this is laid a bed of concrete and the road surface in asphalt. The depth from the bottom of the troughs to the crown of the road surface is about 3 feet 6 inches (1.07 metres) making, with the 13 feet (3.9 metres) depth of the subway, about 16 feet 6 inches (5.1 metres) from rails to roadway.

Where the depth below road surface is greater, a brick arch roof is substituted for the flat trough structure, the former being very cheaper. The height from rail to the intrados of the arch is 14 feet (4.2 metres).

In passing under Holborn and under the Strand, the subway splits into two circular tube ways, each 14 feet 10 inches (4.5 metres) internal diameter. These were driven with a Greathead shield by hand excavation, and are lined with heavy cast iron segments.

In the stations the subway is increased to 30 feet (9.1 metres) in width, with 14 feet 9 inches (4.4 metres) depth to the underside of the roof. The station is partially lighted from the roof to the extent of the overhead island, and it also receives some daylight from the staircase, which is wide and of small depth. It will also be well lighted electrically. The station platform is placed between the up and down lines.

Readers will note from this detailed description that the Kingsway Subway was built to last! It was also built by manual labour. Picks and shovels were the order of the day. It is interesting that, for some of the project, a Greathead shield was used. This method was employed on tube railway construction and was also utilised in the building of the Rotherhithe Tunnel, which opened in 1908. The spoil from the tunnel was carried away in one horse springless dobbin carts and then tipped on a site adjacent to Blackfriars Bridge. In order to aid the equine effort, a traction engine pulling two trailers was also employed on the task. The spoil was then loaded into barges to be shipped down the River Thames to reclamation work at Tilbury.

As construction of the subway was proceeding, the approach tracks along Theobalds Road and Rosebery Avenue to the Angel, Islington were rebuilt for electric traction. Regarding the southern access from the Embankment, the Council were not minded to wait upon the procrastination of Parliament. The Highways Committee resolved to open the subway as far as Aldwych Station in the hope that connecting lines to the other half of the system would be sanctioned in the near future. Just beyond the temporary Aldwych terminus, depot and servicing facilities were installed in the tunnel. These were used for the new, all metal, Class F single deck trams, which were constructed in a batch of 16 by the United Electric Car Company of Preston. Similar looking vehicles, this time built by Brush of Loughborough, formed a group of 34 trams designated Class G. The all metal

construction of both classes was specified to cut down the risk of an on board electrical fault developing into a major conflagration. Traditional tramcars had a high percentage of wooden bodywork, which was impregnated with paint and varnish, and which, in certain circumstances, was eminently combustible.

Top **Car 556 is pictured at the crossover just north of Aldwych Station. This was the end of the line before the opening of connecting tracks to the Victoria Embankment. Note the refuges set into the tunnel walls.** LCCTT

Above **A later view of the southern entrance shows Car 560. Some traces of the former connection to eastbound Embankment tracks can be detected.**

Below **Original specification for Class F car equipped with platform doors.**

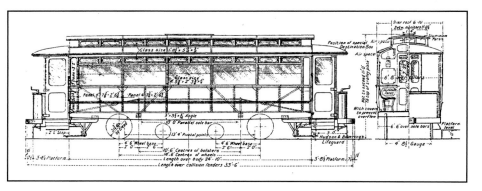

Two official inspections took place, on 29th December 1905 and on 23rd February 1906, before permission was granted for public service. Power for working the trams had to be purchased from the Metropolitan Electric Supply Company, as the new LCC generating facility at Greenwich was still incomplete. The grand opening of the first section of the Kingsway Subway came on Saturday, 24th February, when Mr J. W. Benn piloted a special car, painted blue and gold for the occasion, from Aldwych to the Angel and back. The journey took twelve minutes, which was a marked improvement on previous horsecar timings. Unfortunately after the bigwigs had departed, a rather nasty incident marred the first passenger trip when Driver Walter English was slashed with a whip from a competing

brought to a successful conclusion by the extension along the Embankment and across Westminster Bridge.

After a titanic struggle with the anti tram lobby, the Council's Bill for tramway access to the southern portal of the Kingsway Subway finally passed through Parliament and gained the Royal Assent on 4th August 1906. The fight to get trams across Westminster Bridge had lasted over 36 years! Messrs Dick, Kerr and Company commenced construction work on 3rd September; the tracks were offset to the northern side of the bridge, and against the eastern kerb of the Victoria Embankment. This arrangement left plenty of space for other road vehicles and gave the trams a private right of way in spirit, if not in name. In a lighter vein, rails in Stangate on the

approach to the bridge had to be repositioned and this led to a dispute with Lambeth Borough Council. An underground public convenience recently erected by Lambeth was found to be in the way of the new Vauxhall to Stangate connection. It was therefore demolished by the LCC and they had to pay Lambeth £3,500 for the privilege! Another matter of public convenience was the opening to passengers of the Embankment tramway, which occurred on 15th December 1906.

The entrance to the Kingsway Subway, situated a few feet to the south of the abutment carrying Waterloo Bridge, was joined to the Embankment tramway by a triangular junction. This was referred to in railway parlance as *a cocked hat*, and the rails themselves were inserted into a roadway, which was directly above the underground District Railway. The whole structure was supported by a platform of iron girders. Further back from the entrance, the new subterranean tramway had to negotiate some tricky engineering work associated with the brick arches under Wellington Street. Eventually it was decided not to place a station under the corner of Wellington Street and the Strand. This decision speeded up work somewhat and an official inspection by Col Yorke on 9th April 1908, led to the inauguration of through services the following day. Trams ran from Highbury Station to Tower Bridge, and from Highbury Station to Kennington Gate. The route from the Angel, Islington to Highbury Station was opened on 16th November 1906. The cars working the Kingsway Subway to Highbury Station service were originally kept at a former horsecar depot in St Paul's Road, Highbury. This arrangement continued until the opening of Holloway Depot on 28th November 1907.

horse bus driver. This cost the bus driver his liberty for the rest of the day, because a police constable promptly arrested him. No doubt his passengers were only too happy to take the tram!

Electric conduit tramways had finally arrived in North London, and the impetus was now on the Council to see that the whole Kingsway Subway scheme was

Above **The photographer stands on the old Waterloo Bridge to get this shot of Car 574 as it emerges from the southern portal to the Kingsway Subway. The tracks leading towards the right of the picture were only used regularly in 1909–10. Thereafter they fell into disuse.**

Right **Ready for the off! Just outside Holloway Depot a proud tram crew is depicted on Car 585. The cross capital service from Highbury Station to Tower Bridge Road took between 47 and 50 minutes. There was a tram every six minutes and the through fare was 3d. Just to the left of the destination box one can make out a horizontal metal rod. This was used to strike a signal lever at the entrance to the Kingsway Subway.**
B.J. Cross Collection

TOWER BRIDGE

585

Car 558 is shown further along the route at St John Street by the Angel, Islington. A horse bus and several cabs circle the new electric intruder warily. Apprehension sometimes spilled over into obstruction and violence, when cabmen and horse bus drivers realised their livelihoods were going to be affected by the faster electric trams. LCCTT

Thus, after immense effort, the two halves of the network were finally connected, although only single deck cars could make the full journey. The members of the Council were not content, however, to rest on their laurels, as the other major project, the building of Greenwich Power Station, neared completion. A short technical article, written by Mr J. H. Rider and published in April 1909 served as an introduction to the site.

The Greenwich Generating Station is situated on the River Thames. The site covers an area of approximately three and three-quarter acres (1.5ha), and has a frontage to the river of 240ft (73.1m), to Hoskins Street of 648ft (197.5m), and to Old Woolwich Road of 308ft (93.8m).

The general layout consists of a boiler house 445ft (135.6 metres) long, by 80ft (24.3m) wide, an engine room of the same dimensions, and auxiliary buildings adjoining. The buildings were designed by Mr W. E. Riley, the Council's architect, to the requirements of the author . . .

The four chimney shafts have an internal diameter of 14ft (4.2m), the first two being at a height of 250ft (76.2m), and the last two of 182ft (55.4m). The two latter chimneys were not carried above 182ft (55.4m) in consequence of the agreement with the Admiralty, in connection with the Greenwich Observatory.

Coaling arrangements – a large pier has been constructed, which projects into the River Thames for a distance of about 118ft (35.9m) in front of the river wall. The pier is T shaped in plan, and has a river frontage of 200ft (60.9m), with a width of 40ft 6ins (12.3m) . . . Tracks to the standard gauge of four feet eight and a half inches (1435mm) are laid on the pier, and the coaling wagons are hauled by electric locomotives, the current being supplied through a third rail at 550 volts pressure. The locomotives consist of

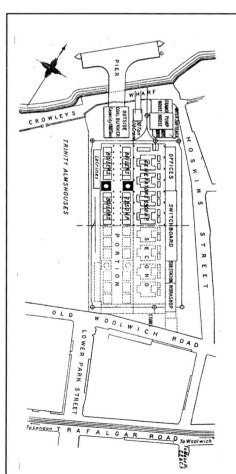

Left **Plan of the first stage of Greenwich Power Station. Note the tram tracks in Trafalgar Road.**

Above **The Tramways Generating Station and its four chimneys dwarf the Trinity Almshouses, Greenwich and the LCC steamboat moored by the pier. On the coaling pier, steam cranes wait for the next barge load of fuel to feed the boilers. Note that the extension towards Trafalgar Road has yet to be built.**
J.B. Gent Collection

Right **The steam powered generators seen here were installed on the advice of J. H. Rider, who based his opinion on good results obtained in a New York power station. The engines are of the vertical horizontal type. Each engine was connected to an alternator, which produced 6,600 volts, which in turn was transformed into 550 volts DC traction current.**
J.B. Gent Collection

ordinary four wheeled tramway trucks, with the usual motor and control equipment, and a light steel house for the protection of the driver. Both locomotives and wagons are fitted with automatic couplers for use in shunting.

Following on from the last couple of sentences, one must presume that the LCC held a British tramway record of sorts. At one time or other the Council ran railed vehicles propelled by horse power, cable, conduit electric, overhead trolley, petrol electric, surface contact electric, third rail electric, and for good measure there was a steam tank engine at Charlton Works!

Mr Rider's article goes on to describe the artesian wells, which delivered clean water to the boilers. These in turn produced the steam to drive reciprocating engines, which powered alternators. The station's output was 6,600 volts, which was conveyed to sub-stations, there to be converted to the traction current of 550 volts DC. Greenwich Power Station opened on 26th May 1906, and during the following year the construction of the second part of the building was put in hand. In early 1909 further generating equipment was installed and the station was fully operational, supplying the needs of the growing tramway system.

The final topic to be covered in this chapter is the construction and opening of a new Central Repair Depot at Charlton, not that far away from Greenwich Power Station. The Council had inspected several likely sites for the CRD and eventually a 6.9 acre (2.8ha) plot adjacent to the South Eastern & Chatham Railway's Angerstein Wharf branch was selected. Construction work began in 1907 and the depot was opened on 6th March 1909. The buildings, which were designed by W. E. Riley, Architect to the LCC, were steel framed with outer walls of plain stock brick. The main works had a projected capacity of 600 cars per annum, but this was quickly found to be insufficient. A revised estimate of 770 trams a year seemed nearer the mark, and permission for an extension was soon granted. The new work plus a railway connection to the SECR was completed by the summer of 1911.

In a paper given at the 1909 annual conference of the Municipal Tramways Association, W. E. Ireland, Rolling Stock Superintendent of the London County Council Tramways set out a description of the Central Repair Depot at Charlton:

The buildings are arranged on a definite scheme for dealing expeditiously with the cars during the two weeks each has to be in the shops for its annual overhaul and renovation.

The Metropolitan Police regulations require the bodywork and painting of each car to be thoroughly renovated once in every twelve months. Advantage is therefore taken of this regulation to systematically overhaul and put into first class condition the whole of the mechanical and electrical equipments of the cars. The layout of the depot is arranged so that regular and synchronous progression of the work in several shops is insured.

Routine for dealing with cars: The works superintendent issues forms, which are forwarded to the rolling stock superintendent, requesting the cars

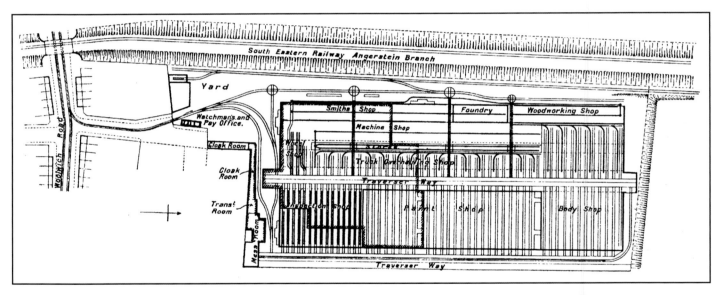

Above **Plan of the Central Repair Depot at Charlton as originally constructed. Note the connecting siding to the Angerstein Railway branch.**

Right **Employees and tramcars line up for a panoramic view of the main traverser at Charlton Works and some of the stabling roads. The workforce is engaged on body repairs; some of the trams have been jacked up to remove their trucks and running gear.** LCCTT

D Class Car 387 has been shunted into the paint shop and is now waiting the finishing touches from the Charlton craftsmen. Adjustable scaffolding either side of the car enabled painters to work more efficiently.

becoming due for renovation in any one week to be transferred from the several car sheds from which they operate in service to the repair depot on the Sunday night. Each car after entering the gateway, shown in the plan view, sheds its plough by means of the special run out arrangement shown. A small steam locomotive then draws the car into the depot through the porch like entrance, and on to a specially constructed shallow traverser, by means of which it is taken into the inspection shop.

Here on the following morning, an inspector carefully examines the car, noting the repairs required, and compiles a detailed list of the necessary work for the information of the superintendent. While the car is in the inspection shop, the brake rigging and other parts of the trucks and the equipment are disconnected, bearing caps and bottom halves of the gear cases taken down ready for dismantling.

The car is again drawn on to the traverser, a pneumatic jack placed under each side of both headstocks, and the body lifted clear of the trucks. The traverser is then moved along the pit, carrying the trucks from beneath the body to a point immediately under one of the lighting wells provided in the floor of the gallery above. Here the motors are lifted by an electric travelling crane running on a gantry above the gallery to the motor overhauling shop, and the trucks sent into the truck shop on the western side of the traverser pit.

The body is then placed upon a temporary truck and taken into the body shop for the attention of body makers and wiremen. The work required on the trucks, motors and bodies usually takes four days to complete, at the end of which time the whole car is reassembled ready for the paint shop.

The paint shop is cleared of its finished cars every Sunday, and the overhauled and reassembled cars placed in readiness for the painters to start their part of the work the first thing on the following morning. The painting and varnishing occupies a week, it being a rule that each week's

output of renovated cars is ready for inspection by noon on the second Saturday following the day upon which they were received at the depot.

This extract gives a broad picture of the functions of the CRD. Obviously, there was a trained workforce attending to various other electrical and mechanical repairs necessary to give each tram a clean bill of health. As can be seen from the accompanying plan, the place had all the skills and the equipment to service any tramcar in the fleet. Work was organised on a modern production line system, and it was organised to ensure that at every stage quality control was paramount.

The LCC had achieved much in the commissioning of the Kingsway Subway, Charlton Repair Depot and Greenwich Power Station. The Council was now a major player in the provision of transport to many millions of Londoners. It had a firm base on which to expand, and the years preceding the outbreak of the First World War would see the brown and cream tramcars multiply and conquer.

CHAPTER FIVE
Tramways Triumphant

Class E Car 733 entered
service in spring 1907.
This type of vehicle and its
body styling represent
the quintessential London
tramcar. Robust and

mechanically reliable with
few frills, these vehicles
soldiered on well into
London Transport days.
B.J. Cross Collection

THE EDWARDIAN AGE ushered in the electric tramcar, and the London County Council, as we have seen, had expended much time and effort in establishing the basis of a tramway network for Londoners. The technology of the conduit was proving reliable, even though construction bills were steep. Traffic receipts were producing a healthy surplus, and competition in the form of horse buses had been swept aside. The frequent electric cars, operating with cheap fares, had taken a large bite out of the revenue formerly earned by suburban steam railways. Increasingly, commuters in the inner London boroughs were turning to the Council tramcars. All signs seemed encouraging, and the publication of the Royal Commission Report had bestowed a leading role on the LCC in the provision of passenger transport for the metropolis of the future.

However, life is rarely that simple. The 1905 report had also revealed that the forces ranged against the tramcar were vocal and well connected in circles of power and influence. Furthermore, the rapid de-

velopment of the motor bus and the ability of this new fangled machine to serve the streets of the West End and the City had given the LCC's opponents ammunition in their fight to keep tramlines out of central London.

The much vaunted LCC housing policy had also run into some heavy weather. The theory of moving families from unsanitary conditions to new cottage estates was a sound one, however, some disturbing evidence was beginning to appear. It seemed that many families who had been rehoused by the Council, were unable or unwilling to pay the new rents. The incidence of moonlight flits rose, as desperately poor individuals returned to the obscurity of the remaining slums. For those single men at the very bottom of the social ladder there were Council run lodging houses where a bed for the night and some sustenance could be had for sixpence. It was clear that, to help the very poorest in society, to give them a roof over their heads, and to encourage employment and industry, a radical rethink was needed. Above all, the

economics of new estates tied to the provision of expensive conduit tramways came under scrutiny.

The LCC surveyed the housing scene in light of past achievements and forthcoming projects. The Totterdown Fields Estate, which had an area of 39 acres (15.7ha) and lay adjacent to a trunk tram route, was deemed a success. Out county estates at White Hart Lane, Tottenham and at Norbury, Croydon were also served by tramways – the former by the Metropolitan Electric and the latter by Croydon Corporation. Those tenants across the boundary contributed nothing directly to the Council's transport coffers, although of course, many out county residents did use LCC trams as part of their journey to and from work.

The task of building decent accommodation for former slum dwellers was a mammoth one. Land was becoming expensive, and indeed scarce, as was the case in LCC territory north of the Thames. Patently, a new cottage estate could not be fitted into the boundaries of Hampstead or Chelsea without an almighty rumpus from existing residents. It made more sense for the planners to cast their eyes south of the river to the green fields of the south-west and south-east suburbs. A tram route linking Putney, Hammersmith and Harlesden was already in an advanced state of preparation. The projected southern terminal on the Wandsworth side of Putney Bridge opened up the prospect of a new tramway connection to a proposed LCC estate in the Roehampton area.

On the other side of South London, the map revealed a vast tract of land stretching in a north-easterly arc from Lower Sydenham to Woolwich. Isolated settlements existed at South End and Grove Park, but otherwise the vista was one of farmland, rough pasture, cornfields and Kentish orchards. The small community of Eltham, which possessed a Royal Palace of some antiquity, was entirely surrounded by woods and fields. The two local authorities whose writ ran in these parts were the Metropolitan Boroughs of Lewisham and Woolwich. Both authorities were sympathetic to the expansion of the tramway network, and as we shall see, the pastures were indeed *rich* for the LCC in these areas.

The scale of priorities not only encompassed housing provision, but also imposed a timetable on electric tramway construction. First on the agenda was the replacement of the existing horse tram routes. It was acknowledged that main traffic arteries with horsecars were an anachronism and that action was needed urgently to speed up the service for the travelling public. The back street routes served by horse trams were now looked on in a different light. It became increasingly difficult to justify expensive conduit conversions for such routes. Added to the cost of the conduit was the necessity of extensive road widening, property demolition and compensation claims, all of which contributed to the final bill. Either the Council had to persuade local authorities to accept overhead wires or other forms of mechanical traction would have to be employed. Then there was the growing menace of the motor bus. Where these vehicles competed with horse trams, passengers preferred the faster form of transport.

The Council was on safer ground when planning new lines to connect existing suburban centres. Electric traction could tackle gradients, which had defeated horsecars. Therefore, work pushed ahead on expanding the network to connect Camberwell with Lewisham via the Dulwich hills. It was hoped that this new territory for electric trams would stimulate urban development and that passenger numbers would rise as a consequence.

The final part of the future LCC scenario concerned through running with other operators. The Royal Commission had already pointed out that transhipment of the travelling public at boundary points caused congestion and no little ill will on the part of the passengers, who then had to pay another fare to continue their journeys. Such a situation was obviously counter-productive and demanded the immediate attention of all interested parties. To the west, the lines of the London United had already secured a foothold in the Metropolitan Borough of Hammersmith. Electrification of the Harrow Road also brought the prospect of company owned tramcars running through Council territory. To the north, the tracks of the Metropolitan Electric were advancing along main roads towards the LCC boundary. To the east, the municipal systems of metropolitan Essex were interested in gaining inner London termini for their

CAMBERWELL GATE, S.E.

3096.
CARD HOUSE.

services. To the south, Croydon Corporation had constructed a main trunk route from Purley to Norbury, and the South Metropolitan Company had pushed tracks as far as Tooting Junction. Finally, in the far southeast, Bexley UDC Tramways had laid rails as far as Plumstead in anticipation of a new LCC through route from Abbey Wood to Woolwich and beyond.

All the surrounding systems were built to standard gauge and were powered by overhead wires. It was down to the LCC to devise change pits or plough shifts to allow through working over the conduit. Of course, any tram used on a through service then had to be converted to run on both conduit and overhead.

As far as the LCC rolling stock was concerned, the fitting of top covers was proceeding according to plan. New vehicles had been ordered and in 1907–1908 the first trams of the new standard E/1 Class had been delivered. Depot and maintenance facilities had kept pace with the expansion of the fleet, and in 1904, a proposal by Mr Fell to build a central repair depot was to be implemented at Charlton next to the Woolwich Road tramway.

Politics also played a major role in the history of the LCC. It is beyond the province of this book to detail all the intrigues in the corridors of power and the voters' response

to them. Suffice to say that every decision concerning the tramways involved ratepayers' money. The allocation of these financial resources became a political hot potato. Critics were swift to cite the spiralling costs of the conduit; they were also quick to spot unnecessary expenditure on planning surveys for tramways in the West End and the City, where the residents obviously did not want the presence of Council tramcars.

Matters came to a head in the LCC elections of 1907. The Progressives, after eighteen years in power, were voted from office. The incoming Moderates or Conservatives were pledged to rein in Council expenditure and to counteract the dangerous trend of municipal trading. It was no surprise that the tramways' budget was subject to close scrutiny. Whilst the new masters could see the wisdom of converting the remaining horse tram routes, they baulked at the excessive costs of the conduit system. The previous concerns of the Progressives, *vis-à-vis* this method of current collection, were now given a hard edge by the Moderates. Clearly, alternatives had to be found quickly. They could involve persuading Metropolitan Boroughs to accept overhead wires – crudely put, if local town halls vetoed the overhead, they wouldn't get the trams! The Council might also encourage those with an inventive turn of mind to come up with a workable method of surface contact current collection, which did away with the need for allegedly unsightly overhead wires. Instructions were handed down from on high to pursue this line of enquiry. In the meantime, every extension was going to be costed to the last penny. The futuristic schemes advocated by the Royal Commission were pushed so far into the future that they disappeared from

view. The Moderates were well aware that this course of action would be a vote winner amongst the well to do in Kensington, Chelsea, Westminster and Marylebone. These influential citizens could now sleep easy in the knowledge that the working class in their tramcars would not assault their bastions of privilege.

Of course, it would be unfair to tar all Conservatives with the same brush. Some members of the Moderates championed what they would have termed a 'more pragmatic approach' to the matter in hand. This is nowhere better illustrated than in an obituary for the late Frederick Houston Carter, published in the Penge Gazette of 15th March 1918. Mr Carter was a prominent Conservative member of the London County Council.

. . . Before he was elected to the LCC, he helped found the Sydenham Ratepayers' Association, at the time when there was a keen controversy concerning the introduction of tramways. He was strongly opposed to the running of trams through high class residential districts, but favoured their introduction into business neighbourhoods, much to their benefit, and he helped carry through the Forest Hill scheme, being present at the last link of tramway construction, which joined up the Forest Hill lines at London Road and Park Road . . .

This sums up the attitude, which would become prevalent among those serving on the Highways Committee. Trams would only run where they would benefit the local populace, and obviously the majority party on the Council would ascribe their own meaning to the word *benefit*.

The list of electric lines, which opened for public service during the first decade of the twentieth century, is impressive. It must not be forgotten that the opening of a new tramway a century ago was an event of some importance. Construction work would attract many sightseers, with children being some of the most attentive spectators. Gangs of labourers lifting heavy rail sections into position would evoke gasps of admiration from the assembled audience. Then the day of the trial run would arrive. Eager eyes would follow the progress of the test tram as it edged its way along the track. Bowler hated officials would leap out at regular intervals to effect checks with fascinating looking equipment connected to meters with clock dials. Instructions would be passed to the motorman and a sudden shower of sparks would mark the emergency use of the magnetic track brake. A few days later, the Board of Trade inspection would bring a stern looking, ex-military gentleman whose task was to check and examine. Sometimes the inspector would descend from the tramcar and engage in conversation with folk whose properties bordered the tramway. During these discussions notes would be taken and a list given to the LCC official on board the tramcar to remedy certain minor features like poorly sited kerb stones or a patch of uneven paving. If all went well, the new section was passed for public service. On the great day, most of the local population were *en fete*, flags and bunting appeared, children were given the afternoon off from school, and even the local band would be roped in for the celebrations. After the arrival of the first car carrying various civic dignitaries, a free for all would develop with numbers of people, especially children, ready, willing and eager to exchange their pennies for a trip on the new electric marvel.

With the Bridges to Tooting route well established and the Kingsway Subway under construction, the Council embarked on a full programme of electrification. On 8th August 1905, the original electric line was extended from Totterdown Street, Tooting to Defoe Road (later Garratt Lane) Tooting. In Tooting Broadway the first section of an intricate four way junction was opened. It seems that the original intention was to run a loop service from Westminster

Top **On 25th April 1907, the Board of Trade inspection of the Lewisham to Lee Green section took place. Class E Car 497 was the chosen vehicle for the test run. Here it pauses at Lee Green terminus seemingly surrounded by most of the male population of the area.**

Centre **Car 456 is depicted in Tooting Broadway at the junction with Mitcham Road. Note the clover leaf car stop sign to the left of the tram.**

Right **The lattice gates to the motorman's platform are closed, as the driver of Car 161 peers round the tram to see what's happening on the other side of the road at Lewisham Obelisk.**
J.B. Gent Collection

via Clapham, Tooting, Garratt Lane and Battersea. Trams from London could terminate either in Tooting High Street or round the corner in Defoe Road. In practice, the curves were found to be too tight for regular use.

Plans were also afoot to provide south-east London with more lines branching from the Camberwell to Greenwich axis. On 30th January 1906, service opened from New Cross Gate to Lewisham Obelisk. Lewisham Road and Loampit Hill were formerly unserved by horse trams because of the gradient from Loampit Vale to Lewisham Road Station. At the Obelisk electric cars met the horse trams on the Greenwich to Catford route.

A significant celebration was fixed for May 1906, when it became possible to cross the Thames by tram. Vauxhall Bridge had been equipped with conduit tracks, which then stretched all the way along Vauxhall Bridge Road to a terminus adjacent to Victoria Station. In the midst of the festivities it was pointed out to the Council that they had forgotten to apply for Parliamentary powers for electric traction on the Vauxhall Bridge. Due to this oversight, horsecars had to be pressed into duty and electric trams did not convey fare paying passengers to Victoria until 5th August 1906. Whilst waiting for Victoria to get officially connected to the network, preparations had been going on frantically in the Greenwich and Lewisham areas. On 10th June, electric trams were extended from the Obelisk to Rushey Green, Catford. The developing shopping areas of Lewisham High Street could now boast the most up-to-date transport system. Horsecars were still retained for the Greenwich South Street to Lewisham Obelisk line, which had to wait a further twenty-two months for conversion. In Trafalgar Road, Greenwich, the first steps had been taken in the reconstruction of the narrow gauge LCC (former WSELT) route to Woolwich and Plumstead. On the

In the south-west reaches of the capital, electric traction got going in the Wandsworth and Battersea areas. On Wandsworth Road near the junction with Cedars Road, D Class Car 333 heads citybound. This class of car was particularly associated with Wandsworth Depot.
B.J. Cross Collection

same day that electric trams reached Rushey Green, cars started running to the foot of Tunnel Avenue, not far from Westcombe Park Station. The situation along Woolwich Road was becoming acute and the Council realised that they had to get rid of the narrow gauge horsecars as soon as possible. Unfortunately, as it turned out, this was easier said than done, and on the route east of Charlton a large amount of road widening had to be undertaken before the project was completed.

Still in the Greenwich area, on 18th June, a branch route was inaugurated from Woolwich Road along Blackwall Lane and the northern part of Tunnel Avenue to a terminus adjacent to the entrance of Blackwall Tunnel. In many respects this was a strange route. Housing was sparse and although the large South Metropolitan Gas Works developed some workmen traffic, a part of the line crossed the desolate Greenwich Marshes, which was almost devoid of habitation. It has been inferred that the Council intended the trams to be extended through the Tunnel to

meet with the Poplar route on the northern side of the Thames. As an aside to this idea, the Council requested a report in October 1908 on the possibility of running trackless cars (trolleybuses) through the Blackwall and Rotherhithe Tunnels.

On the south-western side of the network events were unfolding in the summer and autumn of 1906. On 5th August, trams operating from Clapham Depot commenced service along Garratt Lane from Tooting Broadway to Battersea, Plough Road. This was a natural traffic route, previously

The tower of the Wesleyan Central Hall, Tooting is seen to one side of D Class Car 329 as it journeys along Mitcham Road. Such was the lack of traffic in this era that the photographer presumably felt quite happy setting up his tripod in the middle of the highway. One assumes that tramcars coming up behind him would have rung their gongs softly.

unserved by horse trams. The area was quite built up and the new tram route passed under the London & South Western Railway main line to Waterloo at Earlsfield & Summerstown Station.

Wandsworth Depot was situated in Jews Row. The site of the old horse tram shed was demolished and in its place there rose a structure capable of accommodating 103 electric tramcars. Two traversers were operational within the depot.

When Wandsworth Depot opened on 12th October 1906 it took over the operation of the Tooting Broadway to Plough Road section. The end of the line at Plough Road, Battersea proved to be a temporary arrangement, when on 13th October 1906 electric cars were extended along York Road and Battersea Park Road to the junction of Queens Road. At the same time, tracks were commissioned in Falcon

Road from the Prince's Head, Battersea to Clapham Junction. The link up to existing rails at Vauxhall took place on 22nd December, when through cars proceeded past Queens Road and along Nine Elms Lane to Wandsworth Road and Vauxhall Cross. The Thames-side wharves at Nine Elms were connected to the main line railway; no fewer than six level crossings were formed with the double conduit track of the LCC Tramways. Shunting engines and goods wagons normally had right of way over the electric trams. The Nine Elms North Goods Depot next to the tram tracks was the original 1838 terminus of the London & Southampton Railway

North of Vauxhall, tracks were inaugurated on 8th September 1906, along the Albert Embankment past the historic Lambeth Palace, negotiating the length of Lambeth Palace Road to terminate at

Stangate. The connecting curves to the Westminster Bridge line were opened on 4th February 1907, after the offending public convenience had been demolished. Two weeks after the Albert Embankment rails had been energised, on 24th September to be precise, a connecting service was started from Lambeth Bridge approach to St George's Circus via Lambeth Road. Contrary to LCC policy, there was a short section of single track at the western end of Lambeth Road opposite the entrance to Norfolk Row.

The attention of the travelling public then switched to the rolling hills of Dulwich south of Camberwell. The Highways Committee had given the green light to a programme of extensive road improvements on Denmark Hill, Champion Park, Grove Lane, Dog Kennel Hill, Grove Vale and Lordship Lane. This was a prestige project, which also involved the construction of an electric tramway to serve areas hitherto bereft of reliable public transport. For obvious reasons, horse buses tended to avoid steep hills and residents of East Dulwich had to put up with a circuitous

Top **Dog Kennel Hill, Dulwich, was part of London tramway folklore and always formed part of every enthusiasts' tour of the system. At the top of the hill, to the left of the picture were situated a pedestrian refuge and a gas lamp. This traffic island was subsequently removed before track quadrupling was completed on 23rd April 1912. A Class C car descends towards Constance Road.**
B.J.Cross Collection

Left **Near the foot of Dog Kennel Hill we observe Car 235 about to ascend. From the unfinished state of the roadway and the kerbing it is probable that this view was taken shortly after the tram service was inaugurated.**
J.B. Gent Collection

route to the nearest railway station. Also of significance was that the area's only experiment with horse trams, running on the lines of the London, Camberwell & Dulwich Tramway Company, was a dismal failure and the horsecars packed up after a few months in operation.

Frequent and reliable electric trams would remedy the shortcomings of the past, and on 19th November 1906, passenger service was inaugurated between Camberwell Green and Dulwich Library. The southern terminus was opposite the Plough, Dulwich, but LCC councillors were reluctant to use the names of public houses in tramway destination displays, although of course, certain well known junctions such as the Elephant and Castle, the Plough Clapham and the Bricklayers Arms bucked the rule. This teetotal practice was to last for as long as trams ran in London! For drinkers and non drinkers alike, the new transport facility was very welcome, and passengers were impressed by the seeming ease with which cars tackled the 1 in 11 (9%) grade up Dog Kennel Hill. Four wheel cars of Class C, fitted with top covers and magnetic track brakes, performed the honours on the new route.

It might have seemed that North London was rather a neglected area as far as electrification was concerned. Whilst it was true that the northern connection from the Angel, Islington to the Kingsway Subway was in operation, the momentum for the conversion of horsecar lines only really increased on 15th December 1906, when the Aldgate to Poplar service via the Commercial Road commenced.

The Commercial Road was the main traffic artery from the West India and East India Docks to the City. As such, it saw a constant to and fro of vehicles; many horse drawn carts were heavily ladened with goods and produce. The new electric trams were pitched into this maelstrom of commerce, and their turn of speed showed to advantage.

B.J. Cross Collection

Top **The Plough on Lordship Lane, Dulwich** was a well known bus terminal point. When the trams arrived, the nearby crossover for short working cars was designated Dulwich Library. The temperance faction on the Council was uneasy with the names of inns or pubs appearing on tram destination blinds. Strangely, this puritan tramway tradition lasted well into London Transport times.

Above **Car 300** approaches Lordship Lane Railway Station. The fancy ironwork on the bridge was a sop to local residents who demanded a higher aesthetic style for their railway bridges. Over the intervening years, both tram and train have disappeared from this scene, and the congested highway, which is the A205 South Circular Road, has now transformed this location.
B.J. Cross Collection

Left **Frederick John Horniman** was a wealthy tea merchant and philanthropist. He donated his collection of natural history and objets d'art to the LCC in 1901. The museum bearing his name was erected on London Road, Forest Hill and was reached by a frequent service of tramcars. Outside the front gate an LCC inspector waits for the approaching car.
J.B. Gent Collection

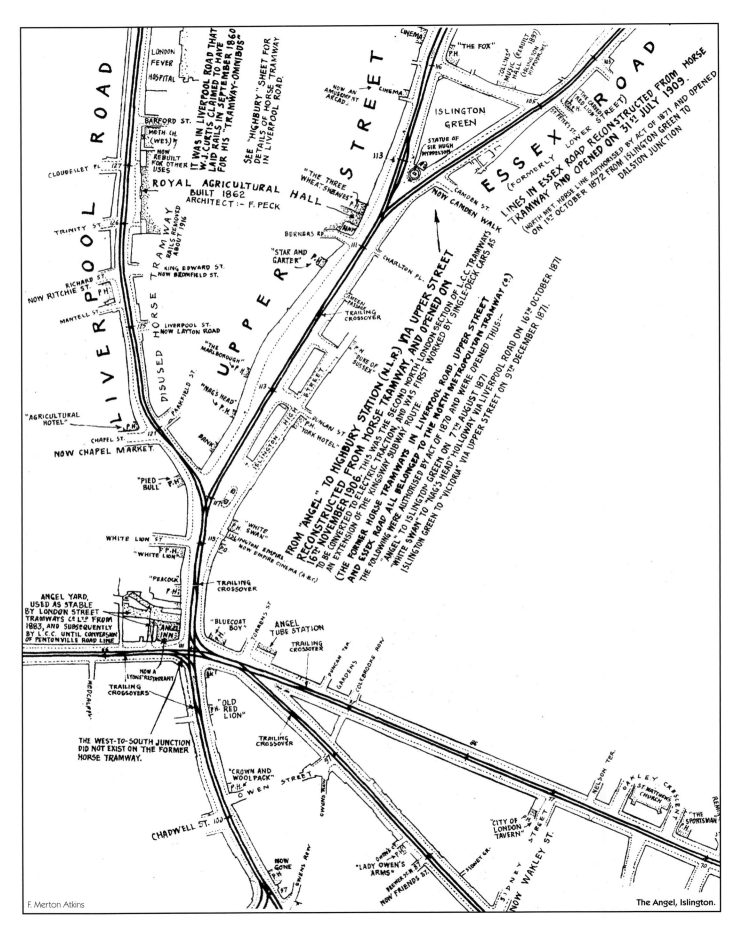

LONDON FEVER HOSPITAL

LIVERPOOL ROAD

BARFORD ST.

METH. CH. (WES.)
NOW REBUILT FOR OTHER USES

IT WAS IN LIVERPOOL ROAD THAT W.J.CURTIS CLAIMED TO HAVE LAID RAILS IN SEPTEMBER 1860 FOR HIS "TRAMWAY-OMNIBUS"

SEE "HIGHBURY" SHEET FOR DETAILS OF HORSE TRAMWAY IN LIVERPOOL ROAD.

CLOUDESLEY PL. 127

ROYAL AGRICULTURAL HALL
BUILT 1862
ARCHITECT:- F. PECK

"THE THREE WHEAT-SHEAVES" P.H.

CINEMA

"THE FOX" P.H.

116

COLLINS MUSIC HALL (REBUILT 1897) (ISLINGTON HIPPODROME)

ESSEX ROAD
(FORMERLY LOWER STREET)

"THE CAMDEN HEAD" (RED LION STREET)

185

163

LINES IN ESSEX ROAD RECONSTRUCTED FROM HORSE TRAMWAY AND OPENED ON 31ST JULY 1909.
(NORTH MET. HORSE LINE AUTHORISED BY ACT OF 1871 AND OPENED ON 1ST OCTOBER 1872 FROM ISLINGTON GREEN TO DALSTON JUNCTION

ISLINGTON GREEN

STATUE OF SIR HUGH MYDDELTON

113

CAMDEN ST.

NOW CAMDEN WALK

TRINITY ST. 126

RICHARD ST.
NOW RITCHIE ST.
P.H.

MANTELL ST.

KING EDWARD ST.
NOW BROMFIELD ST.

LIVERPOOL ST.
NOW LAYTON ROAD

"THE MARLBOROUGH" P.H.

"NAG'S HEAD" P.H.

BERNERS RD.

"STAR AND GARTER" P.H.

CHARLTON PL.

CAMDEN PASSAGE

TRAILING CROSSOVER

111

113

FROM "ANGEL" TO HIGHBURY STATION (N.L.R.) VIA UPPER STREET RECONSTRUCTED FROM HORSE TRAMWAY, AND OPENED ON 16TH NOVEMBER 1906. THIS WAS THE SECOND NORTH LONDON SECTION OF L.C.C. TRAMWAYS TO BE CONVERTED TO ELECTRIC TRACTION, AND WAS FIRST WORKED BY SINGLE-DECK CARS AS AN EXTENSION OF THE KINGSWAY SUBWAY ROUTE.

(THE FORMER HORSE TRAMWAYS IN LIVERPOOL ROAD, UPPER STREET AND ESSEX ROAD ALL BELONGED TO THE NORTH METROPOLITAN TRAMWAY CO.)

THE FOLLOWING WERE AUTHORISED BY ACT OF 1870 AND WERE OPENED THUS:-
"ANGEL" TO ISLINGTON GREEN ON 7TH AUGUST 1871
"WHITE SWAN" TO "NAG'S HEAD" HOLLOWAY VIA LIVERPOOL ROAD ON 16TH OCTOBER 1871.
ISLINGTON GREEN TO "VICTORIA" VIA UPPER STREET ON 9TH DECEMBER 1871.

DISUSED HORSE TRAMWAY
RAILS REMOVED ABOUT 1916

PARKFIELD ST.

"AGRICULTURAL HOTEL" P.H.

CHAPEL ST. 121

NOW CHAPEL MARKET

UPPER STREET

ISLINGTON HIGH STREET

DUNCAN ST.

"DUKE OF SUSSEX" P.H.

P.H. "YORK HOTEL"

"PIED BULL" P.H.

BANK

"WHITE SWAN" P.H.

"WHITE LION" F.P.H.

WHITE LION ST.

ISLINGTON EMPIRE
NOW EMPIRE CINEMA (A.B.C.)

115

120

"PEACOCK" P.H.

TRAILING CROSSOVER

ANGEL YARD, USED AS STABLE BY LONDON STREET TRAMWAYS CO. LTD FROM 1883, AND SUBSEQUENTLY BY L.C.C. UNTIL CONVERSION OF PENTONVILLE ROAD LINE.

"ANGEL INN"

"BLUECOAT BOY" P.H.

TORRENS ST.

ANGEL TUBE STATION

TRAILING CROSSOVER

NOW A LYONS RESTAURANT

TRAILING CROSSOVERS

MEDCALF ST.

DUNCAN TER.

GARDENS

COLEBROOKE ROW

"OLD RED LION" P.H.

THE WEST-TO-SOUTH JUNCTION DID NOT EXIST ON THE FORMER HORSE TRAMWAY.

TRAILING CROSSOVER

86

"CROWN AND WOOLPACK" P.H.

OWEN STREET

OWENS ROW

97

NELSON TER.

OAKLEY CRESCENT

ST. MATTHEWS CHURCH

"THE SPORTSMAN" P.H.

70

CHADWELL ST. 100

NOW GONE P.H.

OWENS ROW

"LADY OWEN'S ARMS" P.H.
NOW FRIENDS ST.

PREMIER ST.

97

SIDNEY GR.

WAKLEY ST.
NOW WAKLEY ST.

"CITY OF LONDON TAVERN" P.H.

77

SIDNEY STREET

REMI...

New junctions were installed at Gardiners Corner, where Commercial Road met Whitechapel High Street, and at the corner of Burdett Road and East India Dock Road, where the unelectrified West India Docks to Hackney Common route crossed the conduit tracks. To accommodate the vehicles for this service, a depot was constructed in Leven Road, Poplar, next to the River Lea. It was connected to the East India Dock Road by a section of single track in Aberfeldy Street. Passengers on this line were eventually treated to the recently delivered Class E cars, which were constructed with fully enclosed top decks. The service actually began with 25 first series E Class cars borrowed from south of the River, as cars of the 602 series were not yet ready.

On 16th January 1907, Aldgate received yet more trams, when the section along Commercial Street, Great Eastern Street, Old Street and Clerkenwell Road opened for traffic. The short section along Grays Inn Road to Holborn terminus was also opened at the same time. This new service effectively skirted the City of London to provide a link between the eastern lines working out of Aldgate and the existing Kingsway Subway route along Rosebery Avenue. No doubt, all this activity by the LCC contributed to the siege mentality of the decision makers in the City of London. However, as events would prove, trams were never extended beyond the Holborn and Aldgate termini.

A clutch of electrified routes followed in short order during the spring of 1907, and the junction at Gardiners Corner would see an increase in tram activity. On 29th March, the short line from Gardiners Corner to London Docks via Leman Street was brought into use. This was followed on the same day by the inauguration of lines running from Old Street to Moorgate terminus at Ropemaker Street. The connecting track from St Leonard's Church, Shoreditch to Great Eastern Street also received its first electric cars. Just over a week later, on 9th April, the sections along Shoreditch High Street to Norton Folgate terminus, and Old Street to Shoreditch Church were connected to the network.

There was another route opened in North London, on 6th February, which was the subject of an ill fated experiment. The section from Stamford Hill to the junction of High Street and Dalston Lane was subject to standard LCC procedure – double track conduit – but the southern portion of the route along Kingsland Road was destined to be different. Stoke Newington Borough Council had twisted the LCC's arm to install side conduit tracks. This was a system, which did without the centre conduit slot. Instead, one of the running rails also served as the slot for the underground conduit. This method of track construction had had varying success in Bournemouth on the South Coast, and in several cities on the Continent of Europe, but it was a novelty as far as the LCC were concerned. To cope with the new route, some Class E cars were fitted with modified plough carriers. These vehicles were kept at Stamford Hill Depot, which lay at the end

of Egerton Road, with a capacity of 140 trams.

At the Stamford Hill terminus the Council's trams met those of the Metropolitan Electric Tramways Company, which had opened on 19th August 1904. There was no through running between the overhead trolley equipped MET cars and the LCC conduit cars. Passengers had to disembark to continue their journeys. This unhelpful situation was of course manna from heaven for the competing bus companies.

The pace of openings north of the River accelerated, and on 18th May 1907, the junction at St Leonard's Church witnessed yet more trams as the section along Hackney Road to Cambridge Heath was energised. City Road from Old Street, along Pentonville Road to Kings Cross Station was next on the list, the inauguration taking place on 29th July. The Angel, Islington was now becoming a centre of tramway activity, and this status was further enhanced on 27th November, when tracks in Goswell Road and Aldersgate Street were made operational. The end of the line at Aldersgate was measured to the inch, right on the city boundary opposite Fann Street. All of which rather sums up the ridiculous attitude, which prevailed at the time. The natural traffic objectives of Cheapside and St Paul's were forever denied to the tramcar. Passengers simply had to get off and walk!

A more rational state of affairs was evident further north, when on the following day to the Aldersgate opening, passenger service was extended to Highgate, Archway Tavern via Holloway Road. The important intersection outside the Archway Tavern was projected to

Car 609 is at the crossover outside the Kings Arms, Kingsland High Street. Short working cars to Dalston Junction would usually terminate here, but at peak times a crossover just south of here at Bentley Road would be used. LCCTT

become a major tramway centre. It was already served by overhead trolley equipped cars belonging to the MET. Their service from Highgate to Finchley had opened on 22nd December 1905. The same lack of intercommunication prevailed here as at Stamford Hill. The final month of the year, on 5th December to be precise, saw the electrification of the rest of Grays Inn Road from Theobalds Road to Kings Cross Station.

The Metropolitan Boroughs north and east of the City now possessed the beginnings of an intricate network of electric tramways. On the south side of the River, in contrast to what was happening in the busy thoroughfares leading to central London, several important suburban extensions were under construction. These lines were tapping new sources of revenue, in the form of mostly middle class commuters. Housewives, who valued the convenience of the electric tram in their shopping expeditions, were also expected to boost the passenger figures. On 4th May 1907, the sedate suburb of Lee Green was connected to the main line at Lewisham Clock Tower. At the terminus by the Tiger's Head, Lee Green, a connecting Tilling's horse bus conveyed people to Blackheath and Eltham.

Other tree lined suburban roads to get the electric traction treatment were East Dulwich Road and Peckham Rye, which acquired tram service on 28th November.

Right **We move north to Stamford Hill to witness the very early days of the LCC route to London Docks. In the background are the overhead trolley equipped tracks of the Metropolitan Electric Tramways Company. As at a number of boundary roads, through tram passengers had to change cars. On LCC territory, tram crews, the police and even the odd postman have time to stand and stare at E Class Car 705.**

Inset **Funeral Card issued to commemorate the imminent demise of horse traction in North London.**

Below **Lee High Road by the former junction with Blessington Road is the setting for this encounter between cars 152 and 213. Note the cloverleaf stop sign to the left of the picture and the police sergeant on bicycle patrol.**

GOOD OLD NORTH LONDON!

In Early Anticipation of the DEATH of the old Trams.

WAITING FOR THE ELECTRIC SHOCK!

The branch to Peckham Rye offered local residents and excursionists a pleasant run from Goose Green, then alongside Peckham Rye Common to the terminus by Stuart Road. A sign of the (political) times manifested itself on 4th April 1908, when the connection between Greenwich, London Street and Lewisham Obelisk opened for traffic. The new regime at the LCC had committed itself to prudent accounting, which ruled out extensive road widening on this essentially suburban route. Single track and loops were retained from the southern end of Greenwich South Street to the corner of Lewisham Hill.

In inner South London the connection between Vauxhall and Brixton via Lambeth Road and Stockwell Road was inaugurated on the same day as the Greenwich to Lewisham link. In some ways this marked a watershed in LCC policy towards tramways. The cool winds of austerity were now blowing through the corridors of power and the trimming of the conduit construction and road widening budgets had become a priority for the members of the Highways Committee.

CHAPTER SIX

Overhead Wires

THE SIGHT OF electric trams powered by overhead wires was a familiar one to town dwellers in many countries. The system had proved reliable, efficient and cost effective and it was adopted all over the British Empire from Reading to Rangoon. Special circumstances were acknowledged to exist in the capital city and the LCC had taken note of the aesthetic feelings of the populace. Unfortunately, feelings – however noble – did not pay the bills, which were mounting with every new tram route. The Council needed to navigate their way out of the narrow channel of local authority intransigence. The idea that every Metropolitan Borough could demand a double track conduit line as of right was clearly a non runner. Common sense had to prevail. The overhead wire system of current collection would have an important role to play in future projects. This important policy decision would require the fitting of trolley poles to some of the new E/1 Class cars, which were entering service.

Aside from cost factors, the use of overhead electrification would bring the LCC into line with all the other tramway operators in London. Through services with dual equipped cars were now a distinct possibility; these connections to neighbouring tramways would address some of the concerns expressed by the Royal Commission. One problem that did have to be settled was the method by which trams passed from conduit to overhead wire current collection. This matter was solved ingeniously by the Council's engineers. They devised a straightforward system of plough shifts, whereby trams could eject and pick up their conduit ploughs with the minimum of fuss or disturbance to following traffic. It was fortunate, that in this case, the LCC did not follow the American practice of excavating a pit under the running rails where a man was stationed to remove each plough. Surprisingly though, the name *change pit* did stick, and was used throughout the tramway era in London.

There was a ready market for overhead trolley fixtures and fittings, including traction standards, so expenses could be kept down by buying in bulk from recog-

nised suppliers. This was obviously not possible with the conduit system. The LCC favoured span wire suspension where the running wire was placed centrally above the running rails. They tried to avoid bracket arm standards, which, although in use by many of the London municipal tramways, had the tendency on double track to pull the overhead wires to one side of the road. The new LCC traction standards were solidly built, possessed a minimum of iron tracery decoration and were painted a shade of medium green. The Council's trams were fitted with swivel head trolleys, which was the norm for Great Britain. This meant that overhead junctions or *frogs* had to have moving blades to guide the trolley head on to the correct wire. Insulated control wires

The crew of London United Car 172 may just be thinking how the task of coping with the overhead trolley system is a lot easier than having to deal with the intricacies of the conduit. They could have compared notes with the motorman and conductor of LCC Car 485, sitting in splendid isolation on the conduit tracks at Merton. This photo illustrates the two systems of traction and the lack of tramway communication at the county boundary.
J.B. Gent Collection

This view of Beresford
Square, Woolwich is
included for its rarity
value. Taken just after the
opening of the Abbey
Wood tram route in July
1908, we observe two
Class D cars fitted with
trolley standards
mounted to one side of
the top deck. Research
has revealed that only
four Class D trams were
equipped in this way –
cars 350, 354, 393 and
343 or 373. The rest of
the local service was
handled by open top
B Class cars, similar to
Car 106, now preserved at
the National Tramway
Museum. Another
interesting feature is the
remaining narrow gauge
horsecar track in the
foreground. These rails
led to the Powis Street
branch, which was
effectively abandoned on
electrification of the main
line. B.J.Cross Collection

Molyneux & Co.   Arsenal Main Gates, Woolwich.

for these pull frogs were fixed to the nearest
available traction standard and it was the
duty of the tram conductor to alight from
the tram carry out the necessary adjust-
ments to the overhead frog. Automatic
points did not feature in the Council's
original plans.

The LCC's first foray into overhead electrification occurred in the Woolwich area.
On 17th April 1908, service was inaugurated from Beresford Square to Plumstead
Church. Single track and loops predominated on this section, in line with the
Council's policy of avoiding expensive road
widening projects. At Plumstead the LCC
tracks were joined with those of Bexley
Council Tramways. The trams of the latter
operator did not look out of place when
compared to the open top, 4-wheel B Class
cars which had been drafted in by the LCC.
A handful of D Class bogie cars also joined
the Woolwich contingent, which were
stationed as a temporary measure in the
old horsecar shed in Lakedale Road,
Plumstead. On 26th July, tracks were
opened from Plumstead Church to the
county boundary at Abbey Wood. Most of
this extension was constructed as double
track. A junction with the Bexley Council
Wickham Lane line was inserted and a
connection was also provided at Abbey
Wood to the new depot under construction.
The date in July was also a red letter day for
Bexley Council, because its trams were
allowed on LCC tracks as far as Beresford
Square. This was a case of allowing a neighbouring operator to reach a natural traffic
objective. It was not through running in the
sense of joint operation between the LCC

and another party. Bexley tracks in
Wickham Lane fell within the boundary of
the Metropolitan Borough of Woolwich, and
therefore could be purchased by the LCC.
However, except for a short lived experiment, the Council showed no interest in
insisting that its tramcars take to the rural
highways of Kent in the direction of Bexleyheath and Dartford.

In an interesting postscript to the deal,
which Bexley worked out with the LCC, the
apparent magnanimity of the Council did
not extend to Erith Council. Their trams
had reached Abbey Wood on 26th August
1905, and the route into Erith was entirely
double track. Any hopes that Erith entertained about reaching Woolwich over LCC
rails were always firmly rebuffed, and the
two sets of tracks remained separated by
the county boundary and a few feet of
asphalt. This dog in a manger attitude
reflected little credit on the LCC, and of
course it later played right into the hands of
the London General Omnibus Company

when they started a direct Woolwich to
Erith bus route.

This latest part of the LCC empire was
separated from the rest of the network by
the remaining narrow gauge horse tram
track in Woolwich Road, Charlton.
Therefore the interesting spectacle of
through conduit/overhead trolley services
did not arise. The situation was similar in
the next major electrification, which
centred on the Hammersmith and Fulham
areas. Here, the two company operators, the
MET and the LUT, had already established
a foothold. It obviously made more sense
not to employ the conduit, where the local
authority had already allowed overhead
wires. Preparations pushed ahead, and on
30th May 1908, the new double track route
from Scrubs Lane, Harlesden to Brook
Green Road, Hammersmith was opened.
London United lines were crossed at
Goldhawk Road and Uxbridge Road,
Shepherds Bush, but there was no direct
connection between the two operators. The

LONDON COUNTY COUNCIL TRAMWAYS.

FRANCO - BRITISH EXHIBITION.

Frequent Services of Cars

ARE RUN FROM

HAMMERSMITH BROADWAY.
HARROW ROAD.
WILLESDEN JUNCTION.
ST. QUINTIN'S PARK STATION,
ETC.,

To and from the Main Entrances to
the Exhibition and Stadium.

For particulars as to services and fares see Tramways Guide,
Route No. 1.

same situation existed at Harlesden where the LCC tracks ended just short of the MET worked lines on Harrow Road. There were no severe gradients on the route and construction was fairly routine – with one exception – the provision of connecting tracks and sidings to the exhibition grounds on the western side of Wood Lane. A double track tramway siding on land adjacent to Wood Lane was planned, but it is debateable whether it was constructed. A railway line for transferring rolling stock was to cross Wood Lane on the level just south of Du Cane Road. This line was agreed and was presumably built, but the connecting double track tramway, which would have joined the railway for a terminal in the exhibition grounds, was rejected as exceeding the powers granted under the 1902 Act authorising the tramway. Objections were also raised by the LCC to LUT proposals for connecting rails from Goldhawk Road and Uxbridge Road. It seems the LCC already had in mind the fact that the LUT lines situated in the County of London were available for purchase in 1909. Whatever the outcome of all these plans, the new

trams were reported to be doing excellent business conveying passengers to the Franco-British Exhibition of August 1908.

Twenty-five E/1 Class cars were allocated to the line, and these were housed at Hammersmith Depot. This building was reached by a single track connection via Hammersmith Broadway, Queen Street and Great Church Lane. The Council finally had a bridgehead in West London, and it was hoped that further cross London links would spring from this auspicious beginning. Not that local residents had long to wait for further construction activity. Work began on the southward extension along Fulham Palace Road to Putney Bridge. Again, the route was double track with no appreciable gradients. Some property demolition had been necessary at the southern end of Fulham Palace Road, and the track construction on Putney Bridge was unusual in that the tram rails were laid outside the crown of the road, close to each footpath. This was known in tramway circles as *gutter running* and had the advantage that passengers boarding and alighting did not have to negotiate other

streams of traffic. The disadvantage came when broken down or parked vehicles obstructed the track. The line took a sharp curve at the southern end of Putney Bridge to terminate in Windsor Street, Lower Richmond Road.

A contemporary article lauds the LCC's latest achievement:

The work of laying the track, which was entrusted to Messrs G. Wimpey and Company, Hammersmith, presented no exceptional features . . . The tracks are paved throughout with wood blocks, except on Putney Bridge where granite setts are employed . . . The line is fed from a substation in Great Church Lane adjoining the car shed . . . The car shed houses cars employed on both the Harlesden and the Putney lines. There is spare ground for the purpose of extension if required, but the building as it now stands can take in 24 cars. It is 210ft (64m) long by 39ft 5in (12m) broad. There are four tracks, each with a pit with brick walls and concrete floor. The total track length in the shed is approximately 840ft (256m).

The substation adjoining presents some features of interest. It is no less than ten miles (16km) distant from the Council's generating station at Greenwich. This is at present the longest transmission in connection with the London tramways. The pressure of the three phase alternating current generated at Greenwich is 6,500 volts, and in the transmission to Hammersmith there is a drop of about 400 volts, or 6 per cent. High tension feeder cables lead from Greenwich to a substation in Wandsworth, which supplies tramways in that district of London. Two separate high tension cables are led from the Wandsworth substation to that in Hammersmith.

This description of the electrical network doesn't sound very glamorous, but the installation of an effective feeder cable system was vital to the efficient running of the

Above **Hammersmith Broadway** is depicted around 1912. This area was well served by electric traction. The London United trams opened their service westwards from Hammersmith to Kew Bridge on 4th April 1901. The District and Metropolitan underground lines had electric trains running from 1905-06, and tube trains on the Great Northern Piccadilly & Brompton Railway were inaugurated on 15th December 1906. The LCC trams appeared last on the scene in May 1908. Cars 978, 1377 and a number of buses offer local residents a choice of public transport.
B.J.Cross Collection

Right **The Star & Garter Hotel and the Young's pub** at the end of Windsor Street, Putney act as a backdrop to LCC Car 1000, which has just arrived at the terminus. A trolley reverser has been included in the overhead wiring. This was rarely used, as LCC crews were firmly wedded to the 'swinging of the pole' philosophy. Horse, electric, petrol and human powered vehicles occupy the carriageway – such was the traffic diversity in this 1909 view. On the right of the picture we glimpse Putney Pier; top deck passengers would have had a fine panoramic vista over the Thames, taking in Bishops Park, Fulham Palace, All Saints Church and Putney Bridge.

LOWER RICHMOND ROAD, PUTNEY.

trams. The success of the Harlesden to Putney operation was yet one more feather in the caps of Messrs J. H. Rider and M. Fitzmaurice, who were proving a sound advisory team.

There were several finishing touches to be put to the Putney – Harlesden line. The bottleneck at Hammersmith Broadway had to be sorted out. This was solved in a somewhat leisurely fashion, and because of the road widening involved, it took until 23rd May 1912, for double track to join the two halves of the route. The LCC's relationship with the MET Company was in general terms a constructive one; negotiations between the two operators were characterised by the idea that agreement on through running would be of mutual benefit to both County Councils – Middlesex and London. The LUT, on the other hand, was regarded by Council circles as a sparring partner, rather than a next door neighbour. Therefore, it was totally in character that, after the purchase of the MET's Harrow Road line by the LCC in October 1909, detailed discussions should be held on connecting the tracks at Harlesden. Impetus was added to this matter, when on 6th December 1910, the LCC purchased the rest of the Harrow Road line from Lock Bridge to Paddington. The route was leased back to the MET and was always worked by that company. Back at Harlesden a triangular junction was

inserted to end the isolation of the LCC Hammersmith service and it was passed fit for use on 25th April 1911.

Hopes had been entertained of future extensions from Windsor Street, Putney in the direction of Barnes or Roehampton. Local opposition caused a Council rethink, and Putney Bridge Road was chosen as the logical next move in respect of a connection to the Wandsworth services. On 30th January 1912, passengers could make the short journey from Putney Bridge to a newly installed change pit at the junction of Putney Bridge Road and High Street, Wandsworth. Although a mere three hundred yards or so separated this terminus from the Garratt Lane route, no joining up of the system occurred for another three years.

Battle lines had been drawn between the LCC and Lambeth Council over the conversion of horsecar lines linking Camberwell with Loughborough Junction, Herne Hill and West Norwood. Prolonged pressure applied by the LCC had resulted in an agreement to use overhead wires on the new routes. On 21st November 1908,

electric service was commenced from the junction with the Brixton lines at Gresham Road, along Coldharbour Lane to join the existing Dog Kennel Hill route just south of Camberwell Green. The first London change pits were brought into operation. One was situated in Gresham Road, Brixton and the other at the eastern end of Coldharbour Lane. Attendants at the plough shifts were required to uncouple or plug in the plough leads as each car moved to or from the overhead trolley section. The sliding plough, which could be easily ejected from the channels of a carrier underneath the tram had yet to come into use. Although the former horse tram tracks used Hinton Road to approach Loughborough Junction, the restricted height of a low railway bridge forced a diversion on the Council. Electric cars would use Herne Hill Road and Wanless Road to regain the West Norwood line at Milkwood Road. This track alteration imposed restrictions on the meeting of the two new routes at Loughborough Junction. Cars entering Herne Hill Road from the east had to swing out into the carriageway wrong road working round the sharp bend until they reached the correct (left hand) track in Herne Hill Road. This awkward arrangement was to last until abandonment of the route in 1952!

Another feature of the Loughborough Junction to West Norwood line was the use of one way single tracks in separate streets. Northbound cars negotiated Milkwood Road. Poplar Walk Road and Lowden Road played host to southbound trams. The prospect of mass demolition along one side of Milkwood Road to accommodate

Car 1551 is seen at Coldharbour Lane change pit. The conductor is at the back of the car ready to hoist the trolley pole on to the wire. His colleague up front will then drive the tram slowly forward to eject the conduit plough to the change pit in the middle of the road. This was a commonplace procedure all over London and barely merited a glance from passers by.
B.J.Cross Collection

double track, was one too horrible for the LCC to contemplate. Besides, this was a good, middle class neighbourhood and the Council did not wish to alienate its potential customers. There was one short piece of single track by Trinity Rise, just south of Brockwell Park, but otherwise the route was entirely double. A depot, situated on the west side of Norwood Road, was opened in October 1909, some months after passenger service began on 30th May. Norwood Car Shed was designed to hold 61 bogie cars, but was never filled to capacity. The end of the line outside the Thurlow Arms was equipped with an automatic trolley reverser, as indeed was the terminus at Windsor Street, Putney. However, LCC crews were creatures of habit and, unlike their Sheffield and Bristol colleagues, they never took to the new fangled device. In time honoured fashion, the conductor insisted on walking the pole round. Eventually, with the arrival of trams equipped with two trolley poles, even the ritual of walking the pole became redundant.

The direct route from Herne Hill Station to Brixton was opened on 5th April 1912. The tracks ran via Dulwich Road and Effra Road. A one way arrangement was employed whereby westbound trams used Water Lane, and eastbound cars travelled along Morval Road and Dalberg Road. A plough shift was installed at the northern end of Effra Road. The citizens of West Norwood now had the choice of two separate tram services into town.

Beresford Square in Woolwich, which had been the terminus for electric cars since April 1908, was the scene of renewed construction work. A single track and loops extension was constructed along the narrow Beresford Street to a point near Ferry Approach (then known as Nile Street). This temporary terminus was later to be the site of Woolwich change pit, and it was envisaged that the remaining length of narrow gauge horse tramway from here to Charlton would be converted to conduit. This short extension opened on 30th November 1909.

On the other side of Beresford Square, a new line branched south; it ascended the slope of the valley of the Thames and struck out along country lanes across Woolwich Common. On this first part of the route there were two sections where the south and northbound lines took separate streets. Again this avoided expensive property demolition. Having reached the crossroads with Shooters Hill, the line resumed its rural progress. It descended into Well Hall, and then climbed a steady gradient on a road specially constructed for the tramway to terminate at the intersection of Eltham High Street. On opening day, 23rd July 1910, the good folk of Eltham were treated to the spectacle of newly delivered M Class cars built to operate on a double trolley overhead wire system. The Admiralty and the Astronomer Royal had required this arrangement, which was very similar to later trolleybus installations. The august institutions of the Royal Navy and the Royal Observatory, Greenwich had served notice on the LCC that they would not tolerate any uninsulated electric traction project within three miles of the Observatory. What this meant in practice was that the normal single wire overhead with return of electric current via the running rails would not be allowed. It was deemed to have a detrimental effect on the Observatory's sensitive instruments. The conduit system was not affected by this ruling.

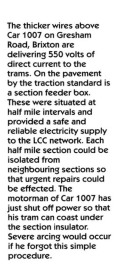

The thicker wires above Car 1007 on Gresham Road, Brixton are delivering 550 volts of direct current to the trams. On the pavement by the traction standard is a section feeder box. These were situated at half mile intervals and provided a safe and reliable electricity supply to the LCC network. Each half mile section could be isolated from neighbouring sections so that urgent repairs could be effected. The motorman of Car 1007 has just shut off power so that his tram can coast under the section insulator. Severe arcing would occur if he forgot this simple procedure.

One wonders whether the LCC pointed out to the scientific authorities that the southern termini of the West Ham and East Ham Corporations both lay within the three mile restricted zone. Perhaps the dreadful effect of stray electric currents was watered down by the River Thames! Whatever the reason, the LCC complied with the Observatory's wishes, but they measured the three mile exclusion zone to the inch, with the effect that the double overhead ended at the Anglesea Road crossover in Woolwich. The final short loop to Beresford Square, via Greens End and Woolwich New Road, was equipped in the conventional way with single wire overhead. On paper this arrangement looked fine, but in practice the LCC had cut off its nose to spite its face. The delay in depoling and repoling at

Anglesea Road slowed down the service. Eventually, on 16th February 1922, the double overhead was prolonged round the terminal loop.

Two further short sections of overhead need to be dealt with in this chapter. On 10th December 1908, at the eastern reaches of the LCC in Lea Bridge Road, the Leyton Council tracks were electrified up to the LCC boundary in anticipation of through running. The connecting rails were commissioned on 1st July 1910, and a change pit was constructed at the junction of Lea Bridge Road and Upper Clapton Road. Meanwhile to the south of the capital, the Streatham route was beginning to make progress towards an eventual link up with the Croydon system. On 31st July 1909, cars began operating from Streatham

Above left **The Effra Road, Brixton connection to the West Norwood route was opened on 5th April 1912. Soon afterwards, E/1 Car 845 is depicted on its way to Victoria. Again, we can note the LCC's reluctance to use single bracket arms instead of span wire construction suspended between two traction standards. Above the running wire are two Board of Trade guard wires, which were installed to prevent wayward telephone and telegraph wires from touching the traction supply and thereby feeding 550 volts to the nearest domestic telephone!**

Above **Many locations featured in this book have changed drastically over the decades, but St John's Church on the corner of Eltham High Street and Well Hall Road remains pretty much as it was in 1910 when this photograph was taken. Again we observe a section box feeding double overhead wires, an arrangement forced on the LCC by the Royal Greenwich Observatory; M Class cars, such as Car 1435, had to operate 'trolleybus fashion' with two poles. Even on the LCC's 'rural' routes, double track and span wire suspension was the norm.**

Above **The plough shift attendant guides a conduit plough from the carrier underneath Car 1012. This change pit opposite Gleneagle Road, Streatham opened with the rest of the route to Hermitage Road, Norbury on 31st July 1909. By this time the LCC was looking favourably at the reasonable cost of** overhead wires, so it was logical that the extension from here to meet the Croydon Tramways at Norbury should be trolley equipped. LCCTT

Above right **E/1 Class Car 1038 has reached the Norbury terminus around the corner from the Croydon Corporation tracks.** F.Merton Atkins

Library to Norbury. The line as far as Gleneagle Road was equipped for conduit. South of the change pit opposite Gleneagle Road overhead wires were employed as far as the county boundary at Norbury. Rather frustratingly, the LCC rails ended within six inches (150mm) of the Croydon Corporation tracks!

The construction of overhead trolley equipped routes represented an interlude in

the LCC saga. Common sense had prevailed and budgetary control had effected changes in the Council's strategy. However, the majority of the LCC's services ran over conduit tracks and the encroachment of overhead wires was only partial. There would still be fierce opposition to anything but the conduit for future connecting lines throughout inner London.

CHAPTER SEVEN
East End Farce

THE LCC OVERHEAD trolley routes were now well established and it would have been thought that an acceptable alternative to the conduit had been found. However, there was one more throw of the cost cutting dice. This time the decision makers were about to take a leap of faith into the relative unknown. They intended to commission a stretch of track equipped with the Griffiths Bedell (GB) stud contact system.

Briefly, the siren song of electric tramways without overhead wires had lured some potential operators on to the rocks. In Britain the use of surface contact electrification was restricted to a handful of towns. Although Torquay, Hastings and Mexborough had all endorsed the Dolter stud contact method, operational difficulties soon became severe. From a start in 1907, Mexborough quit after a year, Torquay lasted until 1911, and Hastings until 1913. The only other town with a substantial investment in stud contact was Wolverhampton. Here, the Lorrain system had a good run for its money and it survived from 1902 until 1921, when the Staffordshire town erected overhead wires.

The LCC opted for the Griffiths Bedell surface contact method of current collection. This had its origins with the firm of William Griffiths & Company, and their principal engineer, B. H. Bedell. Their first, and only, commercial success had come at Lincoln, where the Corporation adopted the new system in 1904. The Lincoln Tramways consisted of one short route connecting the city centre with the southern suburb of Bracebridge. Track was standard gauge and the single truck tramcars were equipped with the GB electrical gear. Service was maintained from 1905 to 1919, when, as in Wolverhampton, Torquay, Hastings and Mexborough, the operator switched to overhead wires.

A. L. C. Fell had set out certain fundamental requirements for efficient operation:
- Certainty of electrical contact between car and stud.
- Certainty of the contact stud being cut out electrically after the car had passed.
- Minimum projection of the stud above the surface of the street, and minimum amount of metal surface exposed.
- Moderate first cost.
- Simplicity and minimum number of moving parts.

These criteria were vitally important, and it must be assumed that they were satisfied in preliminary planning. The Chief Officer and the Council proceeded to act on the scheme. They opted for a short experimental section along the Mile End Road from Whitechapel High Street to the county boundary at Bow Bridge. This was entirely double track, with no appreciable gradients or sharp bends. In short, it would seem that this was an ideal test bed for the GB system to demonstrate its merits. The connecting line along Cambridge Heath Road was also considered for inclusion in the project at a later stage.

Before we tackle the sad history of the scheme, it is worth studying the basic concept of the GB method. The accompanying diagrams and text are taken from a contemporary technical description:

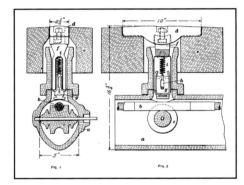

One of the cheapest surface contact systems is that known as the GB system, so called from the initials of its inventors. It is in use in Lincoln. In Figures 1 & 2 the conductor (b) is a one and three sixteenth inch (30mm) steel cable placed in a glazed earthenware pipe (a), about five inches (127mm) in diameter, which is laid underneath the track and is supported on an earthenware insulator (c). This conductor practically takes the place of the trolley wire in the overhead system, and is supplied with current from the generating station in a similar manner. Immediately over the conductor, and at intervals of from six to nine feet (1.8–2.7m), are placed the cast iron studs (d), which are set in granite blocks (e). The studs are constructed so that, when a magnet carried on the car passes over them, a small floating armature (g), housed in a fork (g), is forced against the pull of the spring (i) on to the conductor. The circuit with the cable is then complete and the stud is energized.

In Figure 3 the car equipment of the GB system consists of a means of collecting the current and a magnet for operating the studs. The magnet is fixed rigidly to the car body and is connected to a storage battery carried on the car. A rigid bar (a) runs the whole length of the collector and forms the magnetic poles. The collector consists of a number of iron links (b) suspended from a wire rope, which takes the place of the usual rigid skate. When a stud (c) is magnetized, these links are attracted and bear on the stud, thus conveying the current to the car. When clear of the stud, the links are drawn up out of the way of the paving. This arrangement allows the studs to be placed nearly flush with the roadway.

The theory sounds fine. In practice, the LCC Highways Committee visited Lincoln in the spring of 1907, and this visit resulted in a request for B. H. Bedell to call upon the

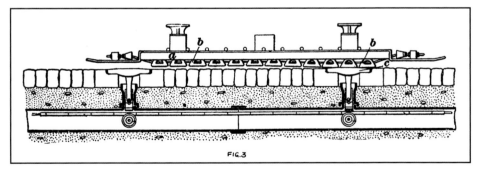

Chief Engineer to the Council. The project started to go wrong right from this first meeting in June 1907. Much to his surprise, Mr Bedell was informed that the installation of the GB system would not be entrusted to the contractor who had put in the Lincoln line. Instead, Messrs Dick, Kerr & Company were the preferred agents on behalf of the LCC. Furthermore, the Council stated that they did not require any more technical assistance from the GB Company. The LCC later changed their minds and asked the company whether they would supply at their own expense a couple of technical assistants to be on hand in case of problems.

The Council was obviously putting pressure on Mr Bedell. It was equally obvious to the LCC that the Griffiths Company needed the prestige of a successful trial in London. Construction of the route began on 7th November 1907, without any GB experts being present. As far as one can tell, the contractors were left very much to their own devices, with only the Council technical drawings to guide them. Away from the track, another dispute was brewing over the collector equipment to be fitted to the test tramcars. The Griffiths Company had been analysing the situation since June 1906, and in July 1907, they had quoted a price of £99 per car. The Council regretted that *'through a mistake, insufficient money had been voted for car equipments'*. This expression of regret left the Company with very little option, but to supply the collector equipment at cost price.

On 3rd February 1908, The Council informed the Company that only one of the 48 equipments would be needed! Again, the GB Company acquiesced and the first car equipment was delivered early in March. There subsequently followed what can only be termed a period of high farce. First, the magnet connection chain had to be altered, and then it was found that the magnet on the collector was not strong enough. Some well meaning Council officials short circuited the magnet, then they removed part of the magnet and nothing worked at all! The tinkering continued – the magnet was deemed to be too short. Two magnets were fitted instead of one. Finally, A. L. C. Fell wrote to the Company saying that the LCC *'considered the Company engineer's presence to be superfluous, when trial runs were being made'*. One can only speculate on the motives behind this statement!

on this one. The design of the paving surrounding the studs and the inadequacy of the electrical insulation came in for some virulent criticism. Short circuits in the studs had caused excessive arcing underneath the three trial cars. To all intents and purposes, the fittings and technical specifications of the successful Lincoln installation had been altered considerably for the Mile End Road test track.

The results of all this were totally predictable. The line opened on 25th June 1908

Not surprisingly, there is a dearth of views depicting the LCC's flirtation with stud contact. In one of the better trial run scenes, Car 910 is doing its best to maintain progress along the highway.

No fewer than 48 car equipments were ordered by the LCC.

The Company then prepared technical drawings and constructed a scale model of the tram trucks and GB current collector. This was all done from their 1906 notes. Mysteriously, the up-to-date truck plans and other technical specifications for the trial car had disappeared somewhere in the post between the LCC Highways Committee and the Griffiths Company. This led to an ill tempered exchange of correspondence, in which neither side were inclined to assume any liability for faults in the installation.

The comedy of errors continued, when in reply to Fell's letter, the GB Company insisted that they had not been consulted on the new design of the magnets, nor would they take responsibility for the fact that the collector gear had been placed too close to the car trucks. They also noted that the collector skate as modified by the Council showed a marked propensity to accumulate a not inconsiderable amount of scrap iron as it trundled along the road.

The construction of the track drew fire from the Griffiths Company. It appears that the LCC and their agents, Dick, Kerr & Company had also departed from the script

and expired almost a month later, on 21st July. The following letter by B. H. Bedell sums up the situation:

On 25th June a service of three cars was started. At the chief officer's request we supplied, at our own expense, two men who could teach the Council's employees how to extract studs and generally deal with the track. The troubles which were experienced were numerous. Short circuits and partial shorts between the magnets and the car were of frequent occurrence, and their effect on the studs was of course very damaging. Large numbers of studs tripped the safety breakers on the cars, and could not afterwards be located, and yet others which sparked on the detector brushes remained undetected, as the action of the safety breakers, which we believe were of LCC design, was very unreliable. Our men noticed that the pitch round the granite stud blocks had sunk away in many instances, and that the passage of a watering cart caused some of the studs to trip the safety breakers. This led us to suppose that considerable leakage must be taking place through the dirt immediately surrounding the studs.

Many studs which remained alive after the cars had passed were extracted, but were quickly removed to an LCC depot, where we could not examine them, so that we were able to gain little reliable knowledge concerning the cause of their failure to act.

On 8th July, we ceased to be able to obtain any information whatever, regarding the behaviour of the system except such as the public generally might glean, for our men were on that day ordered to have nothing further to do with the trams. We were greatly astonished at this, as it had been arranged with the chief officer that they should be employed for three months, and no warning was given that their services were to be dispensed with . . .

The Company wrote again on 15th July, stating that various electrical testing methods used on circuit breakers and the collector magnetic coils were being conducted in an unsatisfactory way. The reply they got from the LCC was short and to the point. The trial was being abandoned. The chief officer regretted that, 'in consequence of accidents to horses and persons, in addition to other defects in the working, it was decided to stop the service and cut current off till further notice'. As a final act of desperation, the Griffiths Company proposed to the Council that complete control of the project be handed over to them. This idea, not surprisingly, fell on deaf ears.

A different tack was then tried. Mr Bedell began a round of telephone calls to important officials in the LCC Tramways. He was assured that in future he would be informed of the dates and times of the tests. Furthermore, he was told that the technical results would be forwarded as soon as possible to his office. In line with recent events, it was not surprising that crucial test data did not reach the Griffiths Company. Repeated requests for this information failed to elicit any constructive response from the LCC.

The trials themselves had been the subject of much local interest. Inevitably the local newspapers fuelled the debate and added spice to the eccentricities demonstrated by the new system of traction. The three test cars would often fail in service. Groups of the fit and healthy were then asked to lend a hand to shove the unfortunate vehicles on to the next live stud. This activity rapidly became a favourite sport with the local men. In fact it was suggested that some of the many public houses en route form themselves into teams to tackle the problem in a more sporting way. Unofficial contests could then be arranged, over set distances, to see who could push the tram furthest and at what speed! Further excitement was added by the passage of a tramcar. The vehicle sometimes caused short circuits, which ignited gas that had seeped from the mains into the GB installation. This was yet another incentive to prove one's manhood – the added risk of getting blown up whilst pushing the tram!

Londoners are quick on the uptake, and the womenfolk along the Mile End Road were not to be outdone by the men. One of the unexpected benefits of stud contact was the pile of scrap iron attracted to the magnets under each tram. At regular intervals this unwanted cargo had to be jettisoned in the middle of the roadway. Women and girls gathered ladies' hatpins, broaches, rings and various other small metallic ornaments. They sifted through the tramway detritus and then recycled it into the local economy!

Half the fun of living on the experimental route was witnessing embarrassing moments like this one. Notice that the motorman, rather inconsiderately, has not got off to lighten the load or to lend a hand. Meanwhile, the assembled spectators are no doubt urging on the manpower traction team to shove a little harder, so that the tram can reach the next live stud. Rapid transit this wasn't, and one can see why the LCC was not going to tolerate the situation for long!

The conventional conduit system is represented here in this 1907 view of cars 622 and 719 in Great Eastern Street. The new LCC trams seem to have attracted an appreciative East End audience! The upper deck slatted ceiling can clearly be seen through the upper windscreen of Car 622.
LCC

The butt of all this ridicule was of course the GB Company and the London County Council. The opposition Progressives had a field day, with Sir J. W. Benn MP leading the attack. He put the total loss to the ratepayers at £300,000, a massive sum in those days. The Moderates appeared to be stubborn to the last and Alderman W. W. Thompson said the Highways Committee had not lost faith in the surface contact system, and he still believed that the installation could be perfected.

An honourable way had to be found out of the impasse, and a solution offered itself in the appointment of an honest broker who could arbitrate between the sides. Such a man was found in the person of W. M. Mordey, President of the Institution of Electrical Engineers. In October 1908, Mr Mordey began his investigation, and by spring 1909, he was making headway. He had succeeded in making the cars operational. He managed a total of sixteen double journeys on both tracks, equal to about 16 miles (25.7km) in the early hours of 5th and 6th March. The system seems to have coped adequately with inclement weather. Mr Mordey noted that ice on the rails and salt, which had been sprinkled on the roadway, did not impede progress. Clearly things were looking up for the GB Company.

Through the month of March, Mr Mordey was assiduous in conducting tests in all conditions. He did receive one setback, when a horse succumbed to an electric shock on the short length of line east of Fairfield Road, Bow. However, the beast suffered only minor injuries and subsequently made a good recovery from its ordeal. Correspondence was exchanged with the Griffiths Company, and on their advice, Mr Mordey changed the insulation material around some of the studs. This seemed to do the trick, and by 31st March, he could

report that the line was in working order and was ready for a further trial. He could also report that he had received several informal visits from Mr Trotter, the Board of Trade Inspector, who had advised on electrical matters. It seems that Messrs Trotter and Mordey had gone over everything with a fine toothcomb and had paid special attention to the elimination of rogue live studs and the arcing from the magnetic skate. After their expert attention, one of the trial cars actually ran at a speed of 24mph (38.6km/h), which was twice that achieved in any of the previous LCC tests.

Mr Mordey was a fair man and he further counselled the LCC that Lincoln Corporation had allowed a trial period of three months of the trams in actual service. During this time the GB engineers had always been on hand to remedy any small faults that had occurred. Significantly, he disagreed with A. L. C. Fell on several engineering points, and he was satisfied that the latter had not based his criticism of the durability of the studs on hard evidence obtained from three and a half years of operation in Lincoln.

It might have seemed that all was set fair for a speedy retrial of the GB system, but the LCC had other ideas. Even while Mr Mordey was writing his report, behind the scenes negotiations were going on between the Council and the Metropolitan Boroughs of Stepney and Poplar. It was agreed that the Mile End Road line would be converted to conduit from Gardiners Corner, Aldgate to Burdett Road. From there to Bow Bridge overhead wires would be erected. On 31st July 1909, the section opened and connecting tracks with West Ham Corporation lines were put in at Bow Bridge.

As might be expected, this left the Griffiths Company furious, and their previous frustration with the LCC turned

into litigation. The Company's anger was directed against Sir J. W. Benn, rather than against individuals of the majority Moderate administration. It was alleged that Sir John had made defamatory remarks about the GB Company. The matter went to court and the Company was awarded £12,000 damages. This award was overturned on appeal, leaving the Griffiths Company with precious little to show for their three year involvement with the LCC.

Party politics lay behind most of the decisions in the GB saga. It must be remembered that the February 1907 election had brought the Moderates to power. They were set on trimming the Council budget, and it is probable that they put pressure to bear on Messrs Fell and Fitzmaurice to strike a hard bargain on the stud contact installation. It seems from the outset that, time and again, corners were cut to produce the desired economic result. What is surprising is that so much bungling from so-called professionals could have been tolerated for so long. The Council seems to have treated the Griffiths Company in a shabby and unworthy manner. Transparent excuses, which verged on the deceitful, were offered for lack of communication by the LCC.

One final mystery concerns the Griffiths Company's legal action against Sir J. W. Benn. One wonders why he was selected when there were other, seemingly more culpable people whose behaviour contributed to the GB farce. It may be that, back in June 1906 when the Griffiths Company was first asked to consider the possibility of car conversions, he implied a confidence in the ability of the Company to supply a quality product. Whatever the reason, the GB system was effectively consigned to the dustbin of history. There were no winners in the conflict, only losers – the ratepayers of London.

CHAPTER EIGHT
Connections

THE PREVIOUS chapters have described events which laid the foundation for the basic LCC network. Tracks now stretched from the Middlesex boundary at Highgate and Stamford Hill, to Norbury in the south. On the eastern side of the county preparations were under way for through running with the municipalities of Metropolitan Essex. In the southeast of the capital there was a connecting line of tramway from Plumstead to Bexleyheath, Dartford and beyond. Finally, in the west, links had been forged with the Metropolitan Electric Tramways Company. Above all, there was now the brand new Kingsway Subway, which joined the two halves of the LCC system.

The period up to the outbreak of the First World War would see the construction of new lines, many of them infilling between trunk routes. The system was now experi-

encing its golden years as the premier surface transport provider in the metropolis. Competition from horse and motorbuses was at a manageable level; many bus operators preferred to remain within the confines of central London, where there were no tramways. The suburban railways had suffered loss of traffic to the electric tramcar, which was cheaper and more accessible to the travelling public. Tube lines and underground railways were holding their own, but again, much of their traffic was confined to central London.

We resume our story on 9th July 1908, at the Nags Head, Holloway, where the LCC electric service to Finsbury Park was inaugurated. The MET had already reached Finsbury Park on 22nd July 1904, but had been obliged to terminate near the county boundary. There was no through running when the conduit equipped LCC cars

arrived on the scene. This situation might seem strange bearing in mind that the two County Councils, Middlesex and London, had been in negotiations for some time. The fact was that the LCC was not prepared, or indeed able, to commit itself to through running. Fitting of trolley gear to conduit cars had to be sanctioned in the Council's budget, and the ironing out of problems concerning the design of future change pits had also held up progress.

On the same day as LCC and MET crews eyed one another across a railless gap at Finsbury Park, electric traction crept a little closer to the City of London. The section from the Angel, Islington to Smithfield via St John Street was opened to passenger traffic. The rails at Smithfield ended just short of the City Boundary at Cowcross Street.

The next few months were crucial in the

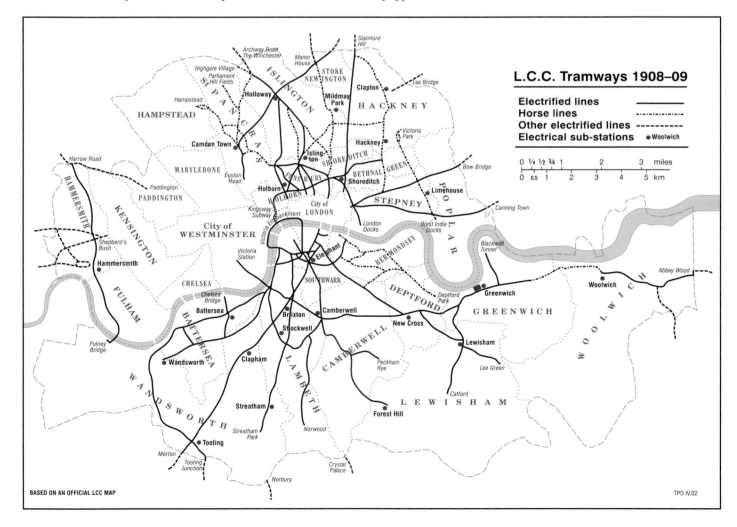

L.C.C. Tramways 1908–09

Electrified lines	———
Horse lines	·-·-·-·-
Other electrified lines	---------
Electrical sub-stations	● Woolwich

BASED ON AN OFFICIAL LCC MAP

TPD IV.02

development of North London, as the Council attempted to eliminate horsecars as quickly as possible. On 15th August, Kings Cross Station was connected to Holloway Road via Caledonian Road. Kings Cross was the centre of further activity on 28th May 1909, when the section to the Farringdon Road junction with Clerkenwell Road was inaugurated. This was followed two months later by the route from Kings Cross to Mornington Crescent via Crowndale Road. This connection opened on 22nd July. Also in 1909, a short connecting line was constructed in Swinton Street; for some reason this was not opened until July 1912. A small extension from Clerkenwell Road to Cowcross Street, Farringdon Road was opened for traffic on 14th May 1910. Again, permission was not granted to enter the City of London and the tracks ended rather uselessly, some way short of the real traffic objectives in Farringdon Street and Ludgate Circus. This tramless gap, which could easily have formed a link to tracks crossing Blackfriars Bridge, was to be the source of

endless frustration to the LCC, but the Council was never able to overcome the absolute veto from the Corporation of the City of London.

Reconstruction in the Camden Town area had also been proceeding apace. Camden Road from the Nags Head to Camden Station opened for electric traction on 11th April 1909. The extension towards Tottenham Court Road followed on 28th May. There was now a trunk route leading from the Euston area out through North London to the county boundary. All that remained was the electrification of the Hampstead lines. These were converted in stages, and although they basically kept to the old horse tram routes, it was confidently expected that the new electric lines would form a bridgehead for future incursions into Northwest London. Unfortunately, these hopes were to be dashed by the intransigence of the local authorities, principally

West Hill, Swains Lane.

the Metropolitan Boroughs of Hampstead and Marylebone, which fought tooth and nail to stop tramways straying over from the neighbouring Borough of St Pancras. Although 'Appy 'Ampstead was designated a favourite playground of Londoners, the arrival of the hordes by tramcar was only tolerated as far as South End Green, a quarter of a mile or so inside the Hampstead boundary. The select areas of Hampstead Village, Belsize Park, Finchley Road and Swiss Cottage remained forbidden territory.

Thus more in hope than in expectation, the LCC embarked on the Great College Street to Hampstead line, which served Kentish Town and Malden Road. This opened for traffic on 10th September 1909. Camden Town to Prince of Wales Road via Chalk Farm opened on 30th November 1909, the same day as tracks from Kentish Town to Archway Tavern via Junction Road were inaugurated. The final section in the local network was the line from Kentish Town to Parliament Hill Fields, Swains Lane. This opened on 20th May 1911. All of the routes centred on Camden Town were constructed with double track. Exceptions to this rule were two stretches of single track in Kentish Town Road and Highgate Road on the Swains Lane route. There was also one way working in separate streets approaching the Hampstead terminus. Westbound cars took Fleet Road, and eastbound trams used Agincourt Road. These two roads ran either side of the new Hampstead Depot, which was opened in January 1914. The fact that this facility, with a potential capacity of 157 trams, was opened later than the local routes adds credence to the notion that the LCC were still optimistic about the chances of further new routes in the area. In reality, the depot was always over half empty and it proved to be somewhat of a white elephant.

Highgate Hill was a bit of a *cause célèbre* in LCC circles. The conversion of the old narrow gauge cable tramway demanded some thought as to the provision of adequate braking on the replacement vehicles. Reconstruction work on the route between Archway Tavern and Highgate Village began in August 1909, and was completed in February of the following year. Trams ascending and descending the gradient were equipped with the conventional magnetic brake plus a newly designed slot brake, which acted on the conduit slot between the running rails. Outside Archway Tavern the conductor of each tram would open conduit hatch plates by means of a lever situated on the pavement. The motorman would then lower the slot brake apparatus in to place. Electric operation commenced on 25th March 1910 as a shuttle service between Highgate Village and Archway Tavern, using specially fitted C class cars from South London. M Class tramcars, which were a 4-wheel version of the E/1 Class bogie car, commenced regular through service on 12th December 1910.

Parts of Shoreditch, Hoxton and Bethnal Green had been subject to slum clearance and new LCC housing schemes. It was now time to add electric traction to the list of modern facilities available for local residents. On 31st July 1909, Essex Road was electrified from Islington Green to Balls Pond Road. On the same day, Cambridge Heath was joined via Mare Street to Hackney. The southern part from Cambridge Heath to Whitechapel Road had to wait until 6th January 1910 for its electric service. Meanwhile, the new car shed at Hackney, with a capacity of just over 100 trams, was commissioned on 31st March 1909. Later in the year, trams running from Hackney would be used on tracks via Clapton Road to Stamford Hill. In the centre of Hackney the presence of narrow streets imposed a one way arrangement on the electric trams. Northbound cars ran via Amhurst Road and Dalston Lane, whilst southbound vehicles made use of Mare Street. All this trackage opened on 23rd September 1909. A connection west of Hackney along Graham Road to Dalston Junction was opened on 20th March 1913. A single line section linked this route with Mare Street. The new double track junction at Mare Street was brought into use on 11th January 1915.

Barking Road, East Ham. No. 3572

The important junction of Manor House on the county boundary with Middlesex was reached on 3rd August 1912, when cars began running via Green Lanes to Mildmay Park, Balls Pond Road. The southern extensions from Balls Pond Road to Essex Road, and to Baring Street via Southgate Road were inaugurated on 26th November 1912. The one way track along Dorset Street (later Dove Road) for eastbound cars was opened on 26th July 1913. The former horse tram route via Bridport Place and Mintern Street was abandoned. Another horsecar casualty in North London was the Liverpool Road line in Islington, which ceased on 19th July 1913. A final effort was made in 1914 to close the remaining gaps, and on 6th March, the short link along Balls Pond Road between Mildmay Park and Dalston Junction was electrified. This was followed on 25th June, by the inauguration of the Highbury Station to City Road line, which ran along Canonbury Road, New North Road and East Road.

Trams serving the New North Road traversed a reconstructed bridge over the Regents Canal Dock, Shoreditch. The bridge attracted publicity as it used the new method of ferro-concrete, which we now know as reinforced concrete. The single 43ft 6in (13.2m) span supported double conduit tracks laid in a roadway 53ft (16.1m) wide. Work began on 5th May 1913 and the structure was opened to traffic on 28th May 1914.

Since the publication of the Royal Commission Report, the LCC had come under increasing pressure to conclude practical through running agreements with its tramway neighbours. We have already seen that in 1908 Bexley Council had pioneered, in a limited sense, an interconnecting service over LCC tracks. The question of how to remove the logjam on through running was aired at the September 1908 conference of the Municipal Tramways Association.

H. E. Blain, General Manager of West Ham Corporation Tramways, read a paper entitled SOME THROUGH-RUNNING PROBLEMS AND THEIR SOLUTION. The debate that followed was spirited, and A. L. C. Fell found himself being criticised by the West Ham and Croydon delegations. The basic argument put forward by several London municipalities was that buses had already done a good job of siphoning off through traffic. Passengers, they noted, were not going to put up with getting on and off different tramcars to cross over gaps in the rails imposed by borough boundaries. The whole situation was verging on the ridiculous.

Alderman H. W. Littler, Chairman of the West Ham Tramways Committee, declared that West Ham's trams were facing intense bus competition. This situation was exacerbated by the fact that the Metropolitan Police was the licensing authority, not the County Borough of West Ham. He then criticised the attitude of the LCC, which compared unfavourably to the willingness shown by other East London tram owning municipalities to come to mutually beneficial agreements.

Steven Sellon of the Tramways and Light Railways Association weighed in with a statement directed at the LCC. He remarked that a passenger aiming to go from Croydon to London by tramcar had to alight from the Corporation tram at Norbury and then had to walk a mile and a half to ask Mr Fell's permission to take an LCC car. There was laughter at this statement, which stung the LCC Tramways Chief Officer into defending his corner. A. L. C. Fell replied to Mr Sellon by saying that the Council had been trying for some time to construct a tramway from Streatham to the county boundary, but these efforts had always been thwarted by the local authority. The Council had just succeeded in obtaining Parliamentary powers for the extension, and until the connection existed, the Council might just as well ask Mr Wilbur Wright (of early aviation fame) to assist!

Mr Fell then tackled the West Ham problem. He stated that the conversion of the horse tramway at Bow had been delayed, and that money needed for road widening in connection with through running to West Ham, might just as well

Thatched House, Leytonstone.

be used for more urgent projects in other areas of the metropolis. His attitude then became more positive and he promised that negotiations with the MET had already commenced, and these would form the basis of future dealings with other interested parties.

The meeting then moved on to the vote of thanks to Mr Blain. The message to Mr Fell and the LCC was loud and clear, and the climate had to be created for full blown co-operation with the MET and several East London municipal systems. Planning became reality on 26th October 1909, when a West Ham car made a test run over connecting rails at Bow Bridge. The purpose of this trial was to check clearances under Bow Road Railway Bridge. The tram was a fraction too tall, but after alterations had been completed to the car, it passed its second test on 17th December with flying colours. Preparations for the ceremonial inauguration of through services were overshadowed by the death of King Edward VII on 6th May 1910. The monarch, who was known as 'The Peacemaker' to his subjects, was very popular and all sections of society mourned his passing.

The somewhat muted day of the link up arrived on 11th May 1910. An agreement with West Ham Corporation, East Ham Corporation and Leyton Urban District Council resulted in two joint services: Aldgate to Leytonstone via Bow and Stratford. Aldgate to Ilford via Stratford and Manor Park. The LCC used standard E/1 bogie cars, whereas the other municipalities stuck to single truck designs.

On 1st July 1910, Leyton was linked to Hackney via a change pit constructed at the Lower Clapton end of Lea Bridge Road. Two tram services were inaugurated: Moorgate to Leyton; Aldgate to Leyton via Cambridge Heath. A number of Leyton 4-wheel cars were fitted with plough gear. They wore a dark green and cream livery, which contrasted with the LCC dark lake and primrose. By this time, repeated coats of varnish had weathered the dark lake to a brown colour.

The third and final connection to East London was opened on 20th December 1912. A change pit was installed at Iron Bridge, Poplar, in advance of the laying of connecting tracks to the West Ham Corporation lines from Canning Town. Trams from West Ham, East Ham and Barking participated with the LCC on the long through service from Loxford Bridge, on the boundary between Barking and Ilford, to Aldgate. A second service was worked from Aldgate as far as Canning Town. Interestingly, Barking Council's contribution to the through service was short lived. In a move that was to foreshadow financial difficulties

of the future, they pulled out of the agreement on 31st May 1914, but allowed East Ham, West Ham and LCC cars to continue running as far as Barking Broadway.

The Metropolitan Electric Tramways Company served main roads in Middlesex, which were natural traffic corridors from North London. At Finsbury Park through running commenced on 1st August 1912. Preparations for the join up had included a new change pit in Seven Sisters Road opposite Blackstock Road, and the purchase by the LCC of the MET track between Finsbury Park and Manor House. Through cars now ran from Euston Road to Palmers Green, and from Euston Road to Enfield. The connection at Manor House to the LCC section of Green Lanes had to wait until 16th August 1914, when Service 51 was introduced from Muswell Hill to Bloomsbury. It should be noted, that from around the autumn of 1912 trams were equipped with numbers indicating which service they were on. LCC lines north of the Thames received odd numbers; those working south of the River received even numbers. The two Kingsway Subway services – Highbury to Tower Bridge Road, and Angel, Islington to Clapham Junction – became 33 and 35 respectively.

Rails linking the MET and the LCC outside Archway Tavern, Highgate had been laid in 1909, but it took until 24th September 1914 for joint services to begin. A new change pit was constructed and the Moorgate to Highgate Service 9 was extended to Barnet. The Euston Road to

THE BROADWAY, ILFORD

Right The Rising Sun Inn is situated on the western side of Epping Forest. Here on Woodford Road in rural Essex the crew of Car 1632 prepare for the return run to town. This was a Sunday extension from the usual weekday terminus at the Bakers Arms, Leyton. The Leyton Council tracks met those of Walthamstow Corporation here, but there was no through running until March 1931. LCCTT

Below Car 1338 has reached the triangular junction at the northern end of Whipps Cross Road. In the background is part of Epping Forest leading to the Hollow Pond. Tracks to the right lead to the Bakers Arms, whilst those on the left lead to the Rising Sun. The tramway along Whipps

Cross Road was later placed on private right of way on the eastern side of the road adjacent to Epping Forest. LCCTT

Bottom From 1st August 1912, tram passengers from Enfield could experience the novel sensation of remaining in one car all the way to Tottenham Court Road. No more would they have to change at Finsbury Park. The trolley of Car 1052 has been swung in readiness for departure southbound from the centre of the market town of Enfield. One little lad sitting at the base of the ornate street lamp seems not all interested in the large brown and cream Council tramcar. J.B.Gent Collection

Walthamstow. Tram Terminus.

The Town, Enfield.

Archway Service 19 was prolonged as far as North Finchley. Thus, the travelling public north of the River had the benefit of an integrated tram system, whereby one fare covered one journey, and one car could be taken from the outer suburban terminus to the gates of the City of London.

The situation south of the Thames was not so advanced, and links to Croydon Corporation, the South Metropolitan Tramways Company and the London United Tramways Company had to wait until the 1920s to come to fruition. One exception to this state of affairs was the case of Bexley Council. Their tracks as far as Bexleyheath Broadway were used by a Sunday afternoon extension of LCC Service 38. The route from Wickham Lane was semi rural and was constructed as single track and loops. At Bexleyheath Broadway there was a kaleidoscope of liveries as the Council's trams met the apple green and cream cars of Erith Council, the dark red and cream Dartford cars, and the chocolate coloured Bexley trams.

Aside from events in North London and the intricacies of through running, there was some substantial route building throughout South London in the years preceding the First World War. On 19th December 1908, the track was extended from Dulwich Library, past Lordship Lane Station and the Horniman Museum, to a terminus outside Forest Hill Station by Dartmouth Road. Not far away in Lewisham, the construction gangs had been busy and on 26th February 1910, the first section of the Brockley route opened from Lewisham High Road to Brockley Lane Station. Northbound cars worked along Shardeloes Road, whilst their southbound sisters used the parallel single track in Malpas Road. The route was extended on 25th February 1911, to Park Road, Forest Hill. This terminus was opposite the Dartmouth Road one, but was separated from it by a low railway bridge in Waldram Road. The direct route from Rushey Green,

Catford to Stanstead Road, Forest Hill was inaugurated on 29th May 1913, and this formed an important link in the network. Further proof of LCC forward thinking was supplied on 5th April 1914, when tramway services were extended along Bromley Road to a new terminus at Southend Village by Southend Lane. The landscape south of Rushey Green was distinctly rural, and passengers alighting at the end of the line opposite the Mill Pond, Southend could be forgiven for thinking they had arrived at the back of beyond.

Over by the riverside, in another part of Southeast London, a long running saga was being played out. It involved the conversion of the ex-WSELT narrow gauge horsecar line. This whole process had lasted far

longer than expected. The main cause of the delays was the narrowness of the road between Charlton and Nile Street, Woolwich. At some places, only wholesale demolition of property would provide enough carriageway width for a new double track electric tramway. Then there was the problem of the Royal Dockyard wall, which had to be set back, stone by stone, to allow free passage of the LCC trams. The new Central Repair Depot, just off the Woolwich Road at Charlton, had opened on 5th March 1909, and a track connection to the temporary terminus at the foot of Tunnel Avenue was urgently needed. A trial car ran on 15th July, and seven days later, the line was opened as far as Rainton Road. Further exasperating months were to follow until

the track was ready as far as the junction of George Street with Chapel Street, Woolwich. On 1st April 1911, passenger services reached the new albeit temporary, interchange point with the horsecars. The patience of the travelling public had been well and truly tested, and it was with some relief that the era of the narrow gauge horse trams finally ended. On 5th April 1914, Woolwich lost its tramway isolation, when the final section of track from Chapel Street to Woolwich Ferry Approach was commissioned. Service 40, which had previously terminated at Woolwich Dockyard, was extended as far as Abbey Wood.

In central London the Council had finally got its way over the widening of Blackfriars Bridge to facilitate a tramway connection from Blackfriars Road to the Victoria Embankment, John Carpenter Street. The sticking point in this dispute to get trams across the Thames had been the ridiculous 300 yards (275 metres) or so of territory belonging to the City of London. True to type, the delaying tactics of the administrators of the Square Mile had frustrated what seemed to be a perfectly logical arrangement. A loop terminus using Blackfriars and Westminster Bridges appeared an ideal solution to speed up tram services, and it would offer greater convenience for passengers. The price exacted on the LCC included an installation of various pedestrian subways at the junction with the Victoria Embankment, plus of course the widening of the bridge to accommodate a double track tramway on the western side of the carriageway. The LCC acted with commendable magnanimity when it invited the Lord Mayor of London to perform the opening ceremony on 14th September 1909.

Top left **Park Road, Forest Hill** positively exudes gentility in this 1911 view. The tram, the cyclists, the ladies and children out for a walk all contribute to an ordered and tranquil way of life in a lost world soon to face the cataclysm of the First World War. There is a conduit plough resting against the section box on the pavement on the left. No doubt in those days the idea of somebody stealing or vandalising the plough was totally alien to society's expectations.
J.B.Gent Collection

Left **Electric trams had only been running through Brockley Cross for just over a year and a half, when Car 110 came to grief on 2nd September 1911 at the junction of Shardeloes Road and Lewisham High Road.** The crowds are out waiting for the LCC breakdown gang to come and retrieve their property.
D.Jones Collection

Nowhere is the cumbersome bureaucracy of legislation more apparent than in the enabling Act to build the short line across Blackfriars Bridge. The Corporation of London (Blackfriars and Other Bridges) Act, 1906 – (6.EDW.7.) covers no fewer than forty pages with eighty sections, many of which are divided up into subsections. Some of the clauses have a faintly eccentric air to them – for example, clauses 50 and 51 state:

Every passenger travelling upon the tramway may take with him his personal luggage not exceeding twenty-eight pounds in weight . . .

The Corporation shall not be bound unless they think fit to carry on the tramway passengers' luggage exceeding twenty-eight pounds in weight nor any parcel or goods.

The spectacle of weights and measures officials weaving in and out of tramcars on Blackfriars Bridge is just a tad ludicrous. The serious point to all this was the time involved in drafting a Parliamentary Bill, and the scope it gave objectors to nitpick each and every clause. Significant parts of the Act cover very unlikely eventualities such as the LCC employing steam locomotives on the bridge (clause 46), or the Council having it in mind to remove all GPO letter boxes in the immediate vicinity (clause 44)!

Elsewhere in south and south-west London construction work on new lines was nearing completion. On 25th January 1909, electric trams began operation on the line from Lavender Hill via Queens Road to a terminus at the southern approach to Chelsea Bridge. Low railway bridges on Queens Road by Silverthorne Road and Southolme Road precluded double deck operation. Cars from Classes F and G worked the new services. This situation lasted until 1927, when tracks and roadway were lowered for double deck operation.

Top right **The saga of the conversion of the Greenwich to Woolwich horse tramway was long and drawn out. The crew of Class A Car 55 pose at the transfer point in Charlton. In the distance is a narrow gauge horsecar waiting to depart for Woolwich.**

Centre right **In this view by the Woolwich Dockyard Gates electric traction has almost ousted its equine predecessor. Road widening and the costly setting back of the Dockyard wall caused interminable delays.**

Right **A scene familiar to all Londoners is the view over Blackfriars Bridge towards the City and St Paul's Cathedral. The newly opened tramway on the bridge probably did not attract much attention, but it provided a vital link for people commuting to and from work.**

On 23rd September 1909, the trunk route from Vauxhall along Wandsworth Road to Lavender Hill, Queens Road was inaugurated. Services commenced running along Lavender Hill to Clapham Junction just over two weeks later on 9th October. The final (interim) terminus of the route was situated on East Hill, Wandsworth and electric cars reached this point from Clapham Junction on 16th December. The new year of 1910 saw the opening of the link, which traversed Queens Road and climbed the hill at Cedars Road, before skirting Clapham Common via Long Lane to arrive at a junction with the original electric line at the Plough, Clapham. This section was opened on 26th February. A final route remained to be opened in the area. This provided another river crossing for the LCC in the form of new tracks across Battersea Bridge to a terminus in Beaufort Street, Chelsea at the corner of Kings Road. The double track on Battersea Bridge was widely spaced leading to another example of gutter running. It was somewhat of a miracle that the LCC did finally manage to penetrate the anti-tram stronghold of Chelsea, but this short line was to be the Council's only success in this part of London.

In the Tooting and Streatham areas new routes were also on the agenda. On 5th November 1910, service started from Streatham, St Leonards Church via Mitcham Lane and Southcroft Road to Amen Corner, Tooting. This line could be considered something of a speculative venture, as Southcroft Road was at this time only a country lane with tram tracks. In fact other vehicular traffic was so sparse

that weeds and various forms of vegetation began to invade the carriageway. However, urban development was never far away, and after the First World War the building boom engulfed the road. On the other side of Tooting, a short extension from Garratt Lane to the county boundary at Summerstown was commissioned on the same date as the Southcroft Road line. At the Summerstown location the conduit tracks of the LCC met the rails of the LUT from Plough Lane and Haydons Road, Wimbledon. No through running was contemplated. The initial service on this line was from Summerstown to Southwark Bridge.

After all this activity, there was one, hitherto neglected area of the metropolis to be tackled. The horsecar lines in Bermondsey and Rotherhithe had the subject of much soul searching amongst members of the Council. On the face of it, it seemed a straightforward job to convert the local system to conduit operation, but the Council was aware of two significant factors weighing against the expense of new electric lines. The area was losing population, and bus competition was increasing. A

study published in 1909 reveals bus routes established in Tooley Street, Jamaica Road, Lower Road, Evelyn Street, Grange Road and St James Road. In Southwark, Bermondsey and the Parish of St Paul, Deptford a steady decline in population had been noted since 1901.

After careful consideration the LCC eventually decided to abandon the back street routes formerly belonging to the London, Deptford & Greenwich Company, even though conduit junctions had been laid at Tower Bridge Road by Grange Road, and at Evelyn Street by Rotherhithe New Road. The Spa Road horse tram route closed on 25th February 1911. The single deck, single car shuttle along Rotherhithe New Road, known affectionately as *the ha'penny bumper*, made its last run from Raymouth Road to Canal Bridge, Old Kent Road on 12th July 1913. The Bricklayers Arms to Rotherhithe line via Grange Road, Southwark Park Road and Raymouth Road was, as we shall see, one of the subjects of the 1914 report. It was finally closed on 30th April 1915, and was the last tramway in London to be worked by horses. The rails were not removed until about 1922.

Back on Tooley Street, the decision regarding electrification had been a favourable one, and preparations began for the conversion. On 25th February 1911, the first section opened from the corner of Bermondsey Street and Tooley Street along past the junction with the Tower Bridge Road tracks to Rotherhithe Red Lion via Dockhead. The western approach to Creek Bridge, Deptford was reached on 22nd

Merton Tram Terminus

June. Meanwhile, work had been continuing on the bascule bridge over Deptford Creek and the line from Greenwich to the east side of the bridge. The link to Greenwich opened on 5th August and through traffic across the bridge was inaugurated on 3rd October. There only remained some fine tuning to be carried out at the London Bridge end of the route. On 28th November 1912, the rails in Tooley Street were prolonged as far as Stanier Street. The final stretch to the terminus by Duke Street was opened on 9th December. Unfortunately, the LCC could not secure permission to connect the Tooley Street line with the Hop Exchange terminus in Southwark Street.

On 10th March 1914, a private and confidential joint report to members of the Highways Committee was introduced for discussion – the title of the report was TRAMWAYS DEVELOPMENT. The 74-page document contained proposals and financial estimates for new services. A prominent theme was the linking of previously *dead end* termini to form through routes.

Part I of the report was headed:

Lines which are immediately necessary to enable the best use to be made of the existing tramway system:

2	*Victoria to Westminster*
2a	*Victoria (Vauxhall Bridge Road) to Buckingham Palace Road*
4d	*Victoria to Hyde Park Corner*
5	*Beaufort Street to Victoria*
5a	*High Street, Fulham to Edith Grove*
5c	*Edith Grove to Beaufort Street*
7a	*Kings Road to Brompton Road*
8	*Uxbridge Road to Hammersmith Broadway*
8a	*Shepherds Bush to Holland Road*
9	*Kensington Road to Kings Road*
12	*Marylebone Road to Harrow Road*
13	*Edgware Road to Kings Cross*
17	*Hampstead Road to Bayley Street*
18	*Tottenham Court Road to Southampton Row*
18a	*Russell Square to Theobalds Road*
22	*Kentish Town Road to Camden Road*
23	*Parkhurst Road to Caledonian Road*
24	*Seven Sisters Road to Crouch Hill*
25	*Holloway Road to Finsbury Park Station*
28	*Charles Street to Charterhouse Street*
29	*Grays Inn Road to Blackfriars Bridge*
31	*Seven Sisters Road to Stamford Hill*
34	*Graham Road to Amhurst Road*
35	*Mare Street to Cassland Road*
37	*High Street, Shoreditch to Cambridge Road*
39	*Aldgate terminus to Aldgate Station*
40	*Aldgate to near Mark Lane Station*
42	*Extension over Southwark Bridge*
44	*Waterloo Road to Blackfriars Road*
45	*Greenwich Road to South Street*
46	*Lee Green to Eltham*
51	*Elder Road to Gipsy Hill*
52	*Norwood terminus to Central Hill*
55	*High Street, Wandsworth to Southfields Station*
62	*Earls Court Road to Brompton Road*

Each of these proposals in Part I was explained in detail with Reasons for Construction, Notes on Special works and Widenings, and the relevant car shed and substation to be associated with the new line.

Part II listed:

Lines which will be hereafter required to meet the transit requirements of the general public by means of tramways:

4	*Hyde Park Corner to Edgware Road (Subway)*
10	*Shepherds Bush, Holland Road to Marble Arch*
11	*Marble Arch to Marylebone Road*
14	*Harrow Road to Cricklewood*
15	*Marylebone Road to Childs Hill*
16	*Chalk Farm Road, Ferdinand Street to Swiss Cottage*
19	*Crowndale Road, Cobden Statue to south side of Russell Square*
33	*High Street, Stoke Newington to Upper Clapton Road*
43	*Southwark Street to Cannon Street, St Paul's Bridge*
47	*Lee Green to Baring Road*
48	*Burnt Ash Hill to Rushey Green*
53	*Herne Hill to Goose Green*
54	*Brixton to Clapham*
55a	*Southfields Station to the county boundary*

P.&S. 2868. JAMAICA RD. S.E.

Fashionable houses and plane trees once lined Jamaica Road by Martin Street. Sadly the depredations of the Luftwaffe and 1960s road builders have altered this area for the worst. In a time before Nazi planes and town planning philistines, Car 1410 trundles sedately in the direction of the temporary terminus at Creek Bridge, Deptford.
B.J.Cross Collection

Part III detailed: *Additional schemes which are very desirable from a tramway point of view, but presenting difficulties which render the prospects of construction remote:*

The penultimate section devoted some columns to the reconstruction of the remaining horse lines. It was felt that the fate of the Southwark Park Road route was still in the balance, as the costs of double track versus single track and loops, and conduit versus overhead were still to be worked out to the satisfaction of the Council and the officers of the Bermondsey Borough Council. On the other hand, the LCC was more positive about the West India Docks to Cassland Road line, although the debate whether to employ conduit or overhead was again holding up a final decision. As regards the Liverpool Road line, the Highways Committee decided to recommend its abandonment.

The final part of the report considered the options for a public transport link through Rotherhithe Tunnel. From Lower Road, Rotherhithe to Commercial Road, Stepney the distance was 2,294 yards (2097.6 metres); from one tunnel gate to the other was 2,086 yards (1907.4 metres) of which 1,621 yards (1482.2 metres) was in tunnel proper. It was immediately apparent that the vertical clearance in a tunnel of 27 feet (8.2 metres) diameter would necessitate single deck tramcars. It was decided that the proposal did not warrant a double track tramway and the Chief Officer of Tramways recommended that '*a service of motor omnibuses would in this case be a suitable system of traction to adopt . . .*'

Of the grand 1914 scheme only tramways 31, 42 and 46 were ever constructed. West India Docks to Cassland Road was electrified via Well Street; the horsecar line in Southwark Park Road was abandoned. The outbreak of the First World War in August 1914 would have profound consequences for Londoners and the whole country, and it put paid to the LCC's expansion programme. As we shall find out in the next chapter, the Council was called upon to shoulder the burden of transporting millions throughout the international crisis.

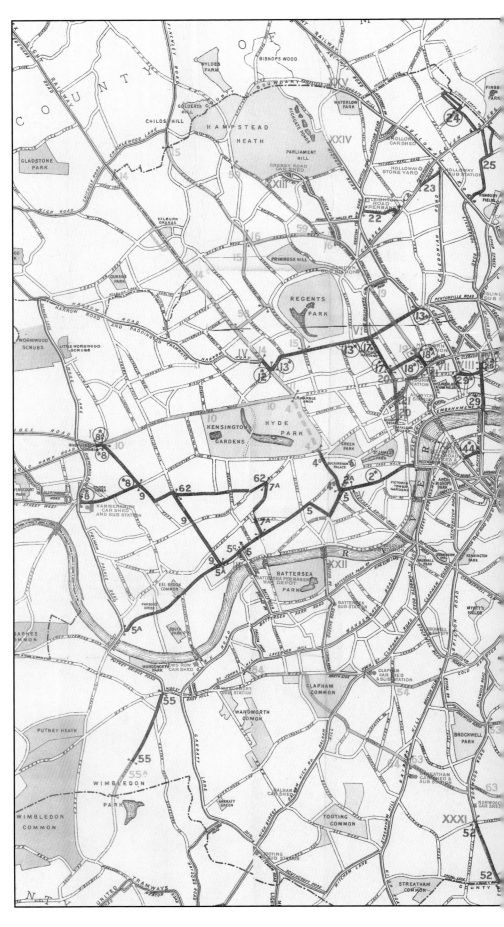

1914 map issued to members of the Highways Committee for discussion purposes.

THE TRAMWAYS OF LONDON

Scale. 2 inches to 1 mile.

REFERENCE.

The existing L.C.C. Tramways are shewn in
FULL RED LINES

Those authorised are shewn in DOTTED RED LINES

Tramways not belonging to the Council are
shewn in FULL BLACK LINES

Those authorised are shewn in BLACK DOTS.

Car Sheds (Electric) .... are shewn thus

Sub-Stations .... " " " "

Permanent Way & other Depôts " " " "

Offices .... " " " "

London County Boundary shewn thus

* Part 1ᴬ Proposed Tramways shewn thus
  Part 1. " " " " "
  Part 2. " " " " "
  Part 3. " " " " "
  Existing Horse Lines " " " "
  Existing Dead Ends " " " "
* Schemes suggested for Session 1915.

CHAPTER NINE
Shouldering the Burden

IN SARAJEVO, on 28th June 1914, a young Serbian student named Gavrilo Princip shot and killed the Austrian Archduke Franz Ferdinand and his wife Sophie. This murder was to set in motion a chain of events which would lead to the cataclysm of the First World War. On 4th August 1914, Great Britain declared war on Germany. Patriotic fervour had been bubbling up for some time prior to the commencement of hostilities and a series of fine summer days had heightened the mood of the populous. LCC tram crews joined in the general wave of euphoria, and it was with some difficulty that many conductors and motormen were persuaded by inspectors not to forsake their trams to join the colours on the spot!

Some members of the Tramways Department who did take the King's Shilling were soon in the thick of the action. The first casualty from the tramways staff came on 23rd August, when Lance-Corporal E. W. Stretton lost his life in the Battle of Mons. A total of 3,507 men employed by the LCC Tramways enlisted during the war. Some 334 men fell in action or died from disease whilst on active service. A significant number perished in June–July and October–November 1918 in the two influenza outbreaks, which swept across the globe. In 1922, the LCC published a bound volume entitled RECORD OF SERVICE 1914–1918, which listed in detail the Council's contribution to the war effort.

On the home front, the events of August 1914 were to cause a complete change in some civilian work patterns, especially amongst those who worked in the armaments industry. The trams were called upon to fulfil an important national function in transporting workers vital to the war effort. Nowhere was this felt more, than in Woolwich, home of the Royal Arsenal. The number of employees on the site numbered around 11,000 in the year before the outbreak of the war. However, at the height of the conflict this figure had soared to some 72,000 men, women, youths and girls. In short, the LCC would have a real job on its hands to maintain and

augment public transport in the area – especially at shift change times in the Arsenal! The main gate to the Arsenal opened out on to Beresford Square, which by 1914 had become a thriving tramway centre for central London tram services, cars for Bexley and Abbey Wood, plus LCC Service 44 to Eltham Church. Access for munitions workers was also possible at several other gates along Plumstead Road, along which ran LCC services 36, 38, 40 and, until 1915, service 42 as well.

It must have been with some relief that, in the nick of time, the LCC had finally completed the electric tramway link between Greenwich and Woolwich. This enabled through services to be run; it provided communication with the rest of the network, which was useful in transferring trams from other areas to cover the growing need in Woolwich. The actual passenger capacity of the local trams had been enhanced by the trailer car experiments, which had been taking place in the area since 20th March 1913. The vehicles

used in these tests are described in more detail in the rolling stock chapter. Suffice to say, that service was commenced on the Eltham (44) and Abbey Wood (42) services. The Eltham route used a loop terminal at Beresford Square, which ensured that no reversing was needed. At the quieter terminus in Eltham the trailer was uncoupled on the double track facing the single track stub terminal. The M Class (power) car would then pull forward, reverse and return to Woolwich. The trailer then had to wait in splendid isolation until another tram appeared up the slope of Well Hall Road. The arriving tram would then push the trailer into the stub terminal, where it would be coupled to the power car. After this operation the pair of trams would return to Woolwich. The Metropolitan Police and the Metropolitan Borough of Woolwich kept a close eye on proceedings, and it was generally agreed that the provision of trailers was particularly effective in the transportation of heavy loads of passengers for short distances. In

All quiet on the Camberwell front, as we survey the inmates of Camberwell Car Shed in 1914. Soon every vehicle will be pressed into service to meet the demands of all out war. Car 1098 has a 92 route stencil – the highest numbered LCC tram service. It was introduced on 28th November 1913 to work from Brixton to Blackfriars via Coldharbour Lane. The service was withdrawn barely two years later. LCC

Munitions workers stream out of the Royal Arsenal, Woolwich. A tram on Service 42 heads for Abbey Wood, whilst two M Class cars on Service 44 wait to transport essential war workers back to their houses and cabins on Well Hall Road. The short stretch from Beresford Square to Anglesea Road was single wire at this time, hence the rather offset looking trolley pole on the nearest 44.

this case, Service 44 was ideal, for it was shortly to become one of the most important lifelines in the war economy.

The rural nature of Well Hall Road was changed forever by a massive building scheme to house workers at the Royal Arsenal. Between February and December 1915, the Well Hall Estate was provided with 1,300 homes built on 96 acres (38.8ha) of farmland. On the western side of the road a settlement called the Eltham Hutments sprang up. These were wooden cabins built as hostels for arms' workers. Trams and trailers were packed at shift change times. Those not able to get a seat would stand in any part of the lower deck where space could be found. This sort of overcrowding became the stuff of legend, and on one car and trailer set, no fewer than 130 passengers were recorded. In the school summer holidays secondary school pupils were also encouraged to join the throng.

They were employed at the Arsenal on an honorary basis as temporary clerks. Their penny tram fares could be paid out of the ten shillings a week honorarium each received.

On the other Woolwich line from the Ferry Approach past Beresford Square and through Plumstead the lack of double track had been causing frequent delays to trams, which had to pass in convoy along single track sections. The LCC applied for special ministerial dispensation to convert single to double track. At a time of national emergency this would seem like a reasonable request. But the scheme fell on deaf ears as far as Woolwich Borough Council was concerned. They demanded the customary (peacetime) demolition of property and expensive road widening before they would acquiesce. This attitude not unexpectedly annoyed the LCC and central government, and the local authority was told in no uncertain terms by the War Department, the Ministry of Munitions and the Board of Trade to bow to the inevitable. The necessary trackwork took place in 1916–1917, but it did not clear away all the single track bottlenecks in Plumstead High Street. Ironically, these sections were to remain until the final abandonment of the first generation system in July 1952.

The mood of the British people, which could be described in 1914 as jovially bellicose, had acquired a touch of realism in the new year of 1915. The hope that the war

Above A population explosion has turned rural Eltham Common into an estate for Arsenal workers. To the left of double trolley Car 1717 are numerous wooden huts and a temporary grocers shop. On the right is the purpose built Progress Estate, which survives to this day, having been granted protected area status.

Right This photograph has considerable historical value. It shows M Class Car 1700 towing one of the first experimental trailers from Charlton Works out into Woolwich Road. Power car and trailer sets were used 'under the wires' on service 42 – Beresford Square to Abbey Wood, and on service 44 – Beresford Square to Eltham Church.

would end by Christmas had faded and the LCC, like other public transport operators, was obliged to make long term plans to cope with an extended international conflict. As the weeks and months passed, and tales of trench warfare became widespread, attitudes hardened and troops going off to the front did not experience the wild social rejoicing of the previous year. Not that the locals were incapable of expressing their feelings. On 7th May 1915, a German U boat sank the Lusitania. Angry mobs took to the streets of the capital, thus delaying many LCC trams. The orgy of violence against shops and businesses which had German sounding names left a trail of destruction and broken glass.

Sporadic enemy bombing raids further compounded the problems of the civilian population. The threat initially came from giant Zeppelin airships, which launched their first raid on London on 31st May. On moonlit nights the airships would follow the course of the River Thames from the North Sea to the capital. The targeting of bombs seems to have been a random affair. In order to keep casualties down, warning of air raids by Zeppelins or Gotha bombers was given by illuminating a series of coloured lamps situated on the nearest LCC Tramways section box. These were positioned on the pavement every half mile, so that traction current could be fed to the conduit or the overhead.

Restricted lighting regulations came into force, and from January 1915, trams were fitted with light shades. At night, the gloom inside the tramcar hampered the work of conductors trying to collect fares. Street lighting was also curtailed, and this resulted in passengers missing their stops. In order to aid the travelling public, the LCC instructed conductors to announce relevant information on stops, services and destinations.

Two track extensions occurred in 1915. On 16th July, the Putney Bridge Road rails and change pit were connected by conduit to Garratt Lane, thus ending the isolation of the Harlesden – Hammersmith section from the rest of the southern half of the LCC system. Almost a month later, on 13th August, service was inaugurated on Waldram Road and Devonshire Road, Forest Hill. The previous termini in Dartmouth Road and Park Road were linked. A short siding was constructed in Park Road to accommodate cars terminating at Forest Hill. They could then stand clear of the main road traffic. Another more minor change happened at the corner of Falcon Road and Lavender Hill, where a double track junction was inserted. This enabled Service 34 to be extended from Clapham Junction to the Plough, Clapham. Wartime conditions meant that plans for other proposed routes had to be postponed until the end of hostilities. In practice, this would mean another five years before any new track projects were undertaken.

Left **Trailer T24 is seen hitched behind a power car at John Carpenter Street, Blackfriars. Services 2 and 4 from Tooting, Longley Road to the Embankment had trailers from July 1913 to May 1922. This particular set looks well filled with commuters on their way back to the suburbs. In response to wartime conditions all day trailer working on Services 2 and 4 started on 30th July 1915. This picture was taken shortly afterwards.**

Below **Yet more queues at Blackfriars wait to board a homeward bound tramcar. Note the difference in roof heights between the D Class car at the head of the queue and the following E Class vehicle. Also noteworthy is the number of women in employment at this crucial time for the nation.**

On the staff front, many of the able bodied young men employed by the LCC had already volunteered for military service. As the war dragged on, so the red tape of bureaucracy became more intrusive. The Munitions of War Act 1915 required all employers to list men in different categories: skilled, semi skilled and unskilled. This official listing particularly applied to those on the tramway engineering side, and a whole range of working people from electricians to permanent way gangers were assigned to the appropriate category. Whichever way you looked at it, the manpower shortage would eventually affect the running of a tramway system, which was already at full stretch. At the beginning of 1915, almost 10 per cent of the LCC workforce were in the armed forces. The idea of employing boy conductors was entertained for a few weeks, but it transpired that this was unworkable. The obvious solution was to offer jobs to women, as was happening in the munitions industry, however the notion of female employment was not one that appealed to the chiefs in the LCC, and they let the matter rest until they were obliged by circumstances later in the year to take action.

Action of another sort was being taken by the male staff in May 1915. A strike flared up at New Cross Depot over rates of pay not keeping up with wartime inflation. Crew feelings were inflamed by the seeming intransigence of the management and of A. L. C. Fell in particular. On 14th May, early morning trams from New Cross ran in very limited numbers. The men had offered to maintain the strategically important Woolwich services, but due to a breakdown of communication between the two sides, even Woolwich bound cars were severely restricted. Attitudes had hardened on both sides, and a deadline of 15th May was set by the Chief Officer. If crews did not turn up to work normally, they would be deemed to have dismissed themselves. Mr Fell went on to say that those men who might be eligible for military service would never be taken back. This statement incensed the strikers who accused Fell of acting as a recruiting officer, when there was no legal obligation for men to join the army. The strike petered out on 5th June. Inspectors and Regulators had maintained some sort of service during the industrial dispute, and LCC clerical staff also helped out where they could. The upshot of all this was that tram crews returned to work reassured that they would receive a war bonus of three shillings a week. But the damage to staff relations had been done, and one must judge whose responsibility it was that communication between the men and management broke down so quickly. Fell's implication that the crews were acting unpatriotically was deeply resented. The men had a right to some protection against rising prices, especially when workers in other industries were earning premium rates.

The intensive service in the Woolwich area offered the spectacle of many tramcars intermingling with military traffic, and in the autumn of 1915 alone there were several accidents and near misses. There was a spate of derailments on the single track sections in Plumstead, followed by a couple of collisions with munitions lorries. A fatal encounter between a tram and a lorry took place on 16th September. The motorman of a tram on Albion Hill was killed in the accident. This was only a snapshot of some of the road traffic accidents, which occurred during wartime conditions. Some blame can be apportioned to newly trained motormen and the gloomy conditions of a partial night-time blackout.

The role of women in the war effort underwent a sea change towards the end 1915. On 12th October, the Germans executed Nurse Edith Cavell. She had been working in a Belgian hospital behind enemy lines and was adjudged by a military court to have aided the escape of Allied personnel to neutral Holland. Her bravery and fortitude in her final hour made her a heroine throughout Great Britain. Edith Cavell's sacrifice was a clarion call to the women of the country. The LCC had already debated whether to employ married women at the CRD in Charlton, but the barriers had already been broken, and it was found that women, irrespective of whether they were single, married or widowed, were adept at many tasks involving intricate electrical repair work. It was only a matter of time before conductresses appeared on trams.

The pressure on the LCC and other all male bastions was immense, but the final nail in the employment coffin came on 2nd February 1916, when the Military Service Act established conscription for all unmarried young men. Now, sheer necessity

forced the Council to take on female platform staff. Conductresses began to appear during 1916; however, the idea of letting women drive tramcars did not take root. The male dominated Tramway Workers Union campaigned vigorously against the training of motorwomen. Inevitably, this rather reactionary stance was reinforced by the Metropolitan Police Commissioner. He foresaw difficulties with female drivers wrestling with handbrakes and panicking when confronted with an emergency. The example of Nurse Cavell obviously had not had much effect on him! Finally, the union threatened an all out bus and tram strike if women were employed as drivers. The LCC took no further action, at this time, but the matter refused to go away, especially when it was reported that a number of tramway undertakings had given jobs to lady drivers. The authorities eventually started to make optimistic noises, and at the end of 1916 this memo was published in the minutes of the Tramways and Light Railways Association:

A significant sign of the times is the decision of the Home Office to authorise the London Commissioner of Police to license qualified women to be drivers of public vehicles including tramcars. Reports are being received that women are giving satisfaction in spite of unfavourable climatic and dense traffic conditions; it is also alleged that neither the existence of gradients nor the question of brakes has had unfavourable results where women have been used as drivers. This testimony as well as the action of the Metropolitan Police will necessarily influence the authorities, and managers may be faced with the alternative of curtailment of services or employment of women drivers.

Day to day working of the system was beginning to suffer not only from a skill shortage, but also from a lack of raw materials. The armaments industry had first call on the steel needed for replacement rails and truck components. A priority system was worked out by the Ministry of Munitions of War, whereby steel and copper could only be released strictly for maintenance purposes only, and then only for routes used to transport munitions workers. As it was, all track repairs had to take place in daylight due to the risk of arc lights attracted the unwanted attention of enemy bombers at night. Thus services were delayed whilst essential maintenance of the permanent way was in progress. PW gangs responded by speeding up rail replacement so that through services could be

Unfortunately the author was unable to find a photograph of his Great-aunt Grace in full LCC uniform, therefore this unidentified lady will have to represent the ranks of LCC conductresses. The navy blue outfit with linen skirt can only be described as practical and utilitarian. Conductresses were sometimes admonished by inspectors for wearing broaches and other jewellery in an attempt to add a touch of style to their appearance.
D.Jones Collection

restored in a matter of minutes. Air raids sometimes caused fatal disruption to the network. On 25th August 1916, during an early morning Zeppelin raid, an LCC all night tramcar was damaged by a bomb at Streatham Hill. Worse was to follow, on 24th September, when Car 1145 received a direct hit. Two crew members and a travelling ticket inspector were killed.

An interesting aside concerning tramway conditions in London appeared in a note published by A. V. Mason, Manager of the SMET Company:

For instance, the war has taught me many things – that women make excellent conductors, and that the average woman is quicker in taking fares than the average man; that passengers unconsciously connive at dishonesty apparently under the impression they save the girls trouble by saying "Don't worry about a ticket"; that half fares for children are popular and remunerative. Another is that a lot of time can be saved and accidents avoided by collecting fares on the platform; that return tickets are a convenience to passengers as well as to conductors, and that the same thing applies to weekly tickets . . .

After the war receipts are bound to drop, but I rather think that expenses, certainly labour, will remain high (and the higher the better from the tramway point of view, that is, of course, if applied to other trades). Material will not drop to the pre-war price for a long time, and repairs will be heavy, as not only have the cars and tracks been overtaxed, but necessarily often neglected.

The second paragraph turned out to be a remarkably accurate prediction for the future.

Throughout the war there had been rumblings from the government about the unnecessary competition between buses and trams on various London routes. The LCC, to its credit, was willing to enter into negotiations with the London General Omnibus Company. The Underground Combine, a powerful collection of transport companies in London, had controlled the LGOC since 1912. The directors of the Combine usually never missed a trick in their own passenger war with the LCC trams. In spite of the national emergency, the Combine reverted to type and stalled the discussions. It seems that the LCOC, and Frank Pick in particular, had been in secret talks with the Ministry of Munitions. It also became apparent that the bus company had pocketed subsidies and extra fuel rations. Towards the end of the war, the whole affair was debated in Parliament and the LCC was able to state that it was never consulted about the subsidies, nor was it privy to other schemes cooked up by Frank Pick. One of these involved the withdrawal of a number of trams along Old Kent Road so that they could be replaced by buses!

On the LCC's southeastern boundary another drama was unfolding. As early as 1915, Bexley Council informed the LCC that they did not have enough trams to cope with the extra passenger traffic generated by munitions workers journeying from Welling and Bexleyheath into Woolwich. An offer of rolling stock to help hard pressed Bexley resulted in cars 823 and 827 being sent over the border into Kent. In the late autumn of 1915, LCC cars 1376, 1378 and 1380 joined their sister trams at Bexley. Unfortunately, the Council's generosity did not extend to the other Kentish neighbour of Erith. A connecting line between the two authorities' tracks at Knee Hill, Abbey Wood, had been the source of debate for many years. Protracted negotiations had been long on pious hopes and short on action. When it looked likely that war conditions would make through running a reality, the atmosphere between Erith and the LCC was clouded by the actions of the LGOC in running a direct bus route from Woolwich to Erith. In the end nothing was settled and the tracks of the two operators remained separate.

Above left **The notes on the back of this card written by photographer O. J. Morris read thus: Streatham, opp. St Leonards Church. Aug. 1916. Trailer T116 forms part of the 18 service from Norbury to the Embankment. Across the Channel in the fields of France the Battle of the Somme was raging with terrible intensity. LCC Tramways employees on active service were in the thick of things. On 8th August, Albert Martin was killed at Mametz Wood, and his sacrifice was followed during the month by J. B. Owens, Sidney Priest, Herbert Miller, F C. Pocock, and on** the last day of the month, David Haslum perished near Longueval – a tragic background to this sunlit scene at Streatham. One can only guess at the mood of Londoners who had suffered bombing attacks by the enemy, which added to the tension of waiting for news of loved ones mired in the trench warfare on the Western Front.
O.J.Morris

Left **We journey on to High Road Streatham by Becmead Avenue. Lighting and blackout restrictions are apparent on Car 529, which has an occluded headlamp mask marked with the fleet number.**

In August 1917, a catastrophic fire wiped out all the Dartford fleet. Bexley stepped in to offer replacement services; it would therefore require even more trams from the LCC to replace the Dartford cars lost in the depot conflagration. An arrangement was concluded whereby all the five E/1 bogie cars were returned to the LCC in exchange for a number of single truck B Class trams, which had been fitted with trolley poles. Five cars were sold to Bexley and a further twelve were loaned to help out with the Dartford crisis. It is interesting to note that, through the Council's largesse, no less than fifty-nine B Class trams were sold to other undertakings. In January 1917, ten cars went to Sheffield, and ten to Rotherham. In November of the same year, six trams were despatched to Newport. Finally, in April of 1918, ten more trams were sold to Sheffield and six trams disposed of to Southampton.

The Greenwich Generation Station maintained power supplies throughout the war. However, it was never an easy situation, as coal supplies could not be guaranteed, and the price of existing stocks rose sharply, especially during 1918. At one point the government obliged the Council to provide emergency electricity to Woolwich Arsenal. Service reductions were enforced to conserve power and routes not considered vital for the war effort suffered. In the Woolwich area the substation in Woolwich New Road had to be rebuilt to cope with the extra load.

Bureaucracy was the bane of many organisations, but a consensus existed that any added paperwork was somehow contributing to the successful prosecution of the war. In short, there was a belief that government interference was necessary to achieve victory. In the midst of all this red tape, the LCC embarked upon a wholesale reorganisation programme. The Council approved the final recommendations in the spring of 1917.

It was resolved that the LCC Tramways Department be reorganised into a three tier command structure. The post of Deputy Chief Officer was replaced by a series of departments under the control of the Chief Officer or Tramways Manager. Mr Fell's immediate subordinates were the respective managers of the Traffic Branch, Electrical Branch, Rolling Stock Branch, Permanent Way Branch and General Branch (clerical work). The Traffic Manager had responsibility for two departments: Development & Planning Section and Operation Section. The Electrical Engineer oversaw the Power Station Section, the Distribution (Southern) Section and the Distribution (Northern) Section. The Rolling Stock Engineer was in charge of the Rolling Stock Section and the Repair Depot Section. Finally, the Permanent Way Engineer looked after the Permanent Way (Southern) Section, the Permanent Way (Northern) Section and the Building Section.

Supporters of this restructuring pointed out the benefits of a streamlined system, which would cope better with the demands

of postwar conditions. They cited a number of statistics to back up their argument for immediate change. We are told that in the year to 31st March 1900, there were 24.375 miles (39.22km) of track open, 117,992,713 passengers were carried who produced a total revenue of £470,098, and the total number of LCC Tramways employees was 2,750. In the year ending 31st March 1914, the traffic figures were very different: 144.83 miles (233.08km) of track were open, 522,209,289 passengers were transported, £2,268,668 was collected from fares and the total number of employees was 12,232. However much these figures suggest a change was due, one is left with the distinct impression that all this upheaval could well have waited until the end of the war. Fortunately, wiser counsels prevailed and implementation of the proposals was postponed. The scheme was finally instituted in July 1919.

The end of the Great War occurred at

11am on 11th November 1918. At around the same time, crowds of workers streamed out of the Royal Arsenal to celebrate. The trams facing them in Beresford Square looked much the same as before the conflict, but the world of London's transport had moved on. The motor bus had proved itself ferrying troops on the battlefield, and bus operators would soon have the opportunity to open up new suburban markets untouched by the tramways. The fight was on to capture the travelling public.

CHAPTER TEN

Tramcars

THE END OF the First World War is a convenient time to suspend the historical narrative and study the rolling stock situation. Basically, an LCC tramcar's main function was to transport people from point A to point B in a cost effective and efficient manner. Modern commentators would probably add another benefit of electric traction – each vehicle was environmentally friendly. This fact was not immediately apparent to our Edwardian forebears who lived in cities with appreciable amounts of atmospheric pollution. As the prevailing wind in Britain normally comes from the west, one finds that smart residential areas were usually situated on the western fringes of industrial cities. The smoke and soot particles then settled on the poorer quarters to the east of the city centre. This pattern was repeated to a degree in London.

Londoners using the trams a century ago were in some respects very different to their modern counterparts. People were of shorter stature and trams were designed accordingly. Anyone of six feet (1.83 metres) or over would have to stoop because of limited headroom from the bulkhead doorframes. Likewise, the spacing of transverse seats restricted legroom for the taller traveller. The seats themselves were wooden and not very comfortable. On the

open top deck conditions could be miserable, and passengers could expect a soaking in wet weather. Ice and snow would add to the fun of those unfortunates sitting outside on the car. Smokers were normally confined to the top deck, and when enclosed upper saloons were fitted to the trams, the fug that built up at rush hours must have been impressive. Rows of cigarette and pipe smokers quickly manufactured an environment rich in carcinogens.

The lower saloon was patronised by non-smokers and, more often than not, contained a higher percentage of ladies,

small children and the elderly. Even here the Spartan nature of the hard wooden benches did not encourage long distance riding. There were no heaters in winter. On the other hand, in warm summers, the lower saloons sometimes became stuffy due to inadequate ventilation. This situation could be partly alleviated by the motorman leaving the front bulkhead door open, although this practice was officially frowned upon.

A hundred years ago, the attitude to personal hygiene was also different to modern expectations. Poverty played a huge role, and many London families did not have access to a bath or adequate washing facilities. Workmen's clothing was made to last and would often remain soiled for weeks. Ladies of a certain social class did use perfume, lavender water and eau de cologne, but most folk did without. Consequently, not to put too fine a point on it, many people smelt. And to cap it all, the original carpet mats on the bench seats had to be withdrawn because they were infested with vermin!

Factors involved in the Council's choice of tramcar included the nature of passenger loadings in London, the terrain over which services operated, the layout of depots, the ease of maintenance and finally, the constraints of the conduit system. It was apparent from the beginning that the Progressive controlled Council would only deal with well established manufacturers. The elected members were concerned that workers employed by rolling stock suppliers achieved an acceptable standard of pay and conditions. The LCC was of course a

Below "Plenty more room on top" is an exhortation beloved by generations of London's tram and bus conductors. The reality of (to modern eyes) cramped wooden seating was rather less than enticing. The prospect of

sitting out here in the rain soon convinced the LCC to bring in an accelerated programme of supplying the fleet with top covers. Note that the backs of each seat can be reversed according to the direction of travel.

Above left The interior of B Class Car 106 shows the perforated wooden bench seats and one lower deck bulkhead with the sliding door open to platform A. Note the swan necked handbrake column on the righthand side of the motorman's controller, and the hatchway in the flooring, which could be lifted to inspect the motors and conduit plough.

Left Above the heads of the passengers in the lower saloon was a splendid array of stylish lamps, polished metal fittings and beautifully crafted carpentry. The roof struts of Car 106 also support the straphangers' handrail. The lampshades affixed to the ventilation strip above the opening top lights give an air of Edwardian elegance.

major customer for any manufacturer and the specifications demanded by the Council's Rolling Stock Engineer had to be followed to the letter.

The earliest electric trams were based on their horse drawn predecessors. Weight constraints limited the design of double deck horsecars, and throughout London the standard 4-wheel open top model, with longitudinal bench seats in the lower saloon and transverse garden seats on the top deck, predominated just before the introduction of electric traction. It was therefore to be expected that the new electric cars would share several design traits with horsecars. The open top was retained and the seating on both decks followed the traditional pattern. Access to the outside of the car was by a reversed staircase from the conductor's platform. Since tramcars are double ended, this style of staircase quickly proved to be an obstacle, which impaired the motorman's all-round vision.

It took the LCC some years to perfect their ideal tramcar for London conditions. Passengers, not unnaturally, tended to avoid sitting on the open top deck in inclement weather. There seems to have been a change in passenger behaviour since horsecar days. The Council quickly cottoned on to the fact that enclosed top decks meant extra revenue. Open balcony and low height styles were tried before success was achieved. Although the LCC maintained quite a large fleet of single truck cars, the 8-wheel bogie car with fully enclosed top deck proved the ideal workhorse for operations all over the County of London, and this standard design appeared in large numbers.

The longevity of the standard design proved a mixed blessing. On the one hand, the sturdy reliable tramcars could be expected to turn out in all weathers and would clock up an impressive mileage over decades of hard work. On the other hand, it was always tempting to delay investment in new rolling stock. This was to prove a fatal mistake for most British tramways. Traditional designs were preserved by the LCC, and when the powers that be woke up to the fact that a radical new approach was needed, it was too late to construct a fleet of truly modern vehicles.

In this chapter we will look at Classes A, B, C, D, E, E/1 and M of the double deck fleet, plus single deck Classes F and G which worked through the Kingsway Subway. All these vehicles represent the traditional era of British tram building, when craftsmanship and attention to detail was entering a golden age. For £717 the LCC could acquire a complete eight wheel tram with bodywork of teak, mahogany, seasoned oak and assorted other timber. Steel framing and angle irons gave each tram body extra rigidity. In short, the Council possessed a public service vehicle of which it could be proud.

Trams were painted in purple lake and primrose livery. Slight changes in colour pigments and successive coats of varnish weathered the livery to a chocolate brown and dull cream combination. In order to save expense, the name of the undertaking was not displayed in large letters on the rocker panel of each car. Instead, the waist panel just under the lower deck window frames featured the gold letters L.C.C. A revision of the livery did occur in the 1920s and this will be described in the relevant chapter.

It is also important to remember that every vehicle in the following list had a two man crew of conductor and motorman. Depot staff were responsible for sending each tram out on the road in a mechanically sound and outwardly clean condition. The interiors of the lower and upper saloons were also cleaned regularly, and it was expected that each vehicle would represent the LCC Tramways in a positive way. Trams that developed serious faults in service were withdrawn to the nearest depot. Crews were trained to handle on the road repairs, and a tool kit was supplied with each tram.

Specimen conduit Car 101

This vehicle, which was referred to in chapter two, was bought from the Westinghouse Company, who had exhibited it at the London Tramways Exhibition of 1900. The car was constructed by G. F. Milnes & Co. and ran on standard Brill 22E maximum traction trucks. It was a traditional open top, double deck design with open platforms. The lower saloon had four windows each side, with eight opening top lights. A partial bulkhead halfway along the lower saloon divided the lower deck bench seats, which were covered by a strip of carpeting material. It is probable that this car was only ever used for test purposes at Camberwell Depot, and that it never entered into the rough and tumble of everyday passenger service.

In 1913 the top deck seating and decency boards were removed and the car was renumbered 110. As a single decker it worked the Queens Road service 32, until it was retired in 1926. The tram was scrapped in 1931.

Class A cars 1–100.

The projected electric services from the bridges to Tooting required rolling stock. Vehicles of class A fitted the bill. They were built at Preston by the Electric Railway & Tramway Carriage Company Ltd, and were delivered in 1903. The lower saloon had a six bay window pattern, and a partial bulkhead in the middle of the car divided longitudinal bench seats. Reversed stairs led to an upper deck with transverse seating. Each tram was licensed for 28 passengers in the lower saloon and 38 on the top deck. No provision was made for a trolley standard on the upper deck, although the cars did have a plug in facility to accommodate the overhead power cable used for shunting cars at Rye Lane and other small depots not equipped for conduit.

Car 18 is shown after some of the top deck rails had been extended to the minimum Board of Trade height of 3ft 6in (1067mm). Two viewing grills have been cut into the staircase risers. Whether this actually increased the motorman's field of vision is debatable – one thing is certain, the reversed stairs were soon replaced by direct ones. LCC

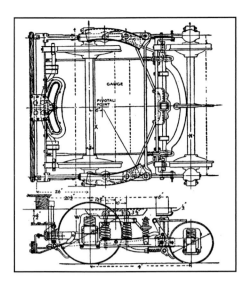

Each tram ran on two Brill 22E trucks, the motors of which developed between them 60hp (60.84Kw). One of the trucks contained a metal extension that formed the plough carrier. Power to the two motors was channelled through a Dick, Kerr DB1 controller situated on the platform at each end of the tram. Because speeds were relatively low – the highest permitted velocity being 12mph (19.3km/h) – it was generally thought that use of a handbrake and a rheostatic brake worked from the controller would be sufficient. However, a number of slow speed collisions cast doubt on the efficacy of the existing systems. Therefore it

became necessary to fit electro-magnetic track brakes, which then became standard for the whole fleet. Their sharp braking effect became a characteristic of the Council's trams, and many visitors to the Capital, who were not used to the antics of LCC trams, would be caught off guard and would find themselves propelled the length of the lower saloon, when the car stopped!

As delivered, the outward appearance of each car featured a prominent display of locations served by the tram route painted on the front top deck canopy above the driver. This was later omitted as cars received advertisements and were allocated to other services. Very soon after the opening of electric services a destination board was affixed to each side of the car. This was complemented by a destination indicator box attached to the top deck railings at either end of the tram. Above each box were three lamps, which were illuminated in a different colour combination for each service. On the left of the rocker panel, just above the trucks, the words

LONDON COUNTY COUNCIL

were painted in black letters. At the other end of the panel was

ALFRED BAKER TRAMWAYS MANAGER.

This was later changed to

AUBREY LLEWELLYN COVENTRY FELL
TRAMWAYS MANAGER,

and in white letters on the side platform bearer was the legend

CLASS A.

What might be termed nowadays consumer pressure forced the Council to

adopt a policy from 1904 onwards of equipping the fleet with top covers. The first design consisted of a covered top with an open balcony at either end of the car. Cars were then classified A1. Low height covers were fitted to some cars on the Clapham routes. The added weight of each top cover increased power consumption, thus obliging the Council to stagger the pace of bodywork conversions, until the Greenwich Generating Station was fully operational.

The second phase of the conversion created an A2 Class car, and the work involved the enclosing of the balconies at either end of the car. This created a fully enclosed upper saloon, but without top deck bulkhead doors, which would have acted as draught screens. The fitting of these doors could not begin until reversed stairs were replaced by the direct type. Around 60 cars of Classes A and D have been converted to direct stairs by November 1907. This task continued through 1908, and the resulting vehicles were allocated to Class A3. When the whole upgrading process was completed just before the First World War, all the class subdivisions were abandoned and each car reverted to plain Class A.

Due to the expansion of the LCC network and the opening of new overhead wire equipped sections, a total of 51 Class A trams were altered to receive trolley poles as well as their original conduit gear.

These vehicles were kept at New Cross and Abbey Wood, and were often to be seen working services 36, 38 and 40. Many A

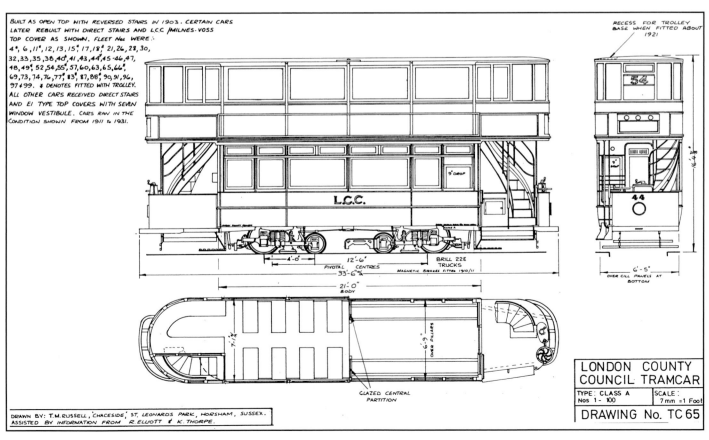

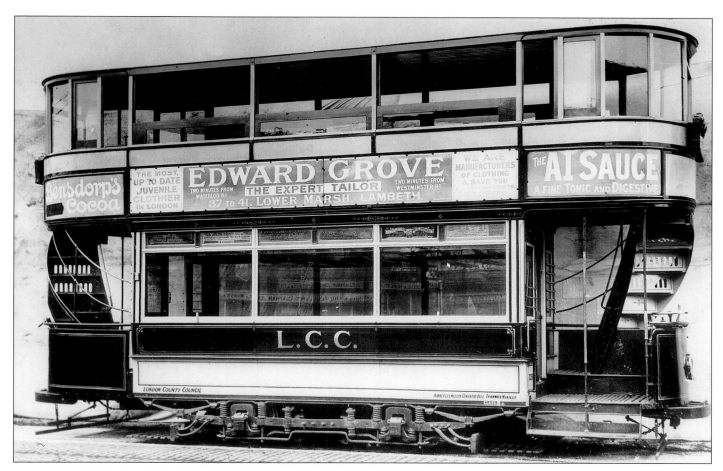

Class cars received new controllers and probably new motors before 1914. Certainly all were converted to Westinghouse T2C controllers and 220 motors following the modernisation of 400 E/1 cars in 1923–25.

The end for Class A came in 1928–31, when cars were gradually withdrawn. The electrical gear and trucks from each car were either salvaged or scrapped. Many body shells survived for decades as sheds on allotments and farms.

Class B cars 102–201.

These trams can be considered a shortened version of the A Class bogie cars. They were built by the ERTC Company, and ran on Brill 21E single trucks. Two traction motors generated 50hp (50.7kW) and seating was provided for 34 on the top deck and 22 in the lower saloon. In many ways these trams were typical of hundreds of other vehicles, which were in service in many British towns and cities. They were designed to be compact cars to be used by the LCC outside rush hours or on lines that had moderate traffic. Their evolution followed that of their eight wheel sisters, with vehicles being allocated to new Classes B2 and B3 (there were very few balcony B1 cars). For the opening of the Woolwich lines in 1908, a Class B4 was introduced. This was an open top B Class with direct stairs and a trolley standard, placed slightly off centre on the top deck. Car 106 of this class has been preserved at the National Tramway Museum.

Over the years the bodywork on this class showed signs of stress and steel body bracing had to be inserted to keep each tram fit for passenger service. However, this was only a partial solution and it became apparent that vehicles were deteriorating quicker than other members of the fleet. By 1914 many were in store, and some were later fitted with trolley poles to be loaned or sold to provincial systems suffering from a rolling stock shortage. In the mid 1920s, a number of these trams were converted into snowbrooms and in this form they survived well into London Transport days. The B Class that were sold to Bexley managed to make it to 1933, when they were all withdrawn and scrapped by London Transport. Some former Class B cars survived in service in Southampton until just after the Second World War.

Car 106 has been meticulously restored by the volunteer labour of the LCC Tramways Trust. The tram now resides at the National Tramway Museum in Crich, Derbyshire. Controller, headlamp, handbrake, direct stairs, metal fender, lifeguard and tray all feature in this view. The destination blind ELEPHANT & CASTLE would not have been used on the original trolley equipped cars, which were confined to the isolated Woolwich outpost based on Abbey Wood Depot.

Class C cars 202–301.

The LCC looked to the Brush Company of Loughborough to supply its second batch of single truck cars. With hindsight this was a good decision as these cars proved sturdier than their B Class sisters. The general design and body style was similar to the previous class. Both B and C classes ran on Brill 21E trucks, but those trams belonging to the latter class received motors, which developed 60hp. During the top cover implementation programme cars were classified C1, C2 and C3 in line with the subdivisions imposed on classes A and B. Trolley poles were not fitted to C Class cars and they never worked outside conduit territory. The main stamping ground of these trams was the Dulwich Hills. Here they worked, in conjunction with class M trams, the services using Dog Kennel Hill. Some sixty cars of this class were equipped with extra mechanical track brakes for their hill climbing duties.

The C Class cars proved more durable than their B Class sisters. Car 296 was photographed at Rye Lane Depot on 31st May 1907. Note the Metropolitan Stage Carriage Licence Plate No. 5586, which was displayed at only one end of the car. *LCC*

One of the author's favourites is this fine study of D/1 Car 371. It represents the acme of Edwardian craftsmanship. Surely in no other era could a public transport vehicle retain such style and utilitarian elegance. The striking dark lake and primrose livery with gold lettering would have enhanced many a South London High Street. *LCC*

They proved tough, reliable little cars, but they produced an uncomfortable ride when driven at speed. This was a characteristic of many 4-wheel, single truck cars, and LCC engineers conducted tests to ascertain how they could alleviate the problem. They pioneered a system of shock absorbers and dampers, which reduced the oscillation between axles and truck, and between car body and truck. This work was carried out in 1924–27 and was reported to have been reasonably successful. Some trams from classes C and D were also equipped with motors and controllers from E/1 Class cars.

Replacement of this batch by more modern vehicles occurred in 1928–30. Many of the class ended up being towed to the ex-LUT Depot at Chiswick. Here they awaited buyers. Car bodies were priced at £5 each. Some eighteen cars were converted to snow-brooms.

Class D cars 302–376, 377–401.

On first appearance these vehicles looked very similar to cars belonging to Class A, however there were important differences in truck design and manufacture. Vehicles from Class D rode on McGuire bogie trucks. The decision to go for the McGuire trucks was probably taken to evaluate their performance. Unfortunately, this type of bogie was never very popular anywhere else, and the Council had to maintain a restricted spares policy when the trucks needed repair. This meant in practice that cars 388 and 392 were eventually retrucked using the tried and tested Brill 22E.

Cars 302–376 were built by Brush in 1904. The remainder of the order was contracted out to the British Electric Car Company at Trafford Park in Manchester. Seating capacity was 38 outside on transverse seats and 28 in the lower saloon on bench seats. Modifications to this class followed the pattern of other classes and vehicles were designated D1, D2 or D3, as appropriate. Four D Class cars – 350, 354, 393 and either 343 or 373 – were sent to Woolwich to help out on the Abbey Wood

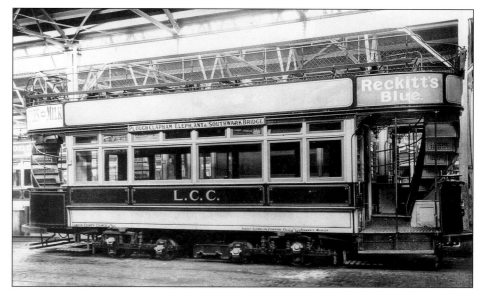

Right **A member of Class D rests at Clapham Depot. Noteworthy features of this double truck vehicle are the magnetic brakes suspended between the driving and pony wheels** of the maximum traction trucks, and the plough carrier attached to the righthand bogie. This view dates from 1906.
F.Merton Atkins

route. They were reclassified D4. They remained in open top condition with direct stairs and the trolley standard placed centrally, but to one side of the top deck. Eventually all car subdivisions were scrapped and 24 trams in this class received trolley poles. Disposal of the class followed the usual routine and cars were delicensed and sold off in 1929–31.

Class E
cars 402–426, 427–551, 602–751.

This class of tram can be considered to have pioneered the typical Capital City Style, which became distinctive to the LCC Tramways. The Council accepted the tender of Hurst, Nelson & Co. of Motherwell, Scotland, to supply the first 150 cars of this class. The lower saloon contained four large windows each side and seated 30 passengers. The upper saloon was fully enclosed and accommodated a further 46 people. This produced a welcome increase in seating capacity over the earlier cars. The height of each car at fifteen feet nine inches (4.8 metres) from rail level to roof was to ensure that E Class trams could pass under Clapham Road and Balham railway bridges.

Construction of each car involved a steel underframe, which supported a mainly wooden body. The driver's platforms were still in an unvestibuled and unglazed condition, thus affording the crew only minimal protection against the elements. The Metropolitan Police were still adamant that no partition, glazed or otherwise, should separate the driver of a bus or tram from the road ahead.

Maximum traction trucks were manufactured by Mountain & Gibson of Bury, Lancashire. They were designated McGuire, Mountain & Gibson Type 3 bogie trucks and were produced in significant numbers

for the LCC. At one stage the manufacturers managed to turn out over 700 trucks in a year. One truck in each pair carried a metal extension in which was housed the plough carrier.

The order for the first 150 cars was placed in August 1905, and delivery began early the following year. It was intended that the first batch – cars 402–551 – would work south of the River Thames, principally out of Clapham Depot. Some vehicles from the 460–490 series started life at New Cross when the Catford to Vauxhall route was extended to Victoria, but most of these later went to Clapham.

The introduction of the E Class pioneered tramcar design features that were to become "the metropolitan standard", and were to last until the end of the tram system in July 1952. The maximum traction trucks have the familiar London look. Bored passengers could read advertisements in the lower saloon top lights for Hyde's Bird Seed and Box & Co. and other local businesses. The tool kit marked with the fleet number is stored under the stairs to the left of the driver. Finally, we note the top deck sliding window used often by youngsters to poke their heads out to get a better view of the scenery.

Partial bulkheads divided seating on the lower deck of this Class A or D car. One wonders if this was a device to stop a least half the passengers sliding into the other half when the driver made an emergency stop! At least, the hardness of the wooden benches was mitigated by the carpeting material embossed with the LCC monogram. Unfortunately, this material had to be withdrawn from the trams and burnt, because, according to official sources, 'it became infested with vermin' – so much for the exciting life led by our forebears!

The series 602–751 was ordered in March 1906 with North London in mind. Stamford Hill and Poplar depots were to receive the new vehicles.

It has been established that these vehicles were delivered without bulkhead doors at the top of the upper deck stairways. This situation was unsatisfactory as it allowed an uncomfortable through draught of air that could reach gale proportions in the winter. Research suggests that cars from about 700 onwards were delivered with top deck bulkhead doors and the situation was gradually rectified, and eventually all cars were equipped with top deck doors.

The fitting of trolley poles, on the other hand, took a little longer, and from 1920 onwards most of this class received the necessary equipment so that they could work all over the network. These vehicles were robustly built and were well maintained by the LCC. They all passed to the LPTB in July 1933.

Class E/1
cars 752–1001, 1002–1051, 1052–1226, 1227–1426, 1477–1676, 1727–1776, 1777–1851.

These trams were the mainstay of LCC operations and constituted a stable, standard fleet for almost the entire life of the first generation London tram system. In outward appearance and mechanical performance they owed much to the satisfactory results obtained from Class E cars. Experience of the E Class in service had suggested to the LCC engineers some fine tuning to the basic design. In the E/1 these practical results were realised by the inclusion of a superior method of body trussing to eliminate stresses and strains, wider corner pillars in the lower saloon and modified M&G trucks. Seating was for 32 on the lower deck and for 46 in the upper saloon.

A decision was reached to keep the overall height of these cars to a minimum; this was in line with Council policy that many of these cars were to be fitted with trolley poles. There was a problem with clearances under Clapham Road and Balham railway bridges. Normal height top covered cars of classes A to D could not pass under these bridges. When trolley poles needed to be added to Clapham route cars in 1921, the pole on the first experimental car had to be offset, away from the crown of the roof, in order to clear Balham Bridge. The problem was finally solved when the roadway was lowered (see p.103). Other design features included destination indicators mounted in teak weatherproof cases. Illuminated service numbers in the end window of the upper saloon were added towards the end of 1913. Lifeguards were of the swinging gate and tray pattern and every car was equipped with an oak toolbox. This contained a feeder pillar key, a jack capable of a maximum lift of five tons, one two pound hammer, one pair of conduit hatch lifters, one screwdriver, a pair of pliers, a pair of India rubber gloves, ash strips for putting ploughs in at a live hatch, one adjustable spanner, one chisel, one shackle, a tin of disinfectant powder, a plough lifting rope and one wood block. Each E/1 tram was also kitted out with a crowbar with the top end made to fit the jack, a point lever, a flexible steel towrope, assorted hooks and a towing chain!

The first order was placed with Hurst, Nelson on 21st February 1907. Delivery was scheduled to commence from 20th May. The order for next batch of cars – 1002 to 1051 – showed a significant confidence in the skill and reliability of the Council's own direct labour department. They were constructed at the old North Metropolitan horse tram works in Union Road, Leytonstone. The decision to construct tram bodies at Leytonstone was partly due to the fact that the

London County Council Maximum-Traction Truck. — In Fig. 10 is shown a centre-bearing swing-bolster maximum traction truck, which is specially fitted. with a plough carrier, for use on the conduit system of the London County Council Tramways.

The side elevation, plan, and half-sectional elevation are shown, respectively, in views (a), (b), and (c). The bolster a is a hollow casting that extends nearly the full width of the truck between the side bars b. The car body rests on the top quadrant or swivel plate c, which is pivoted to the lower swivel plate d at the pivotal point e. The lower plate d, in turn, is hinged to the bolster at f, so that the swivel plates may rock slightly, if necessary, to equalize the distribution of the load on them. An additional rubbing plate or side cushion g is bolted to each end of the bolster to balance the car body. The nests of helical springs h under each end of the bolster rest on spring planks i, which are in turn hung by links j to brackets k on the transoms l. The whole weight of the car is thus transmitted through the springs h to the transoms l, which are rigidly bolted to the side bars b of the truck frame. The side bars are themselves spring-borne by the helical springs m on the top of the axle boxes n, o.

The brake blocks p, q are applied to the respective wheels by exerting a tension on the brake pull rod, which is not shown, but which is pivoted to the central point of the link r. The driving-wheel brake blocks p are attached to the curved brake beam s, and the blocks and beam are hung from the end sill t of the truck. The pony-wheel brake blocks q are attached to the brake beam u, and are hung from one transom by means of the brackets v. Since there is not room for the motor to be hung between the axles of the truck, the motor support w is carried on the spring pillars x, and these are in turn bolted to the end sill t. Extensions b' of the side bars b of the truck form the side frames of the plough carrier. To allow the truck to swivel freely on curves, and in order that the plough may readily be removed from the car, the runners y, which support the plough, stretch right across the truck, while the electrical contact bars z are 4 feet 5 inches long. The contact bars are curved away toward the ends to provide an entrance for the collector springs with which the plough is fitted. In many cases collector springs are not used, and connection is made to the plough by means of flexible insulated cables.

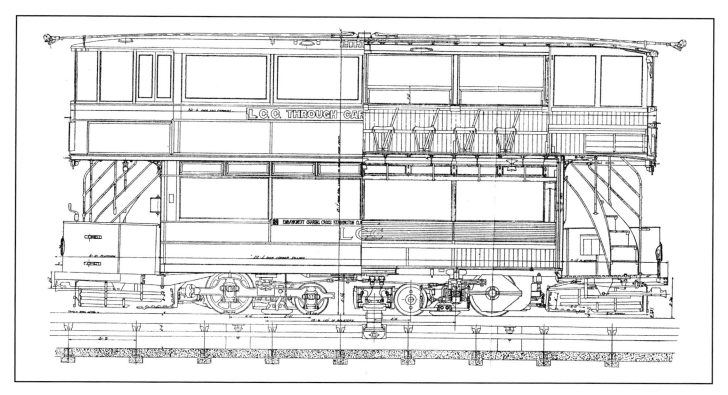

LCC had inherited a number of ex-North Metropolitan employees and large quantities of seasoned timber, originally intended for the building of new horsecars. Some voices on the Council urged that all tram construction be kept in house, but this was not possible due to the constraints of the Union Road Works, which could only handle six cars under construction at any one time.

The order for cars 1052–1226 was placed about the same time as deliveries on the February order started to filter through. This latest batch started to arrive at the turn of the year 1908/9. On 29th June 1909, the LCC approved the financing of another 200 E/1 class cars. Previous batches had varied in the provision of trolley equipped cars – in the series 752–1051, only 977–1001 had been given overhead equipment. Most of the 1052–1226 series were conduit only. Cars from the series 1227–1426 were all dual equipped for trolley and conduit. Cars 1350–1353 were triple equipped – conduit, single wire trolley and double wire trolley for the Eltham to Woolwich service. The last order before the war resulted in cars 1477–1676 being delivered from Brush in 1911–1912. It should be mentioned that Hurst, Nelson were also working on the 4-wheel version of the E/1, which was classified M, at the same time as they were fulfilling the main orders for bogie cars.

After the war the LCC returned to the tried and tested design and commissioned further cars of this class. This time the order was split. Brush built 75 cars, while Hurst, Nelson supplied 50. The batch from Loughborough was numbered 1777–1851 and the HN cars received the numbers 1727–1776. Delivery was spread from 1922 over to the following year.

Above **Side view of a standard E/1 car with half cut away to show seating – note the plough in position.**

E/1 Car 1262 is pictured in Holloway Depot by the tram washing apparatus. In pre mechanical days it was reckoned that one person could clean four trams per night. This particular vehicle is from the 1910 batch of 'standards' and has already lost the three coloured light display above the destination blind. The Venner number stencil, which measured 26½ inches (673mm) by 8½ inches (216mm), can clearly be seen in the top deck window. Service 27 ran from Edmonton to Euston Road. LCC

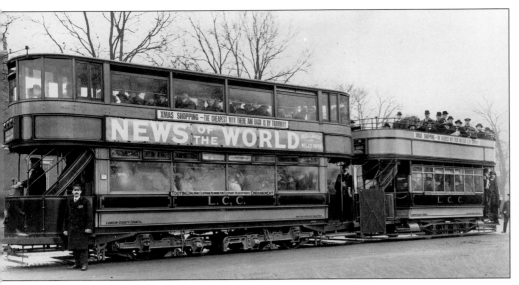

Class M
cars 1427–1476, 1677–1726.

These trim and sturdy vehicles were in fact a shortened version of the standard E/1. Their main claim to fame was the special single truck on which each car rode. This was manufactured from pressed steel and was connected to the underframe by a swing bolster mechanism normally associated with bogie cars. This method of truck attachment produced a distinctive swaying motion in the tram, which was unlike that of other, more conventional 4-wheel trams.

Cars were built by Hurst, Nelson, with the exception of specimen Car 1427, which was constructed at Leytonstone in 1909. The first batch was delivered in 1910, and

cars 1428–1437 were equipped with double trolleys and put to work on the Eltham service. Each car seated 24 in the lower saloon and 38 on the top deck. Highgate Hill was the recipient of cars 1438–1476. Tramcars working this gradient were fitted with a conduit slot brake as an extra safety feature. Brush-built cars 1677 to 1726 acquired the epithet of Dulwich cars, because they were allocated to the Dog Kennel Hill routes. In the 1920s, in common with trams of Class C, these cars received dampers to counteract excessive body movement and oscillation from the trucks.

The traditional double deck fleet operated by the LCC served its purpose well, but as we shall see in a subsequent chapter, the aspirations of the average passenger, as regards standards of comfort, rose after the First World War. The LCC was slow to meet the challenge, as indeed were a significant number of British tramways. The resulting pullmanisation programme will be described later. Suffice to say here that classes E/1 and M were well maintained and were compulsorily transferred to the LPTB in 1933.

Services working the Kingsway Subway had to be equipped with single deck cars. The design of these vehicles reflected American practice in that passengers could board or alight from either side of the tram. This facility was obviously useful at the island platforms in the Kingsway Subway. The original concept of single deckers seems to modern eyes a totally sound one, but for operational reasons these trams were before their time. The vast majority of the cars owned by the LCC were double deck, and over the years, the pressure built up for a standardised fleet. Had a 1911 experiment succeeded, in which cars 575 and 572 were coupled together, then the future might have been different.

Class F cars 552–567.

These trams were constructed by Dick, Kerr & Co at Preston. They were delivered in 1905–1906, and were of composite metal construction. This method was employed to reduce the fire risk that a conventional wooden bodied car might suffer. Some wood was used in the construction of the seats, but it was treated with a special fire retardant compound. The practical use of steel sections and aluminium panels for the bodywork resulted in a solid, serviceable and reliable vehicle. Seating on two facing longitudinal benches was for 36 people. Cars had both top lights and a clerestory roof to ensure adequate ventilation. The bulkheads of this class were made from steel panels and did not contain windows. This class lasted until withdrawal in 1928–1930; the electrical equipment was salvaged after disposal of the bodies.

Class G cars 568–601.

Very similar to their F Class sisters, these vehicles also sported metal bodies, but this time with glazed bulkheads. They were built by Brush and ran on M&G maximum traction trucks. Some single deck trams entered service from Clapham and New Cross Depots in 1907, pending the completion of the Kingsway Subway in April 1908. These vehicles continued to work for some years from Clapham and New Cross on the two subway routes. As

Right Car 600 is nearing the end of its days. Note the LONDON THROUGH THE AGES poster on the bulkhead window. This was an effective use of publicity to encourage tramriding. Destiny later decreed that this particular car would escape the immediate fate of the other single deckers and it was taken to Holloway Depot for use as a tool van.

regards the rest of Class G, with the exception of car 600, the bodies were all sold off after withdrawal from service. Car 600 was retained as a tool store at Holloway Depot.

Petrol Electric cars P1–P3.

The LCC was nothing if not inventive in its desire to reduce costs on the electrification of less remunerative routes. One target in mind was the horse car line from South Hackney to West India Docks (Service 71). The three metropolitan boroughs of Hackney, Bethnal Green and Stepney had consistently refused to grant the LCC permission to erect overhead wires on this route. Conduit construction was ruled out

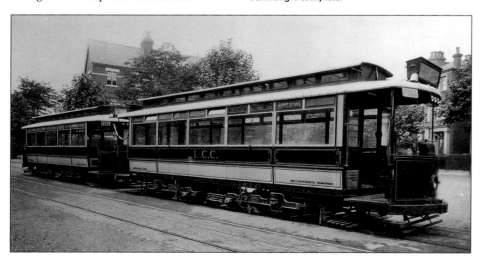

by the LCC due to the expense involved. The Council had already suffered the embarrassment of the GB surface contact fiasco, so they must have been somewhat wary of any large scale experimental projects. The next foray into the realms of cost cutting only concerned three vehicles, which were the subject of an experiment into the practical use of petrol electric tramcars. It was mooted that a light 4-wheel car, powered by the Tilling Stevens system, might just do the trick on lightly trafficked lines. A conventional petrol engine, which developed 40hp (40.5kW), was installed under the stairs on one platform. This engine was linked to a generator that produced around 350 volts for the car motors. Provision was made in the design for an alternative power supply, when the car was not operating in petrol electric mode. Presumably a plough carrier and a trolley mast could be fitted as required.

On 7th May 1913, trials took place in and around the Central Repair Depot in Charlton. Contemporary reports suggest that the signs were hopeful, but later trials over Service 70 from Tooley Street to Greenwich proved less than satisfactory. Cars P1–P3 were withdrawn to Marius Road Depot, where they were partially dismantled. They eked out the rest of their existence shunting trailer cars within the confines of the depot.

Trailer Cars T1–T8, T9–T158.

It was apparent in the second decade of the twentieth century that, at peak periods, the LCC could do with some extra passenger capacity on trunk routes. The practice of using trailer cars was widespread in many countries, and it seemed a good idea to try it out in London. Eight former North Metropolitan horsecars were rebuilt as trailers and trials were conducted in 1913. Trailers were used as experimental units on services 44 and 42 in Woolwich, and on services 2 and 4 from Merton to the Victoria Embankment.

Results of these tests were reasonably encouraging and the Council was persuaded to order another 150 purpose built vehicles from Brush of Loughborough. Cars T9–T158 were delivered from January 1915 to

Left The petrol-electric cars P1-3 looked very similar to trailers T1-T8. One obvious difference was the provision of an independent source of motive power. The engine was at one end of the car together with the generator and at the other end (depicted here) could be found a radiator and a Solex fan mounted on the shaft of a small series wound electric motor.

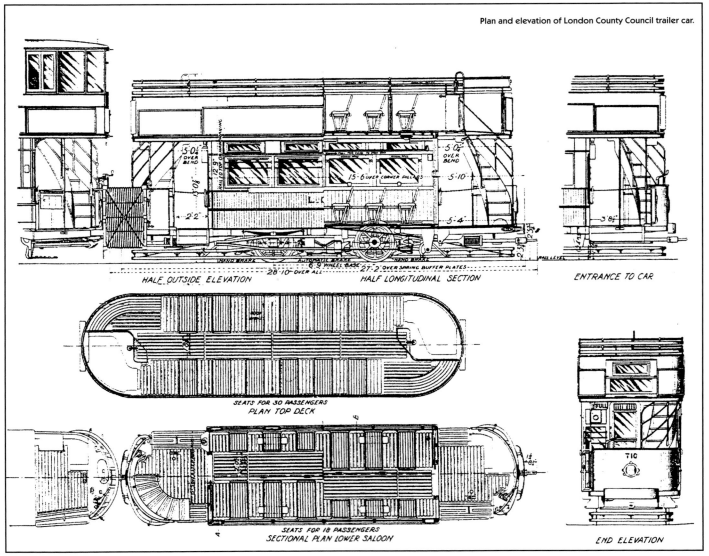

Plan and elevation of London County Council trailer car.

HALF OUTSIDE ELEVATION   HALF LONGITUDINAL SECTION   ENTRANCE TO CAR

SEATS FOR 30 PASSENGERS
PLAN TOP DECK

SEATS FOR 18 PASSENGERS
SECTIONAL PLAN LOWER SALOON

END ELEVATION

October 1916. Wartime production difficulties were cited as a reason for the delay in supplying the trailers. They were set to work on the services already mentioned, plus the 64/84 from New Cross Gate to the Embankment, the 70 from Greenwich to London Bridge and the 40 from Abbey Wood to the Embankment. All seemed to go to plan, with the trailers fulfilling their primary function of transporting war workers and London commuters.

The return of a peacetime economy brought changes to traffic patterns, and the 1921 order for 125 new E/1 trams effectively doomed the trailers. The service along the main trunk routes was speeded up with traditional single unit cars, and the trailers were withdrawn in 1923–24.

Works Cars.

Ancillary vehicles were vital for the effective operation of a complex tramway system. Works cars were employed to ferry supplies from depot to depot, and to convey maintenance equipment to permanent way renewal sites. In summer road watering duties were undertaken and in winter the snowbrooms made an appearance. Class H cars 01–04 were single truck water tank cars. Car 01 was fitted with double trolley poles for the Eltham route. Class J cars 05–06 were single truck stores vans. Class K cars 07–010 were stores vans. Class L cars 011–012 were open vans used to transport wheelsets, motors and axles from the CRD to other depots. They rode on unusual Warner radial trucks. Class L/1 cars 013–014 were stores cars constructed on trucks removed from B Class passenger cars. At one stage these two trams were coupled together as emergency staff cars for the workers at the CRD. Class L/2 Car 015 was constructed out of C Class Car 273, which had survived as a double decker until 1929. Its main function was to transport sand from the several LCC wharves to outlying depots.

A total of twenty-one B Class cars were converted to snowbrooms. The top decks were removed and a large rotary brush was installed under each platform. Similar treatment was meted out to eighteen C Class cars, which were fitted with snow ploughs. The use of all these snow fighting vehicles was very restricted, and their appearances were reserved for emergencies only.

The LCC also owned, at one time or another, just over fifty motor vehicles. The functions of some of the road service fleet were similar to their railbound stores car contemporaries. However, as internal combustion engine technology advanced, the Council came to rely more and more on these vehicles to carry out routine tasks, one of these was to act as tower wagons for overhead wire repairs.

Finally, we are presented with a mystery. In June 1910 a Contract & Specification document was issued for tram-building firms to submit tenders for 50 single-deck cars of the Class N bogie type. This was, in fact, a single-deck version of the standard E/1. Research has so far failed to unearth the car plans of this unique class or the reasons for wanting to order this type of vehicle.

In reviewing the rolling stock, it becomes apparent that the LCC was well placed in terms of vehicle numbers to face the expected post-war upturn in passengers. Such optimism proved to be illusory and it became increasing obvious during the 1920s that the LCC, together with every other tramway operator in the metropolitan area, would have a fight for survival on its hands.

The LCC had its own standard gauge, third rail electric system for conveying coal from the Thames wharf to Greenwich Power Station. The two vehicles depicted here were the forgotten members of the works car fleet. R.T. Horne Collection

The trackwork within Charlton Works could accommodate standard gauge railway flange widths. This Andrew Barclay built 0-4-0 saddle tank locomotive was photographed in March 1931 as it neared the end of its working life. Steam traction was employed to shunt tramcars around the Central Repair Depot. H.C. Casserley

CHAPTER ELEVEN
A New Beginning

THE YEARS from the end of the Great War in 1918 to the start of the Depression in the early thirties have been variously described as *The Jazz Age*, *The Roaring Twenties*, or more prosaically, *The Years Between the Wars*. London society reflected the fads and fancies of the western world, as prosperity gradually returned to the capital and *the Bright Young Things* basked in the spotlight. Listening to popular music, following fashion, dancing to live bands, shopping in department stores, watching professional football and hiking across the countryside were some of the cultural activities that blossomed in the 1920s. Charlie Chaplin, a former frequent user of LCC trams from Kennington, was pulling in audiences at the new cinemas, which were appearing all over the capital.

Eminent personalities in political circles spoke of '*new beginnings*' and of '*homes fit for heroes*' to sweeten the return of many soldiers to what were practically slum conditions. The policy makers in Whitehall were dominated by paradoxical desires – on the one hand they wanted to make Germany pay for its aggression, and on the other, they wished to improve international relations so as to avoid the carnage of another world war. Many intellectuals, politicians and trade unionists were influenced by the workers' state that was being created in the Soviet Union. The relationships between capital and labour, private enterprise and state intervention became important issues in an era of radical activity.

In outer London boroughs the suburban middle classes came of age and the private motoring era began to have an effect on the streets of the metropolis. Slum clearance projects were reinvigorated, and the construction of large council estates on green field sites, such as Downham and Becontree, promised decent accommodation for working people. Over half of the nation's population took the first step on the road to emancipation in December 1918, when women over 30, who were householders, received the vote. Full adult female suffrage had to wait until July 1928.

In spite of the increase in ownership of private cars, the vast majority of Londoners used public transport. Technical advances in the design of the motor bus were to propel this vehicle to the top of the passenger carrying league. A hybrid called the railless tram or trolleybus was also in the throes of development, and the success of the 1922 tram to trolleybus conversion on a route in Birmingham raised a few eyebrows amongst transport managers.

After the First World War the Council dispensed with the services of women conductors. In those days of restrictive employment laws the dismissal of the female workforce was judged as expedient, bearing in mind the number of male employees who would be returning to their former jobs from active service in the military. Car 240 is pictured at Peckham Rye terminus.

A report presented to the LCC on 15th July 1924, was headed TRAMWAYS, TROLLEY VEHICLES AND MOTOR OMNIBUSES COMPARED. It concentrated mainly on the experience of Birmingham Corporation, and on the traffic figures from Bradford and Leeds. Alfred Baker, manager of the Birmingham system and former chief officer at the LCC, summed up the situation:

In anticipation of an extension of an existing tramway, where it was reasonably probable that tramways would be required at some future date, I would use the trolley omnibus. I would use the trolley omnibus in substitution for a single line of tramway where the traffics are light, or where it was not possible to double the track, particularly when faced with reconstruction.

On routes in suburban districts where some sort of transport is necessary and where there is no likelihood of trams being required, I would certainly use the petrol omnibus. I would use the petrol omnibus in running cross country routes and in connecting up the outer termini of tramways.

I desire to repeat and emphasise that, for the transport of large masses of people expeditiously and cheaply, the humble tramcar has no competitor and still holds the field.

The conclusion to this report mentioned the possibility of further research into the running of trolleybuses as connecting services to the Council's tramways. The thought was also planted that a trolleybus route could precede a full blown tramway. As it was, the LCC had already tested the water with tentative plans for a trolleybus route from Lee Green to Crystal Palace and West Norwood, but the project fizzled out.

Clearly, the tramcar was going to come under increased scrutiny as the decade wore on. Its mass transit capabilities in shifting large crowds were not in question and in this respect the LCC seemed to be on safe ground. The Council tramways system was patently geared to the volume market, as it were. However, on the edges of the County of London, many tramways, both municipal and company owned, were feeling the pinch. Underinvestment in new rolling stock and track layouts had been chronic, and it quickly became clear to decision makers that the benefits of maintaining electric traction along narrow streets were debatable. Indeed, as we shall see, the dismantling of tramways in London commenced outside the LCC area, and from the late twenties onwards, the writing was well and truly on the wall.

After the enforced postponement of expansion plans in the war years, the Council was quick off the mark in peacetime. On 18th February 1919, the Highways Committee approved an application for Parliamentary powers to link several inner London termini. Substantial street widening on the proposed routes was deemed unnecessary and it was calculated that through running cars would show a

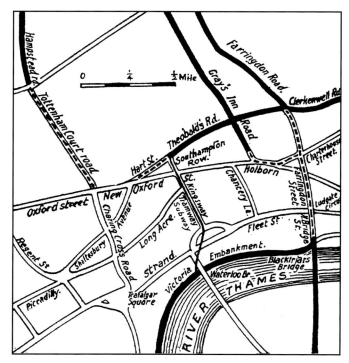

Top **Continuing the Charlton theme, we now find ourselves at the Central Repair Depot. Next to Class A Car 29 and, partly obscuring an E Class tram, is horse drawn Tower Wagon 183. The date of this view is given as 1st March 1924. If this is correct, then these cars would be waiting for a mechanical overhaul and a repaint.**

Above **Quiet days outside St Laurence's Church, Catford, as a near empty E Class Car 426 waits for departure to Victoria. The year is 1923 and later that autumn the LCC will be called upon to transport football fans to Charlton Athletic's new home ground at The Mount, Laleham Road. Fortunately for the history of the peoples' game, disastrous financial results caused Charlton to move back to The Valley, easily accessible by LCC services 36, 38 and 40.**
N.D.W.Elston

Left **Plan of the proposed central London extensions – March 1919.**

97

Left If the projected link up between Holborn and Farringdon termini had gone ahead, then MET trams working over LCC metals would have avoided the time consuming shunting manoeuvres at Holborn. Note the tied down trolley pole on this tram, which was running on conduit track at the northern end of Grays Inn Road near Derby Street. This Service 59 tram is working from Holborn to Edmonton Town Hall, and MET Car 245 was supplying the motive power. The route had been worked alternately by the LCC and the MET, but a pooling agreement between the two operators resulted in Service 59 being run by the MET from 1924.

Below left Views are rare of the City terminus at the Queen Street Place approach to Southwark Bridge. Cars 1833 on Service 6, and 1378 on Service 46 are queuing to use the reversal stub occupied by the tram in the distance.

symbolism of the occasion was completely lost on the Lord Mayor of London, Sir Alfred Bower. The main gist of his speech seemed to centre on the fact that large crowds wouldn't have to walk across the River in inclement weather. They could now take the Council tramcar instead. No allusion was made to the City's implacable hatred of this form of transport.

A survey of the fleet, conducted for a magazine article in May 1919, revealed the existence of 1,375 bogie cars, 242 single truck cars, 50 steel Kingsway Subway cars, 158 trailer cars, 8 stores vans, 4 water vans and one rail grinder. The use of trailer cars has already been mentioned in the previous chapter, and these vehicles came into public focus in the autumn of 1919. A national railway strike began on 27th September and lasted until 5th October. During this time the LCC Tramways were called upon to perform heroic feats of crowd shifting. Lines of passengers locked out of Charing Cross Station formed queues on the Embankment. The *coupled cars*, as they were called, came into their element and were praised for the effectiveness with which they dealt with the rush hour problem.

Although the 1919 proposals had run into the sand, ideas for track extensions in other parts of the capital fell on fertile soil. In the late spring of 1920, the LCC and MET rails were connected at Stamford Hill. Before the inauguration of through services the side slot conduit in Kingsland Road was replaced by the more normal centre slot variety. On 2nd June, Service 49 from Liverpool Street was revised to terminate at Edmonton Town Hall instead of Stamford Hill. LCC cars shed their ploughs at a change pit just north of the junction with Amhurst Park.

South of the River, the LCC was about to realise a dream that had first appeared in the South London Tramways Bill of 1873. Amongst other lines, this bill had proposed a cross country link between Lee Green and Eltham. The horse tramway, which the promoting company had envisaged, only ever existed on paper. The idea then lay dormant until conduit tracks reached Lee Green and the twin wire overhead Service 44 climbed the hill to terminate at Eltham Church. A connection now seemed a logical

surplus over working expenses. The first new tramway was a natural connection between the two halves of the system. It was to run from existing tracks on Blackfriars Bridge via New Bridge Street, Ludgate Circus and Farringdon Street to link up with the tramway in Farringdon Road. A second new line was proposed via Charterhouse Street, Holborn Circus and Holborn to the tram terminus at the foot of Grays Inn Road.

The idea of getting trams closer to the main shopping areas of Oxford Street and New Oxford Street was the basis behind a proposal to extend the Hampstead Road tramway the length of Tottenham Court Road. A second proposal concerned the prolonging of tracks in Theobalds Road to a new terminus at the corner of Hart Street and New Oxford Street. It was also suggested by the Council that the Aldgate terminus be moved a short distance across the City of London boundary towards a new stopping place outside Aldgate Station.

It might be supposed that the feeling of national unity in a common purpose engendered by the recent war would have

produced at least a consensus on these extensions. Sadly, the protestors returned to their time honoured stance and Parliament threw out the proposals, mainly because the local authorities objected. Thus another golden opportunity to facilitate cross London passenger traffic was lost, and this setback finally convinced the LCC that further plans for central London were pointless. Clearly, the energies of the Council were better directed to improving the outer London network, and with this in mind, powers were sought for a suburban link between Seven Sisters Road and Stamford Hill. This new line was to run along Amhurst Park and was to be equipped with overhead wires. Success was forthcoming on this proposal, although the line was not opened for another five years.

One minor success scored by the LCC was the construction of tracks over Southwark Bridge to a new terminus in Queen Street Place. Did some wag in the LCC fix the opening date of 14th July 1925, to symbolise the metaphorical storming of the Bastille of privilege that was the City of London? If this was the case, then the

next step in the works programme. As with all new lines, objectors had the opportunity to write to the local authority concerned, in this case the Metropolitan Borough of Woolwich. One such complainant, who lived in a big house on Eltham Road, asserted that the arrival of tramcars outside his front door would encourage *'all manner of urchins and the working class'* to pilfer fruit from his apple trees! One can assume the objector's point of view was noted, and that a fixed stop was not placed in the vicinity of his front wall.

A new change pit was constructed outside Lee Green Fire Station and double track was laid along Eltham Road past Eltham Green to the temporary end of the line outside the gates of Lyme Farm, Eltham. As the name of the terminus suggests, the major part of the extension was rural in nature and on fine summer days, cars on Service 46 would carry a fair number of hikers and excursionists out to see the countryside. Double trolley wires were employed throughout in accordance with the standing orders of the Royal Greenwich Observatory. Trams were permitted to be driven at a heady 20mph (32km/h) along most of the route. Colonel J. W. Pringle of the Ministry of Transport inspected the line on 26th November and public service commenced three days later.

The remaining tracks on Eltham Hill into Eltham High Street had to wait for road widening to be carried out. Eventually, on 25th February 1921, only a few yards separated cars on Service 46 and those on Service 44 in Well Hall Road. The connection round the corner of St John's Churchyard was finally opened to traffic on 22nd March. Through trams now ran from Southwark Bridge to Beresford Square. They were designated Service 46. Surprisingly, Service 44 survived, as a short working of the 46, throughout the rest of the LCC era until the final day of tramway operation in July 1952.

In the south-western reaches of the system, Wandsworth East Hill was finally joined to tracks in the High Street on 4th August 1921. This was a logical connection, which enabled services 26 and 28 to be extended to connect with the Hammersmith lines.

Across in East London, the rails along Grove Road and Burdett Road had been lying derelict since the withdrawal of the horsecar service on 11th August 1914. Plans to electrify this route had stalled because of the local councils' opposition to anything other than the conduit system. It seems that the stubborn town halls were informed in no uncertain terms that if they didn't agree to drop the conduit demand, then the line would go the same way as its contemporaries in Bermondsey. Total abandonment loomed large and this prospect concentrated the minds of the elected officials wonderfully and conversion to electric traction commenced in 1920.

The new line had several interesting features. It was equipped with overhead wires and possessed two change pits, one at the Hackney end of Well Street and the other at the junction of Burdett Road and East India Dock Road. Cars working through South Hackney navigated a figure of eight section on one way single track in Lauriston Road, Church Crescent, Cassland Road and Terrace Road. Finally, if proof were needed that the money really had run out for expensive demolition projects, then one needed to look no further than the southern half of Grove Road. Here the electric track was fitted into the existing road layout. The budget did not run to widening the carriageway and the trams were forced into a single track and loops arrangement. The section opened on 28th July 1921, to be followed on 1st December by the inauguration of connecting curves from Graham Road into Mare Street, and from Mare Street into Well Street. This allowed Service 77 to replace Service 71. It ran through from Aldersgate via Dalston, Hackney and Burdett Road to West India Dock.

The other tramway event in East London was the near collapse of the Leyton system. This had been on the cards for some time, and the LCC already had contingency plans to maintain existing through services. The Council worked out a deal with Leyton whereby they undertook to work and

Above right **The extension of Service 46 from Lee Green to Woolwich via Eltham was an immediate success. Double trolley E/1 Car 1369 makes its way along Greens End towards Beresford Square. The Royal Arsenal Gate is in the distance. The 54 bus loading at the side of the road has a long pedigree; the route is still operational, although nowadays much of central Woolwich is a traffic free zone.**
D.Jones Collection

Right **Pictures showing Service 77 in LCC days are very rare. The figure of 8 single track section – southbound via Cassland Road, Terrace Road and Lauriston Road; northbound via Church Crescent and Lauriston Road – was a unique feature of this postwar electrification. A northbound car has just crossed the southbound track and is now running along Lauriston Road. The van on the left of the picture is parked outside the Albion Public House.**
G.N.Southerden

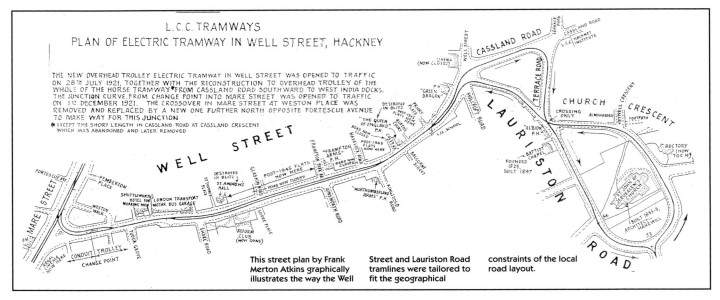

L.C.C. TRAMWAYS
PLAN OF ELECTRIC TRAMWAY IN WELL STREET, HACKNEY

THE NEW OVERHEAD TROLLEY ELECTRIC TRAMWAY IN WELL STREET WAS OPENED TO TRAFFIC ON 28TH JULY 1921, TOGETHER WITH THE RECONSTRUCTION TO OVERHEAD TROLLEY OF THE WHOLE OF THE HORSE TRAMWAY FROM CASSLAND ROAD SOUTHWARD TO WEST INDIA DOCKS. THE JUNCTION CURVE FROM CHANGE POINT INTO MARE STREET WAS OPENED TO TRAFFIC ON 1ST DECEMBER 1921. THE CROSSOVER IN MARE STREET AT WESTON PLACE WAS REMOVED AND REPLACED BY A NEW ONE FURTHER NORTH OPPOSITE FORTESCUE AVENUE TO MAKE WAY FOR THIS JUNCTION
* EXCEPT THE SHORT LENGTH IN CASSLAND ROAD AT CASSLAND CRESCENT WHICH WAS ABANDONED AND LATER REMOVED

This street plan by Frank Merton Atkins graphically illustrates the way the Well Street and Lauriston Road tramlines were tailored to fit the geographical constraints of the local road layout.

maintain the Leyton lines for ten years from 1st July 1921. Leyton Council retained ownership of the track and agreed to finance any future repairs to the permanent way. On this topic it is worth noting that the tram tracks adjacent to Whipps Cross Road, on the edge of Epping Forest, were placed on a private right of way confined to tramcars.

As regards rolling stock, no less than nineteen Leyton cars were withdrawn and replaced by twenty E/1s, which were transferred to Leyton Depot. LCC trams now operated, in conjunction with those of West Ham Corporation, Service 7 – Bakers Arms to Victoria & Albert Docks via Stratford – and Service 8, connecting the same two termini, but routed via Forest Gate.

Although the elected members of Leyton Council were mightily relieved to get out of the tramway business, they didn't quite manage to wash their hands completely of the whole affair. Rather perversely, some local councillors still acted as if they were doing the LCC a favour by letting them run *their* trams! Several times during the twelve years of LCC stewardship, they managed to persuade the LCC to listen to their pleas. Consequently, when a scheme was suggested in 1926 to close Leyton Depot in Lea Bridge Road and transfer operation of services 7 and 8 to West Ham Corporation, all hell broke loose. Fears were expressed that the LCC was divesting itself by stealth of its Leyton appendage. Public opinion forced a change of heart, and anyway, West

Ham later acknowledged that they didn't have the spare capacity to run the services single handed. A further storm blew up in 1928, when the LCC, mindful of savings to be made in manpower, sacked seven men from Leyton Depot. The installation of new car washing equipment had effectively made them redundant. Local indignation was again aroused and the furore reached right to Joshua Kidd Bruce, the General Manager. Fortunately, wiser counsels then prevailed and a face saving agreement was worked out with Leyton whereby other work was found for those who had been dismissed.

On the streets of East London and along many tram routes in other parts of London competing buses added to the traffic congestion. The drivers of these vehicles sometimes took risks to snatch passengers from other companies. Collisions between rival operators occasionally provoked a bout of fisticuffs in full public view. The situation was aggravated by the apparent acquiescence of the Metropolitan Police, who were the licensing authority. Concern was expressed in Parliament and matters came to a head with the passing of the London Traffic Act 1924.

Although the legislation was principally directed at bus companies, the power to restrict bus operation along certain thoroughfares certainly helped the tramways. The act specifically mentions that restrictions should apply where the existence of established alternative passenger transport facilities along a particular street rendered further bus competition unnecessary. This new law gave some respite to the hard pressed tramways, but the sword swung both ways. Having disposed of a number of annoying competitors, the London General Omnibus Company emerged stronger and fitter. It was now able to devote more resources to the improvement of bus designs and to the development of new routes, which served growing suburbs beyond the tram termini.

It was alleged that Ministerial intervention in the London Traffic Act had saved the tramways. Lack of revenue would eventually force the LCC and other tramway owning councils into a position where they would not be able to service their debts. The burden would then fall on the ratepayers. It was also argued that if many miles of tramways went out of business, cheap fares for workmen and others would become a

Into East Ham territory by Woodgrange Park Station, we observe LCC Car 1168 on the through 63 service from Aldgate to Ilford Broadway. Competition is apparent in the form of General bus B 612 on route 25. Tram, motor bus and suburban railway all offer the potential traveller a choice of destinations at different fares. Throughout the twenties local authorities, highway engineers and town planners were locked in discussions to decide how to optimise public transport arrangements. Unfortunately, in the long run the tram lost out.

thing of the past. Thus the poor would suffer by the wholesale conversion to buses.

One of the recommendations contained in Section 1 of the London Traffic Act was the establishment of the London and Home Counties Traffic Advisory Committee. This gathering of the great and the good from the worlds of local government, public transport, road haulage, the police and the main line railways was convened in a worthy attempt to sort out the growing traffic chaos. They published an annual report detailing the progress, or lack of it, of various pet schemes devoted to speeding up the motorist. When tramways did feature in their deliberations, they were stigmatised by the so-called coefficient of obstruction. This quasi-scientific mumbo jumbo designated, one presumes on a scale of one to ten, the electric tramcar as 9, the motor bus as 4 and the taxicab as 1. All of which provided a perfect justification in the increasingly anti tram propaganda emanating from motoring associations and the underground railway and bus companies. This sliding scale of highway obstruction did have its lighter side, when, on a tour of LCC tramway installations, the manager of Calcutta Tramways remarked that an elephant sitting in the middle of the road merited an 11 on the scale – errant pachyderms were obviously a problem for some tramways of the Raj!

The first two annual reports from the London and Home Counties Traffic Advisory Committee deserve further scrutiny. As befitted a serious study of traffic problems, the 1925 offering from the Committee was packed full of text, maps and diagrams illustrating the ideas of contemporary experts. When the reader actually cuts through the verbiage, the suggestions and action plans seem less convincing. This was disappointing, and one might be forgiven for thinking that, in local authority offices and government circles, the report was probably filed rather quickly. The bus companies demonstrated a range of emotions over the restricted streets order of the 1924 Act. Predictably, some wanted it scrapped immediately, and presumably they were less than impressed by the fact that some 600 streets, where trams operated, had been declared or were about to be declared restricted. From the tramway point of view there was an interesting discussion document on the future of the Elephant and Castle congestion black spot. Repositioning of tram tracks seemed to be the favoured option here. The same solution was proposed for the Hay Market, Aldgate, where the tram rails were splayed either side of the market activities. Finally,

passenger figures were included for a major traffic census of public transport corridors in London. LCC trams appeared in three of the surveys – Ilford Broadway to Aldgate, Barking Broadway to Aldgate and Wimbledon Station to Kennington Gate. The percentage of seating accommodation occupied in trams and buses on departure from selected loading points on these trunk routes demonstrated a remarkable uniformity. This was further proof that buses were now able to offer a service on a par with their railbound competitors. Rather ominously, the chart of accident statistics at the end of the Report gives a special section headed Tramway Accidents. In 1925 there were no less than 143 out of a total of 462 street accidents, which were attributed to the presence of tramways on the capital's highways.

The 1926–1927 Report seemed a little more focused than its predecessor. Main congestion spots were listed and suitable remedies suggested. The main thrust of the Report was to encourage cooperation

A congestion trouble spot in anybody's language was the five way tram junction at Gardiners Corner, Aldgate. LCC cars and trams from other East London municipalities mix with buses, carts and vans coming from Commercial Road and the Docks. This view was taken on 12th July 1912, but even ten years later the problem here was acute and deliberations began on how best to tackle the situation.

between transport providers to solve the ever growing traffic problems. The phrase 'co-ordination of passenger services' begins to take on a life of its own; we see here the concrete beginnings of a movement towards the formation of the London Passenger Transport Board. Other important ideas to be aired were the provision of a bus, tram and tube interchange station at Manor House, and measures to solve congestion at the Elephant and Castle, Bricklayers Arms, New Cross Gate and Camberwell Green – all major LCC tramway junctions. It was acknowledged that the LCC was doing something about Whitechapel High Street and the Aldgate Hay Market, and the elimi-

PECKHAM RD, S.E.

670.Z.   **HOUSES OF PARLIAMENT & WESTMINSTER BRIDGE, LONDON.**   BEAGLES' POSTCARDS.
THE BRIDGE IS ONE OF THE HANDSOMEST IN EUROPE AND FORMS A FITTING APPROACH FROM SOUTH OF THE THAMES
TO THE HOUSES OF PARLIAMENT, WESTMINSTER ABBEY AND THE WEST END OF LONDON.

Left The competition for road space would result in the elimination of the electric tramcar. Here in Peckham Road, is Car 504 obstructing or obstructed? The mass of motorised vehicles in front and the oncoming motorcycle and sidecar have made alighting from the tram a hazardous business. The LCC did try to install pedestrian loading islands at important junctions, but the effort was too little too late.
J.B.Gent Collection

Below left This view is familiar the world over. It also lends credence to the planners' arguments about traffic congestion. The double tram track on the north side of the bridge should have been made into a dedicated right of way. As it was, the buses, lorries and private cars normally steered clear of the lines of approaching tramcars, but this lane discipline sometimes broke down to the detriment of all concerned.
B.J.Cross Collection

this ground alone it appeared desirable that the reductions on each route should proceed in stages.

The text continued in a similar vein, describing the off peak situation and alluding several times to the requirements of the travelling public. The damage had been done to the LCC and other metropolitan tramway operators. The bus companies must have found all this music to their ears, as it appeared that the anti-tramway lobby was gaining in influence. Indeed, this judgement by the Committee is crucial in understanding the events, which led to the downfall of the London tramcar. It must also be understood that many of those using public transport, particularly the elderly and mothers with small children found it much safer to board a bus, rather than step out into the carriageway to try to get on a tram. Obviously, loading islands and pedestrian refuges would have alleviated this problem, but the provision of these vital ingredients for public safety was sparse or non-existent on many major tram routes.

Fierce omnibus competition was a factor cited in a financial analysis of the Council's tramways. Another factor, which limited traffic receipts, was that large areas of central London remained unserved by trams. Looking at the figures in the round, there was still a steady growth in the undertaking. In 1914, traffic revenue per mile of single track was £7,871; this was set against total capital expenditure of £13,028,119. The net deficit was calculated at £88,526. In 1922, the per mile revenue had increased to £17,382 and the total capital expenditure amounted to £15,283,020. However, the deficit at £88,757 was similar to the one incurred in 1914. The reason for this unsatisfactory situation can be deduced from the expenses for labour and materials per car mile. In 1914 this figure was 2.83 pence, but by 1922 it had shot up to 7.458 pence. This reflected wartime and postwar inflation of wages and materials.

The plight of the LCC was contrasted with that of Glasgow Corporation, which managed a surplus of £152,724 in 1922. Clearly something was amiss in the capital. The difference in profit and loss terms was partly due to reasons already stated and to the fact that the conduit system was starting to become a major financial

nation of some single track on the Albert Embankment, but the widening of Old Street/Kingsland Road intersection to permit *'the segregation of interlacing tramway lines at this point'* had to await the provision of sufficient funding. The free for all at Tooley Street terminus was another seemingly intractable problem. The broadening of Grays Inn Road by the tram terminus was yet one more project caught up in the financial queue.

The debate about restricted streets rumbled on, and the Committee seemed inclined to recommend a reduction of bus services along many principal tramway routes. However, the watchwords remained *'caution and consensus'*, which attitude inevitably delayed decisions.

The LCC wrote to the Committee complaining about this tardiness in implementing measures that would give their tramcars some degree of protection from omnibus competition. The Committee replied in these terms:

The Council (LCC) considered that the reductions so far proposed in the number of omnibus journeys along tramway routes during rush hours was less than was justified, having regard to the accommodation available in tramcars and the number of passengers carried. While recognising that the reductions proposed during the rush hours were less than could be justified on the basis of the loadings, we considered that the reductions in omnibus journeys should proceed slowly and be spread over a wide area, in order to avoid, as far as possible, any serious displacement of labour, or the infliction of serious hardship on the omnibus proprietors involved. It appeared to us that to reduce a service of omnibuses on any route to the limits indicated by the returns of loadings would be likely to involve considerable risk of the available facilities being rendered inadequate for the actual requirements of the travelling public. On

liability. The first doubts now began to emerge regarding the long term viability of the LCC system. The spectre of wholesale fleet renewals and the financing of new lines to serve the expanding suburbs began to exercise minds at the new LCC headquarters of County Hall. The first part of this fine building, which was situated on the east bank of the Thames next to Westminster Bridge, was opened by King George V in 1922, and it provided a suitably impressive home for London's local government.

Speeding up the service after the withdrawal of the trailer cars involved the use of the latest batch of E/1 cars 1727–1851, which was delivered in 1922. These vehicles stole a march on the other LCC classes by reason of their superior acceleration. They were equipped with two trolley poles, one for each direction of travel. The TRAMWAY AND RAILWAY WORLD of 13th April 1922 carried a particularly interesting article on the engineering problems associated with lowering of track under bridges:

To enable cars equipped for both the overhead trolley and the conduit system to pass under railway bridges on the Clapham and Balham High Roads, the double tracks of the London County Council Tramways have had to be lowered. It was determined to do this without interfering in any way with the tramway traffic – a very difficult operation, which was carried out without injury either to men, to the rolling stock, or to the permanent way. The awkwardness of the problem will be realised by the fact that 68 cars were running per hour for about five hours of each day, and 40 cars per hour for the remainder of the day. During the night four hours were available with only a half hour interruption by the night car services, and on Sunday, there was no traffic between 1a.m. and 7a.m. At the Clapham Road bridge under the SECR the line had to be lowered 8 inches (203mm). This involved altering the tracks for 200 yards (182.8 metres), including the level portion under the bridge and the two approach gradients.

The article goes on to discuss the meticulous planning of the placing of individual rails to avoid the interruption of services. The whole operation was directed by General Manager A. L. C. Fell and was carried out under the supervision of Mr J. Welling,

the permanent way engineer. A gang of 33 men was employed and the task took 51 working days to complete.

The relationship between the LCC and the London United Tramways was fraught and complicated. One suspects that the municipal idealists in the Council were nettled by the apparent early success of the company operated LUT. Coupled to this, was the fact that LUT tracks had been laid in the Metropolitan Borough of Hammersmith – tracks, furthermore, which had used the overhead wire system of current collection, not the favoured conduit. Negotiations between the two sides for the LCC to acquire LUT assets situated in the County of London had been rumbling on for years. A deal seemed to have been hammered out in May 1917, but a natural break in its implementation was forced by the war. With the return of peace, the LCC finally decided to carry out the agreement, which basically concerned tracks in the Borough of Hammersmith and the transfer of ownership of Chiswick Depot.

The irony of the situation was that the much lauded LUT of earlier days had now fallen from grace and was showing its age. So much so, that when LCC rolling stock engineers inspected the 45 trams they had just acquired from the company, they decided they were below standard and the cars were eventually sold back to their original owner. Old LUT trackwork had to be inspected and repaired, and a new double track connection was inserted at Hammersmith Broadway. This allowed Service 26 to be extended over former LUT metals to a new terminus at Kew Bridge.

The junction at Hammersmith Broadway was one of the congestion black spots highlighted by the Second Annual Report of the Traffic Advisory Committee. A traffic census was taken in the area which revealed that trams formed 10 per cent of the traffic in Brook Green Road (buses 23%), 9 per cent in the Broadway (buses 22%), 11 per cent in Queen Street (buses 17%) and 17 per cent in Beadon Road (buses 2%) on the LUT terminal loop. Ironically, one the main

Above right **A lively throng of trams is observed at the corner of the Victoria Embankment by the famous statue of Queen Boudicca. By modern medical standards the claim by the tobacco advertisers on the side of the tram beggars belief. No doubt the smokers sitting in the upper saloon would have believed every word of it!** Hulton Getty

Right **Although Newington Green may have seen better days, the place still has a faded elegance in this 1925 view. The motorman of Car 1281 is deep in thought as he trundles past the letterbox on the corner of Mildmay Road. The image of the tram in the dappled sunshine and the sleepy midday atmosphere contribute to a fine study of interwar London.** N.D.W.Elston

proposals in a new traffic scheme to avoid conflicting vehicle movements, was to re-route everything via the one way loop using The Grove, Beadon Road and King Street, which had been pioneered by the electric tramways.

Chiswick Depot proved to be a mixed blessing for the LCC. Although the building was of great architectural interest, the rails and some of the infrastructure were showing signs of deterioration. The site was intended as an adjunct to Hammersmith Depot; however, it quickly became apparent that regular use by LCC bogie cars would be too risky. Much of the depot track had been laid on wooden sleepers and many of these had rotted, thus making the permanent way rather less than permanent. An ad hoc arrangement was worked out, whereby Chiswick became a storage centre for de-commissioned trams whose days of active service were over.

In South London the joint agreement took a different form, in that the LCC and LUT seemed to be working together when their respective lines were connected at Tooting. A change pit was constructed and services 2 and 4 were extended on 2nd May 1922 from Merton to terminate at Wimbledon Hill. This was a logical step because it enabled LCC trams to reach the natural traffic objective of Wimbledon, without passengers having to change at the county boundary in Tooting. The new arrangements also held out the promise of through running over purely LUT rails in the direction of Kingston and Hampton Court. Both parties realised, that during the summer months, a direct connection between the Victoria Embankment and Hampton Court could be a money spinner in terms of the tourist excursion trade.

Again, nothing was ever done in a hurry, when it came to decisions between the LCC and the LUT. This state of affairs was even more apparent when one realises that an original through running test had taken place way back in August 1912! Let the report from the WIMBLEDON BOROUGH NEWS for 23rd August 1912 tell the story:

An important early morning test was carried out on Friday to determine the adaptability of the London County Council tramcars for travelling over the lines of the London United Tramway Company, which stretch from Tooting, where the LCC system ends, to Wimbledon, Kingston, Hampton Court, and other places beyond.

The test was made in order to discover whether it would be possible for Londoners from south of the Thames to travel all the way to Hampton Court without changing cars.

The Council car chosen for the test, which began at midnight, was fitted with an overhead trolley pole. It was run from the public track to that of the company without mishap, and travelled safely to Hampton Court and back, completing a journey of 20 miles (32 km).

The experiment was so satisfactory that

tram travellers will look forward with keen interest to the day when arrangement will be completed for a permanent connection at Tooting and a continuous through running of County Council trams to Hampton Court.

In spite of the genuine hopes of the reporter, it took until the 22nd May 1926, for the Saturday and Sunday route extensions of services 2 and 4 to take effect. The Merton to Summerstown shuttle Service 81 continued to be operated – usually by a solitary company tramcar. This vehicle had to be driven all the way from Fulwell Depot to take up duties. The isolated section of Service 81 along Haydons Road and Plough Lane was the scene of LUT trolleybus trials in 1922–23. These were inconclusive and the company tram service lasted until 16th April 1931, when a change pit was opened at Plough Lane and LCC Service 14 was extended along Haydons Road to a terminus in Wimbledon. An interesting aspect of this route was the running of Wimbledon Stadium specials by the LUT. Spare cars would be sent over from Fulwell to join the LCC tracks from Wimbledon to Haydons

Road. Here the slower company cars were subject to a war of words or worse from LCC motormen. It was not unknown for an LCC driver to come up close behind the LUT car ahead and bump it fender to fender in an endeavour to provoke the LUT driver into greater velocity!

A stadium of somewhat larger dimensions than that at Wimbledon, formed part of the British Empire Exhibition at Wembley. King George V declared the Empire Stadium and the exhibition grounds

Transport Guide to the British Empire Exhibition 1924.

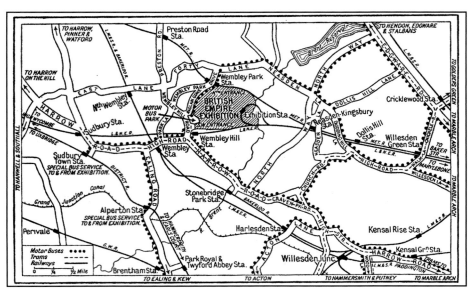

open on 23rd April 1924. Three days later, Wembley Stadium was overflowing with football supporters cheering on their team at the FA Cup Final. Not unnaturally, these new public attractions put pressure on the MET and LCC to provide suitable tramway connections. Service 30, which worked via Hammersmith, was extended over company tracks as far as Wembley Hill Road, on the MET Sudbury route. The exhibition closed on 1st November 1924, then reopened for a final summer season in April 1925. The whole site was subsequently dismantled, leaving Wembley Stadium as a permanent monument to the 1924 event.

The pace of events overtaking the LCC Tramways had exacted its toll on the health of the Chief Officer and General Manager, A. L. C. Fell. He retired on 31st December 1924, and was replaced by Joshua Kidd Bruce, who was appointed Acting General Manager. On 21st July 1925, this status was upgraded to General Manager. His impact on the organisation was mainly felt through the fleet renewal programme, popularly known as pullmanisation (qv).

On the eastern side of the capital mounting concern was being expressed about traffic congestion and the lack of transport facilities to the new LCC estate at Becontree. These worries were explained to a public enquiry, which was held in March 1926. All forms of public transport linking London with the Lea Valley, the boroughs of metropolitan Essex, and the growing suburbs of Ilford and Romford came under scrutiny. Tramways had been part of the scene for a long time and the main aim of the Inquiry in this sphere was to investigate complaints of overcrowding at peak times. Another perennial source of friction was the complaint by the LCC, West Ham Corporation and other tramway operators about the wasteful bus competition they had to endure. The representative of the LCC also suggested that an express tram route from the Docks to Becontree, routed along the Barking Bypass, would provide a much needed facility. East Ham Corporation

The gap between the LCC Tramways and lines belonging to Croydon Corporation is about to be bridged. The symbolism of the occasion is rather marred by the years of petty disputes, which through caused these few inches to remain unbridged for so long. The situation here at Norbury was at least remedied to the passengers' satisfaction. At other places in London the impasse of abutting tracks and no through running was to last a little longer. *LT Museum*

seemed to have a similar scheme in mind when they suggested that tram track be laid from Bow Road to Barking on top of the mound covering the Northern Outfall Sewer.

The final recommendations issued by the Inquiry were very disappointing from the tramway point of view. It was suggested that new railways would be best suited for the Becontree Estate, thus putting paid to any embryonic tramway plans. A corridor of land between Fitzstephen Road and Ilchester Road had been earmarked for a rail line. In fairness, the bus companies had already targeted the estate, and the presence of the nearby District Line, opened on 12th September 1932 from Barking to Upminster, added to the public transport facilities on offer. Finally, the inquiry came down on the side of Ilford in resisting any overtures from the LCC, East Ham and West Ham to participate in through running. This decision must have come as some relief to the LCC. According to the Council's Highway Committee minute books for 4th June 1925 to 17th July 1928, meetings with Ilford Council representatives had taken place on an informal and formal basis no less than seventeen times!

Ilford then got cold feet and pulled out of further negotiations – the word parochial obviously had beneficial overtones in those parts!

On 23rd March 1924, the connecting tramway from Seven Sisters Road via Amhurst Park to Stamford Hill was inaugurated. This important link speeded up east to west tram traffic and afforded yet another connection to the tracks of the MET. The new lines were equipped for overhead trolley operation, and a change pit was constructed at the eastern end of Amhurst Park.

South of the River Thames, frantic activity had been going on in the Croydon area to bring the main line from Norbury to Purley up to scratch. Rails were repositioned and relaid; the overhead was renewed and traction standards renovated. Acceptable proposals had been offered by the LCC to Croydon, and on Sunday, 7th February 1926, through services were opened between the metropolis and its Surrey neighbour. All seemed to be coming up roses, until Croydon Corporation voted on 29th March to close their Addiscombe tram route. This abandonment, which in fact didn't take place until the following year, was a grim sign for the future.

In the 1926 report of the Royal Commission on Cross-River Traffic in London, which mainly concentrated on the provision of new bridges across the Thames, the case on competing forms of transport was stated concisely:

It is clear that the railway and the tram are not retaining their hold on the affections of the public to the same extent as the omnibus, the business of which has been multiplied fourfold (since 1911), and which carries almost one half of London's travelling population . . .

The prospects were ominous for the tramcar in London.

Once the Croydon to Embankment service got going it was a great success. LCC Car 1249 is depicted on London Road by the railway bridge at West Croydon Station. The connecting curve in front of the photographer leads to SMET tracks in Tamworth Road. Trams have since returned to the area and Croydon Tramlink now serves Tamworth Road.

CHAPTER TWELVE
Uncertain Times

AFTER THE First World War, unrest in the coal industry was never far from the surface, and a series of strikes and lockouts had the effect of galvanising the trade union movement. During the mid-1920s the government and employers became equally obdurate. The country was set on a collision course. Appeals for moderation failed and the General Council of the Trades Union Congress asked between 1,500,000 and 1,750,000 workers to come out in support of the miners. The first (and last) general strike in Britain's history was due to start at one minute to midnight on Monday, 3rd May 1926. The first wave of workers included those employed in transport services, power generation, printing, construction industries, iron and steel manufacturers and chemical plants.

The tramway and bus workers of London obeyed the call of the TUC.

Late on Monday, 3rd May, the government invoked the Emergency Powers Act, which gave them the right, amongst other things, to commandeer trams and to take over transport vehicles. The rank and file of the LCC crews refused to cross picket lines on Tuesday, 4th May, and the Council was faced with an indefinite period of no tram service. Cars stayed firmly in their depots. The gates of the Kingsway Subway were locked and an eerie silence fell over once bustling streets. Incidents of clashes between strikers and police in the metropolitan area were reported during the day. At one stand off near the Poplar end of Blackwall Tunnel, strikers were making motorists get out of their cars and walk

through the tunnel! A police baton charge resulted in a number of casualties being admitted to Poplar Hospital. The robust attitude of the police was shortly to be felt by tramway workers.

During Tuesday, officials from the LCC, acting under instructions from the majority party on the Council, devised a contingency plan to maintain some sort of tram service

The wet weather seems to have driven all the passengers from the open top decks of the competing Tilling and London General motor buses. Here at Lewisham Clock Tower the tracks split – to the left trams can go to Woolwich and Eltham via Lee Green; to the right Car 203 will wend its way in the direct of Catford. Service 62 ran solely on conduit tracks, therefore trams did not need a trolley pole.
LT Museum

during the Emergency. They invited staff that remained loyal to the LCC to return to work. Protection was to be offered and temporary accommodation provided in selected depots. The response was poor. Although a number of university students, whose sympathies lay with the political Right, had volunteered for transport duties, the LCC wisely turned down their offer of support. On the other hand, the management of the London General Omnibus Company welcomed any sort of volunteer, and they managed to get out around 86 buses over the next two days.

Whatever the strategy, the LCC did try on Wednesday and Thursday to break the strike. However, before the action started, officials had received at least one well written and polite note from a striker. The anonymous writer informed his employer that 'with great regret' he and his fellows would be fixing metal objects to the conduit slot to impede the progress of any renegade tramcar. He went on to say that the LCC as a municipal organisation should be supporting the rights of the workers in the face of government. The author of this missive was spot on when he described the proposed tactics of striking tramway crews. A metal bolt attached firmly between the edges of the conduit slot was a very effective deterrent, but was obviously of no use on overhead wire equipped routes.

On Wednesday afternoon, a skeleton service of twelve cars left Camberwell Depot. Although at least one round trip was made to the Embankment, the atmosphere turned nasty and the strike breaking trams were soon safely back within the confines of the depot. Attempts were also made at Clapham and at New Cross to run a service of sorts, but the attitude of the strikers, backed up by the local populace, became distinctly hostile. Tram windows were broken and attempts were made to seize the volunteer crews. Outside Clapham Depot several charges were made by mounted police and a number of tram staff received baton wounds. The mood of the crowd was ugly and civil unrest spread to other parts of South London. On the other side of the system there is some evidence to suggest that several trams were run from Hammersmith Depot. This had the advantage of not being tied to the conduit.

On Thursday, 6th May 1926, the level of violence increased when a pitched battle was sparked off at the Elephant and Castle. This important tramway junction was the scene of a number of confrontations during the General Strike, and on this Thursday, tramway workers, dockers, power station workers and railwaymen took on the forces of law and order. Other incidents occurred

at Tooley Street and Poplar. A bus driven by a volunteer ploughed into the crowd and caused the first fatality of the strike. The LCC strike committee was in touch with other workers from municipal and company tramways. It was noted that on Friday, groups of individuals had halted trams in Cardiff, Hull and Glasgow.

The government acted on Saturday, 8th May, to move foodstuffs from the London Docks. An armed convoy was planned along the East India Dock Road. This prompted a discussion amongst Poplar Depot men whether they should place trams as part of a barricade, but the idea was dropped because concern was felt that the tramcars were in fact municipal property, and, as such, belonged to the people. Had the LCC been a private company, no doubt the men would not have had any qualms about using the fleet to block the highway. The convoy passed at around 11.20am. The use of troops was especially poignant as many of the striking workers had served in the colours during the war, and were well used to military discipline.

The Sabbath Day arrived, and true to the British way of life, the traditions of Sunday observance prevailed across the capital. Striking tramway workers and others who had served in the forces were instructed by the TUC to wear their military service medals and ribbons. This seems to have had an effect on many of the middle class, especially when the smartly dressed ex-soldiers turned up for church services. This was nowhere more apparent than at St Mark's Church, Kennington – the home church of the LCC Tramwaymen's Brotherhood. This charitable foundation organised an annual church parade of LCC crews in uniform, with the Tramways Band in attendance. During the Great War the Brotherhood took on the re-

sponsibility of trying to alleviate the conditions of tramwaymen's families, whilst the breadwinner was away fighting at the front.

After leaving church many LCC men learnt that the London Underground was offering an improved service. This news must have come as a blow to their hopes of solidarity amongst London's transport workers.

By Monday, 10th May, the mood of the country seemed to be changing, and a desire for a settlement of the nation's ills became widespread. The enthusiasm amongst many of the strikers was undiminished, but it dawned on some that the employment of troops and the government's firm control of the situation had made the chance of a victory very slight. The LCC tramway union officials, who had been looked on to set an example for other municipal tramway employees outside London, were still receiving progress reports from around the country. On Tuesday, news came in of the *Battle of Lewes Road Tram Depot* in Brighton, where a force of 350 police had clashed with strikers. The LCC men could only express their solidarity with their south coast colleagues. However, on the following day the strike began to crumble. Representatives of the TUC met the Conservative Prime Minister, Stanley Baldwin, and the two sides began to work out a compromise agreement. The Minister of Labour, Sir Arthur Steel-Maitland had already put out a statement that 1,194 buses were running on London's streets, and that a return to work was already taking place. There was to be no victory for the TUC. Defeat was effectively conceded on Thursday, 13th May, and the government, in an unaccustomed show of conciliation, ordered that no victimisation should occur after the end of the strike. Returning strikers were advised not to set

One of the most violent areas during the General Strike was here at the New Kent Road by the Elephant and Castle. Normal service has been resumed in this view, but scenes like this remind us how reliant the average Londoner was on a frequent and reliable tram service.

Blackfriars Bridge. London

about volunteers, and employers were reminded that they should take back strikers on 'fair and equable' terms. What this meant in practice for LCC crews will be revealed later.

That so many bus workers had capitulated in the eyes of the tramwaymen, left a lasting rift between the two sets of employees. This distaste was enhanced by the LGOC's issuing of printed certificates thanking their voluntary workers for 'coming to the support of the Country in a serious crisis'. Language of this sort was like a red rag to a bull for all the LCC crews who had stayed out.

Ironically, the miners' strike continued until November 1926, but the General Strike had effectively run out of steam by Friday, 14th May. Meetings between LCC officials and union Representatives had taken place on the Thursday and Friday. An agreement was worked out, whereby dismissal notices to the strikers were withdrawn and reinstatement of crews would begin immediately. Over the weekend, services gradually returned to normal.

On 21st May, Sir Oscar Warburg for the LCC issued the following statement:
In the case of men who resumed work immediately after the strike, the period during which they were on strike is not to be deemed a break in service.

If there are any cases presenting special difficulties as regards this matter, the heads of departments concerned are to report the facts so that any necessary decision may be given at the present time.

In any case in which holidays or sick pay are granted in accordance with scales depending on the length and continuity of service, the period of the strike is to be ignored in calculating the holidays or sick pay of individuals who went on strike.

The above decisions are to be communicated to the individuals concerned and it is to

TRAM TERMINUS TOOTING JUNCTION

be made clear to them that by withdrawing their labour they forfeited any claim to these privileges, but that on this occasion the Council has decided to restore them.

Thus the LCC showed a modicum of magnanimity to its tramway employees. But the whole affair left a lasting mark on British society. Most returning LCC tram crews never again spoke to any of the small number of volunteers; such was the depth of feeling. The General Strike proved, if indeed proof were needed, that the supposed national unity engendered by the First World War had evaporated into a dog fight along class lines. The actions of strikers and volunteers in 1926 were to last long in the communal memory, and industrial relations were permanently influenced by the events of May 1926.

The day-to-day business of running the LCC trams reasserted itself and active steps were taken to investigate the viability of new tramway routes. The minute books of the Highways Committee are littered with correspondence related to proposed extensions. The list includes: Grove Park Station to Eltham, an extension towards Bromley, Norwood to Crystal Palace, Southend Village to Grove Park, Park Street (Camden Town), Euston Road and Marylebone Road, Hampstead Heath to Heath Street, Westmount Road and Westhorne Avenue (Eltham), and a series of plans for new lines over the projected St Paul's Bridge and a rebuilt Lambeth Bridge, plus a number of tram subways in the central area.

A tramway connection between the end of the LCC track at West Norwood and the South Metropolitan terminus at Crystal Palace had been in the air for some time. The process was lent impetus by the events on 4th November 1926, when LCC and SMET rails were joined at Tooting Junction. The sum of £1,650 was allocated for the construction of a new change pit to allow LCC Service 6 to use the overhead wire equipped tracks of the SMET. Since

the South Metropolitan Company did not have any suitable vehicles for through running, only LCC standard bogie cars were used on the Service 6 extension to Mitcham Cricket Green.

Although the Tooting connection seemed to go smoothly, there was endless bickering between the Metropolitan Borough of Lambeth, the Metropolitan Borough of Camberwell, local residents action groups and the LCC. This stymied progress on the Crystal Palace link. The route chosen, via Auckland Hill, Gypsy Road, Dulwich Wood Park and Farquhar Road was the subject of some debate. At one point, a single track one way scheme was proposed, using St Louis Road and St Gothard's Road. Time, money and effort were expended and all for nought – the line was never built!

A letter dated 13th January 1926, was sent by Cawston Estates to the LCC. It suggested a new tram route via Calmont Road and Elstree Hill on the Lewisham/

Bromley boundary. This would have been a useful bridgehead for a tramway invasion of Bromley. But the residents of the Kentish market town were already well served by buses and the Southern Railway, and the prospect of an LCC involvement in the local transport provision did not appeal.

A similar request was received in a letter dated 6th June 1927, in which the Eltham, Sidcup and District Trades and Labour Council asked for a feasibility study to be carried out on running trams the length of Westmount Road, Eltham. Not very far away in Woolwich, the local council suggested that the terminus of the *Eltham* trams in Beresford Square be diverted to Cross Street (later General Gordon Place). The Chief Officer of Tramways reported on 21st July 1927, that the Council was not in favour of this move. He also suggested that Woolwich Council shift the street market from Beresford Square to Cross Street, in order to make more room for the tramcars!

Above **The tramway junction at the crossroads of Shoreditch High Street, Hackney Road, Kingsland Road and Old Street was renewed in 1927-28. Car 647 on Service 55 is heading for Bloomsbury, whilst Car 795 is working Service 49 to Liverpool Street.** G.N.Southerden

Left **London County Council Car 1780 is on London United Tramways territory in Worple Road, Wimbledon. Note the rather ornate track signal attached to the traction standard at the corner of Arterberry Road. The 'signal passed at danger' debate was rarely serious on street tramways, which normally relied on line of** sight and the common sense of the motormen. If two trams arrived at either end of the single track at the same time, the London bound car took precedence. The route extension from Wimbledon to Hampton Court provided passengers who boarded at the Embankment with the pleasure of two crossings of the River Thames – at Westminster Bridge or Blackfriars Bridge and at Kingston Bridge. The route could also claim a British tramway record of sorts in that it passed through four counties – London, City of London, Surrey and Middlesex. G.N.Southerden

Although many proposed routes never left the drawing board, there was one Southeast London project, which was occupying more attention than all the other schemes put together. This was the link from Southend Village through the new Downham Estate to Grove Park Station. From there tracks would drive north and east to cross Service 46 at Eltham Green and to proceed along the proposed Westhorne Avenue to a final connection with services 44 and 46 at Well Hall. On 11th November 1925, the Town Planning Committee suggested to the Highways Committee that all new tramways through housing estates be laid on grass track in the centre of the roadway. This method of segregated, reserved track tramway construction was employed to great effect in many provincial cities, principally Birmingham and Liverpool. It would have fitted the bill admirably in Grove Park and Eltham. However, the LCC were not about to take any risks. The results of running cars along the reserved track at Whipps Cross Road were inconclusive, and it was feared that wide roads with median strip tramways would somehow damage social cohesion in new estates. But the decisive factor was money. Fewer problems were posed and it was less expensive to build a single carriageway road with conventional tram tracks. With the maintenance bill for the conduit an ever-present headache, the Council erred on the side of caution.

The new work was caught up in the advance planning for the South Circular Road (A205). This new highway had appeared on a plan published as long ago as 1911. The then London Traffic Branch of the Board of Trade had pencilled in several new trunk roads including the North Circular (A406), Western Avenue (A40), Eastern Avenue (A12) and the Rochester Way (A2). The fact that the LCC proposed to use part of the South Circular from Baring Road to the junction of the new Rochester Way, added to the consultation exercises with local and national authorities. It should be noted here that every other tramway operator in London, with the exception of the Walthamstow/MET link, had long since given up on extension plans. The prevailing philosophy in the Ministry of Transport was antipathetic to trams, and as we shall see, the officials were not too happy that the LCC proposed to use a section of one of the MoT's new showpiece superhighways.

South of Lewisham, the first stage from Southend Village to Grove Park formed part of the transport provisions for the residents of the new Downham Estate. A change pit was planned for the western end of the future Downham Way. The track from there to Grove Park and Eltham would be equipped with overhead wires, as would the new route on Westhorne Avenue. Rather cheekily, the LGOC wrote to the LCC asking when Downham Way would be fit for a motor bus route – the Council replied in stern fashion by invoking the London Traffic Act 1924, and applying for this particular thoroughfare to be designated a restricted street. The London General and their nuisance omnibuses were not going to spoil a purely tramway celebration! On 28th September 1926, the first section opened from Southend Village to Road Number Eleven, Downham. Road Eleven quickly metamorphosed into Valeswood Road, as more housing was erected on the vacant site. On 28th July 1927, services were extended to a terminus opposite Southover. The intermediate target of Grove Park Station was reached on 15th November 1928.

Tramway schemes presented for approval during the parliamentary session of 1928 included the rebuilding of the Kingsway Subway to take double deck trams, and the promoting of a bill for a

Above **The Downham Cottage Estate was commenced in March 1924, and it was always intended that the Council's tramways would play a major role in its development. Part of the 54 route through the estate came within yards of the County of Kent. This was the nearest Bromley got to having trams. Note the standard LCC two storey house of brick construction. In total 6,071 dwellings were erected to take the overspill from London. Weekly rents varied from twelve shillings for a two room flat to twenty-one shillings for a five room house – all this and the added convenience of Car 1358 right outside your front door!** G.N.Southerden

Right **The end of the line at Grove Park was meant to be a temporary terminus before tracks struck northwards and eastwards to join up with Westhorne Avenue and Eltham Hill at the Yorkshire Grey. The dream ended with the coming of the LPTB and its pro-trolleybus policy. Such things were in the future, when Dr Hugh Nicol photographed Car 1033 on 11th January 1930.** H.Nicol / National Tramway Museum

Class D Car 327 was
withdrawn from service on
29th January 1931. Here it
is seen on 13th May 1929
in York Road. H.Nicol /
National Tramway Museum

tramway between Grove Park and Well
Hall, Eltham. The Ministry of Transport
were not happy with the Council's
proposals to run trams along the new South
Circular Arterial Road, and this caused the
project to be held up. In the case of the connecting line from Baring Road to Eltham
Green this delay was to prove fatal for the
LCC's plans. Eventually, this Ministry
inspired stalling caused the Council to seek
a direct meeting with Councillor William
Barefoot of the Woolwich Metropolitan
Borough Council. On 29th December 1927,
the worthy councillor wrote to the LCC
suggesting that the section serving the new
estate in Eltham (Westhorne Avenue) be
given priority. On 18th January 1928, the
Council received notification from the
Ministry that it was unlikely that the
building works and new railway bridges
associated with the South Circular Road
would be finished according to schedule.
One wonders whether this was a ploy by the
Ministry of Transport to keep trams off
their brand new road. In the event, credit
has to be given to Woolwich Borough
Council who practically bullied the LCC
into making advanced plans for the
Westhorne Avenue line.

On the fares front, the LCC trams were
still very good value for money, and an
inquiry into travelling facilities in Southeast London came up with some interesting
comparisons. The journey from Charlton to
Charing Cross in 1926 was analysed
according to the method of transport used
by the passenger. The Southern Railway
train single fare was one shilling, the return
was one shilling and elevenpence, and the
workmen's return was eightpence. The
fares by bus were sevenpence single; there
were no return or workmen's fares on offer
from the bus company. The LCC tram to the
Embankment trumped the lot. A single cost
fivepence, a return eightpence, and a
workmen's return sixpence. The distance
from Charlton to Charing Cross was 7½
miles (12km).

From the same Advisory Committee
Report came the following statement:
*We recognise that would be passengers
frequently experience difficulty in
boarding omnibuses and tramcars at
such points as New Cross Gate and the
Elephant and Castle, owing to the fact
that these vehicles have been completely
filled by long distance travellers, but we
consider that the remedy lies not in the*

*provision of further vehicles to traverse
the streets, but in bringing all forms of
public transport facilities in London
under public control, in order that their
operation may be complementary rather
than competitive, and so arranged as to
meet the requirements of the travelling
public.*

This awfully long sentence contains the
nub of the argument – some form of co-
operation was needed to streamline
London's public transport. The Conservative majority on the LCC had been looking
at ways of divesting itself of its tramway
obligations. A private holding company
formed by the amalgamation of the LCC
Tramways, the Combine (the London
Underground Group of companies – LGOC,
MET, SMET and LUT – to name but four),
and the municipal owned tramways,

appeared a likely solution to the problem.
However, just as the Labour Party had
opposed the London Traffic Act of 1924, on
the grounds that '*it was conferring a virtual
omnibus monopoly on the LGOC and its associated companies*' – so the future Labour
Government of 1929 was less than enthusi-
astic about committing local authority
assets into the hands of the capitalists. Two
enabling Bills presented to Parliament in
the Session of 1928–29 sought to form a
common management between the LCC
and the Combine. It was also proposed to
set up a common fund and a system of
apportionment of receipts and expenses.

The London Labour Party and the
London County Council Labour Party
fought the Bills tooth and nail. There was
no love lost between the London Labour
Party's chief protagonist, Herbert

Nearing the end of its
working life, Car 240 quits
the quadruple track
section at the foot of Dog
Kennel Hill. The field on
the right was part of 15
acres (6.07ha) acquired
by the LCC in December
1929 to provide twenty
blocks of flats in a slum
clearance programme.
Soon, new HR/2 trams
would be giving residents
a quality ride into town.
G.N.Southerden

Morrison, and Lord Ashfield, chairman and spokesman for the Combine. This seemingly implacable hostility between the two was not to last, and, as we shall see, the relationship mellowed over the next couple of years.

One of the many arguments against the Bills was that the LCC Tramways would be handed over to private directors. The proposed unitary transport authority, chaired by Lord Ashfield, would have twenty representatives on its directorate. The LCC were promised only two seats on the board. The Bills also did not make clear what would happen to the £17million worth of ratepayers' money, which had been invested in the LCC Tramways.

The temperature of the political climate rose, when London Labour MPs forced two all-night sittings of Parliament, on 6th–7th November and on 11th–12th December 1928. Passions had been aroused in the defence of the LCC trams. The ruling Municipal Reform Party (conservatives) on the Council seemed to be quite happy to get shot of their tramway commitments. At the Annual Conference of the London Labour

Top left **Out in the suburbs of Metropolitan Surrey we observe Car 1100 as it approaches the crossover by the Red Deer in South Croydon. The section of track along Brighton Road was well maintained by Croydon Corporation and car crews could usually make up time on the run to Purley.** J.B.Gent Collection

Left **The original iron suspension bridge at Lambeth was built in 1862 and closed to vehicular traffic in June 1910. Clearly this situation was not in the best interests of cross-river communication, and work started in 1930 to** construct a new Lambeth Bridge. The tram tracks at the junction of Lambeth Road, Lambeth Palace Road and the Albert Embankment had to be realigned. In spite of the critics of the conduit system, the Council built this temporary track whilst civil engineering work was proceeding. H.Nicol/National Tramway Museum

Below **Before the Aldgate/Whitechapel Market scheme got going, the LCC produced several plans of the location. This one shows the Gardiner's Corner layout and the obstruction caused by the hay carts.**

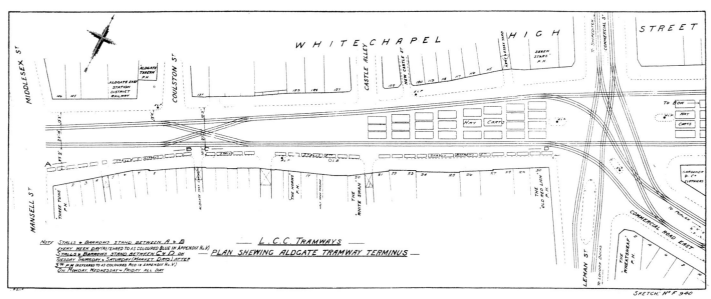

Right The rails beside the former haymarket at Whitechapel were realigned between August and October 1929. The wonder was that it had taken so long to remove this source of congestion, but the wheels of bureaucracy grind exceedingly slow. The LCC permanent way crew obligingly stand still for the official photographer whilst a stream of motor traffic flashes past. We are in an era well before plastic cones, reflective barriers and police speed cameras. A single rope and a couple of red flags were deemed sufficient in 1929. LT Museum

Bottom right The late twenties style of LCC flats may look rather stark to modern eyes, but they served a purpose in rehousing the poor. Here at Stamford Hill the Council's artist has added the necessary tramway to the drawing.

Party, on 1st December 1928, the following resolution was adopted:

That this Annual Conference of the London Labour Party, widely representative of the London Labour, Trade Union, Co-operative and Socialist Movement, expresses its alarm at the proposal of the LCC to transfer management of London's municipal tramways to a private trust.

This conference, speaking in the name of a very considerable section of the travelling public, strongly condemns the decision of the Municipal Reform majority on the LCC to proceed by way of a Private Enabling Bill virtually to hand over the Council's tramways to the Traffic Combine . . .

This conference, whilst affirming its belief in the necessity for the co-ordination of all London passenger transport facilities on a basis which is consistent with the public interest, contends that this is not possible through Private Bill legislation. It therefore declares that the problem must be dealt with by a Public Bill, and that such a Bill must provide for the effective public ownership and/or public control of all the passenger transport facilities within the London traffic area . . .

Various delaying tactics were employed during the spring of 1929, and the Bills were effectively lost after the election of the second Labour Government on 30th May 1929. Herbert Morrison, now Minister of Transport in the new government, promised the House of Commons that alternative proposals would be considered. This obliged him to consult with '*Lord Ashfield and his wicked Combine*' – Morrison's own words. This period of active ministerial consultation lasted until the Labour Government fell in August 1931. In the meantime an event happened on the New York Stock Exchange. From 24th October to 29th October 1929 panic gripped Wall Street and the ensuing Crash effectively caused a worldwide depression. Unemployment soared in industrialised countries and Great Britain quickly followed suit. Although London never reached the appalling rate of 80 per cent unemployment experienced in Jarrow, the chill winds of the world crisis made the economic prospects of a new decade – the 1930s – seem particularly unattractive.

CHAPTER THIRTEEN
Never a Dull Moment!

PREVIOUS CHAPTERS have already alluded to a strict hierarchy in society. In the early part of the twentieth century this social structure was reinforced by the British class system. The prejudices produced by such a system of birthright and wealth impinged on the daily existence of millions. Knowing one's place in the order of things was considered to be part of the social survival kit. The London tramcar also had a role imposed on it by the combined pressure of snobbery and restrictive legislation. This unholy alliance prevented the LCC Tramways from achieving their full potential.

As we have noted from the evidence presented to the Royal Commission, vested interests and the affluent regarded the trams as vehicles of the working class, and their presence was not welcome in residential areas. The horse bus and its motorised successor were regarded from early on as the natural public transport vehicle for large areas of central London. Indeed, the exclusion of the tramcar was so total that many foreign visitors to the capital who stayed in the West End, went home convinced that tubes and buses serviced all the requirements of the travelling public.

In his 1930 work entitled DAS LONDONER VERKEHRSWESEN (London Transport), Kurt Moehl makes the following statement:

The London tramways cannot be compared in any way with the comprehensive bus network. The length of the tramway system at 558 km is only a third of the bus system . . . In the last few years London's tramways have been subjected to heavy competition from buses. This has affected all development schemes, and an expansion of the tramway system cannot be expected.

Continental observers were left with the impression that London was a special case, splendid in its isolation, not only in its lack of tramways, but also in its insistence on employing double deck vehicles – all definitely out of step with the rest of the world! However, on the other hand, London has a knack of generating its own unique rhythm and variety. During the first three decades of the twentieth century, those visitors who did step out of the narrow confines of the West End and the City would have found a vibrant society well served by the LCC and its tramcars.

The LCC workforce was almost entirely male. Unmarried women were only employed in specific clerical jobs. When a female employee got married, it was expected that she would leave her employment with the Council. The only known motorwoman on the LCC was the enigmatic Lillian Lawrence who drove Class C cars from Rye Lane Depot for a spell in 1904. Lillian dressed as a man and was accepted as such by her colleagues. She eventually

Left **The lad selling copies of The Star has been included in this view of London Life – No. 16 The Electric Tram. The motorman's right hand rests on the handbrake and his left grasps the controller handle. Open platforms were fine in summer, but their attraction diminished in the cold and wet. The Metropolitan Police were loath to authorise enclosed vestibules on tramcars in the London area.**
J.B.Gent Collection

Far left **The conductor receives the same postcard treatment as his driving colleague. Note the ticket punch, the whistle and the broad leather strap holding the cash bag. The weight of 'coppers' (pennies and halfpennies) needed a substantially made satchel. The conductor was also expected to assist passengers on and off the car, to answer questions about destinations and stops, and he was required to run 'a tight ship' whilst the motorman attended to his driving duties.**
J.B.Gent Collection

LONDON LIFE. – No. 16. THE ELECTRIC TRAM.
BEAGLES POSTCARDS.
THE TRAMS ARE OF THE GREATEST CONVENIENCE TO THE THOUSANDS OF PERSONS TRAVELLING IN LONDON, PARTICULARLY TO CONVEY THE WORKERS TO AND FROM THE CITY.
BELOW THE CAR IS A SAFETY DEVICE TO PREVENT ANY PERSON FROM BEING RUN OVER, SHOULD THEY ACCIDENTALLY BE KNOCKED DOWN IN FRONT OF THE CAR.

10513—24 LONDON LIFE. L.C.C. TRAMCAR CONDUCTOR. ROTARY PHOTO. E.C.

achieved fame as Curly Lawrence, builder and designer of miniature steam locomotives.

Staff relations were very formal; colleagues at work would refer to one another by surname or by rank – Motorman Smith, Inspector Jones etc. This rather stilted atmosphere was mitigated somewhat by the chance to rub shoulders with others in the sports and social clubs run by the Council. The morale in some of the smaller depots and at Charlton Works was generally better than in the larger establishments like New Cross or Holloway car sheds. However, inspectors and senior staff set the tone, and if they were judged to be fair with the men, then they received the respect they deserved. Conversely, any official who crossed the boundaries of fairness quickly became the focus of animosity, and it can be said that these individuals were feared and hated in equal measure.

At the start of the electrification programme the Council liked to regard itself as a model employer. Gone were the harsh conditions associated with the horse tram companies. In their stead was a code of conduct, which was supposed to bring out the best amongst tram crews and supervisory staff. This was the ideal, but in practice any minor infringement of the rules could result in instant dismissal. Union activity in support of better conditions was patchy. The Amalgamated Association of Tramway and Vehicle Workers (AAT) provided some measure of help and advice for its members, although the impact it had on the employers was minimal. What the LCC management wanted they generally got. The public face of the LCC centred on a fair wage for a fair day's work, and visiting politicians were spun this line. Indeed, the Council sometimes went out of its way to stress the reasonable nature of the conditions of the job, but in truth the fine words and pious hopes of the members of the Highways Committee amounted to little. A tramway man's ten hours labour per day could be spread over fifteen to sixteen hours, with at least eight hours between duties. The average spreadover, according to a report issued on 9th February 1905, was twelve hours twenty-eight minutes. Motormen and conductors were subject to a rigorous list of rules, which were enforced by senior staff. Ticket inspectors (often called jumpers) also kept an eye open for anything amiss with the tram and its crew. Smoking on duty was a cardinal sin, as was turning up for work unshaven or dishevelled. Each driver was expected to keep a safe distance from the car in front, in order to avoid the offence of close poling. The official version reads thus:

No carriage using a tramway shall follow another carriage using the same tramway at a less distance from such other carriage than fifty yards (45.7 metres), except at traffic junctions or on single lines of tramway unless directed to do so by a properly appointed official of the Council, but this shall not be deemed to alter or diminish the powers of the police in controlling the traffic.

So ran edict 30 on page 46 of the October 1932 Statutory Rules and Orders – the latest edition of a booklet with which every crew had to be familiar. The eighty-four pages contained lists of byelaws, speed limits, regulations and penalties for non compliance. Woe betide any crew member who was caught *in flagrante* or who was tempted to argue the issue with an inspector. The alleged miscreant was then reported or booked by the inspector. This resulted in a reprimand by the Charge Depot Inspector. Any serious offence like insubordination usually meant the sack. The LCC could afford to adopt this policy, because for every job on the trams, there were two or three men only too willing to claim their place in the sun.

Each aspiring motorman had to be well schooled before being allowed out in charge of an LCC tramcar. At the driving school within the confines of Clapham Depot a rigorous routine sorted out the sheep from the goats. Trainees were put through their paces on a skeleton single deck tram whose 4-wheel truck rested on rollers. Thus the car could be driven by the trainee, without the fear that it would career out of control amongst the rest of the rolling stock. Instructors kept a close eye on the class and after three days theory and practice a new

Some posed pictures of this era catch the subjects in an almost unnaturally sullen demeanour – this one is no exception. Perhaps the fixed expression is a habit learned by having to remain still for a time exposure. Whatever the reason, the motorman of D Class Car 399 has a face reserved for castigating cabbies that stray on to the tracks in front of him! The conductor is more photogenic and obviously takes all this in his stride.

The novelty of the new electric trams has worn off and they are now a means to an end – getting to work on time. Workmen (and women) crowd aboard waiting cars at Rushey Green on 18th April 1912. An inspector waits in front of the lead tram to signal the right of way to the driver. LCC

boy would be sent out on the road with an experienced driver. On passing out day the trainee driver was examined by a police official who posed various questions and arranged for an emergency stop of the tramcar to test the motorman's competence. If all was well, then the driver joined the ranks of the other LCC motormen.

The London County Council Tramways Motorman's Handbook lists over thirty pages of do's and don'ts for the driver to remember. Basically he had to be familiar with all the mechanical aspects of the car. He had to be prepared to isolate a fault and to deal effectively with it. The conduit and trolley systems, controllers, resistances, motors, circuit breakers, canopy switches, lightning arresters, brakes (hand and magnetic), sand gear and trucks – all had to mastered and understood.

A good driver always had to get on with his conductor. This relationship was crucial to the efficient running of the car, and several lasting friendships were built up with the motorman and conductor working as a team. Erratic driving did not help the conductor's job, and the misjudgements of a careless motorman had an effect on the passengers as well as on the conductor's ability to collect fares in a civilised manner. Some inspectors used to book conductors who had not punched a ticket at the correct place. The excuse that the driver braked hard at the time, throwing the conductor off balance, did not cut any ice with officialdom.

At peak hours the LCC sometimes employed snatchers to help regular conductors. A snatcher was a qualified conductor who used to go from car to car collecting the fares. He would sign the regular Conductor's waybill on each tram, before he transferred to another tram. On the Victoria Embankment and at other city termini, the loaders or dispatchers also pitched in to aid the hard pressed tram crews. These men were the forerunners of the modern crowd squeezers employed in such countries like Japan, to ensure that everyone is crammed in so that the car doors can close. Of course on the LCC there were only open tram platforms and no car doors, and no standing passengers allowed in the early years, so the process was perhaps less brutal!

The loaders began duty at 4pm and clocked off around 7pm. They were each equipped with a whistle to communicate to the motorman. One or two quick blasts on the whistle indicated departure or an emergency stop because someone had fallen off the back of a moving tram. Alertness was needed to check all was well, and knowledge of destinations and services was also required. The loader would often have to field questions from uncertain travellers who were anxious not to get packed on the wrong car.

As well as inspectors, there were the regulators. These gentlemen were stationed at fixed points on the system. During an eight hour shift each regulator was delegated to

Above **This is the lower deck of experimental HR/1 Car 1852. Whilst the vehicle may be a 'one off', the scene is distinctly mundane. A conductor selects a ticket from his rack to give to a fare paying passenger. The LCC publicity poster on the bulkhead adds colour to the lower saloon interior.** B.J.Cross Collection

Right **People who pontificate on the modern lack of manners might like to consider this free-for-all as trailer T69 is besieged by homeward bound commuters. Such scenes were common during industrial disputes, which resulted in strikes affecting the suburban railways. Since the buses and tubes couldn't cope, the much maligned tramcars took the brunt of the surge and eventually got everyone home in one piece!**

Order is restored as a couple of LCC inspectors shepherd queuing passengers on to Car 1424. This and the previous picture were taken at the Blackfriars end of the Victoria Embankment.

control the flow of tramcars and to ensure that regular timekeeping was adhered to. His job also included giving instructions to motormen to get a move on in case of late running. Cars could also be turned short on the instructions of a regulator. The tram would then be reversed and returned to service in an attempt to cope with peak hour or changed traffic conditions brought about by a hold up on the road. The regulator also gave window orders to conductors. A four finger sign from a regulator meant that the conductor was authorised to open the eight main top deck side windows to a depth of four inches. Similar signals indicated fully open or shut as the weather conditions dictated.

Of course the tramways could not function without the attentions of all those employed to service and maintain the permanent way. Gangers, labourers and paviours worked long hours to keep rails and conduit in good order. Track relaying at major junctions presented numerous headaches for the police and the Council. Often work would go ahead all day and all night if a particularly complicated layout like Gardiners Corner, Aldgate needed renewing. Conduit cleaners armed with specially engineered mirrors, which could reveal any obstacles or faults below the road surface, carried out inspections of the conduit regularly.

Apocryphal stories abound of all manner of objects that turned up at the bottom of the conduit. On 1st October 1930, the great British love of animals came to the fore

when a black and white cat was retrieved from the conduit in Shardeloes Road, Brockley. It was alleged that it had been stuck under the roadway for a total of seventeen days. In spite of his ordeal, Timothy the cat basked in the publicity of his release. Aside from live captives, LCC reports list coins, rings, articles of jewellery, walking sticks, children's hoops, bits of iron bedsteads discarded from rag and bone carts, bicycle parts, steel bars, chains of various descriptions, shoes and pairs of false teeth – all found lurking at the bottom of the conduit! We are not told whether anyone turned up at the lost property office to claim this treasure trove of detritus.

The AAT's supremacy in the union field was challenged by the emergence of the London and Provincial Licensed Workers Union (L&P). This had grown up with a

more militant, hands on approach than the AAT. Although the LCC's conciliation boards were a step in the right direction, the case for the tramway workers to receive enhanced pay for an eight hour day on a twelve hour spreadover took some achieving. Also there was a call for wages to keep pace with inflation, which was especially serious during the years of the First World War. Industrial action occurred in May 1915, when the L&P issued a call to arms to the tramwaymen of London. The course of the strike has been described in another chapter, but it is worth noting that both the AAT and the L&P members felt very aggrieved at the situation and the subsequent lock out by the management.

The sufferings experienced by civilian and soldier alike in the Great War caused some social conventions to be modified. After 1918 the working people of London were certainly more politically aware, and this newfound unity was mirrored by increased union activity. The amalgamation in 1920 of the AAT and the L&P to form the United Vehicle Workers was part of this process.

Employment prospects for returning servicemen varied. The author's grandfather was not untypical, in that no job awaited him on his homecoming from the Royal Navy to North London. His sister, Grace, who had worked on the single deck Kingsway Subway cars, was released from her wartime employment, and was not able to secure a permanent LCC post for her brother. This was contrary to the impres-

We don't know the occasion being celebrated in this photograph. Was it a retirement or an award ceremony? Is the chap with the book about to engage in a 'This is Your Life' speech? The human aspect of working for the LCC Tramways comes out very well in this view. Conductors, motormen, inspectors and depot officials all look suitably dapper. Pride in one's work and one's appearance was an Edwardian virtue encouraged by the Council. LCCTT

sion that family involvement in the LCC was an advantage in securing employment. Clearly, conductresses who had soldiered on bravely during the war years did not merit any special treatment after international hostilities had ceased. The majority of returning tramwaymen, on the other hand, were reinstated by the LCC, and the author's grandfather eventually got work as a station porter on the LNER.

There was a trade slump in 1920–1921, which affected the social and political climate in Britain. This nationwide downturn in the economy probably had less impact in London and the Home Counties than it did in some of the hard pressed industrial centres of the nation. This pattern was to be repeated throughout the twenties and into the Depression of 1929–33. The unemployment rates in the capital never reached the disastrous levels of many northern cities, which relied on heavy industry. In spite of this general resilience, the figures coming out of the Head Office of the LCC Tramways at 23 Belvedere Road, S.E.1, projected a gloomy outlook. The trams clawed back some of their market share by 1923 and the situation then stabilised, but the golden years of a job for life on the tramways had gone for good.

The National Joint Industrial Council for the Tramway Industry (NJIC) had been constituted in 1919 and, as a result of negotiations with the employers, a forty-eight hour week had been granted to tram crews. The establishment of the Metropolitan District Council of the NJIC took the pressure off the LCC in that the Council could now deal with a nationally recognised body. However, the inconsistencies within the metropolitan public transport sphere remained. In 1922 the top weekly rate for

an LCC motorman or conductor was seventy-nine shillings (£3.95). This compared with the London General Omnibus Company's top rate of 100 shillings (£5) for a driver. This obvious disparity in pay between tram and bus crews was to drag on for another thirty years!

This strange situation was compounded by the fact that tram and bus workers were organised by the Transport and General Workers Union on very similar lines. Union branches were based at depots and delegates were sent by the rank and file members to attend the Trams Council of the T&GWU. The Trams Council together with the Central Bus Committee and a representative from the taxicab drivers made up the No.1 Area Passenger Trade Group Committee of the Union.

In 1931, in the midst of the Depression, the earnings of the LCC tramway man had actually fallen to seventy-two shillings (£3.60) per week. Looking in the sales column of a daily newspaper would have quickly crushed any thoughts that a motorman or a conductor might have had about joining the motoring fraternity. A secondhand Austin 16 Tourer was priced at £225, and a new Armstrong Siddeley Saloon could be purchased for £425. At almost the lowest end of the earnings scale, a refined housemaid could expect to receive the sum of seventeen shillings (85p) per week. It doesn't take a maths' genius to work out that a very large percentage of the capital's workforce would have to rely on public transport for the foreseeable future. It also becomes crystal clear that one had to be well heeled to join the ranks of the private motorists. These few motorists began to dictate the transport policy for London and

the rest of the country. In the eyes of the Automobile Association and their fellow travellers the tramcar had to be hunted to extinction.

However, the LCC tram did have its friends and the humble railbound servant of the people does appear in various literary guises. Sometimes the sheer presence of a multitude of trams inspired the observer to record the wonder of the scene. One such observer was Richard Church, who penned this down to earth tribute of rush hour at Camberwell Green in THE GOLDEN SOVEREIGN, published in 1957:

A generation of citizens is already growing up which will not know the London dominated by the equalitarian tyranny of the LCC trams, those dull brown, top heavy canisters on bogie carriages with massive iron fenders at each end, which in their thousands carried the workers in their millions day by day, hour by hour, into and out of the centre of London, from home to work, from work to home, winter and summer, the year round, in a ceaseless shuttle of clangour and grind, the deep and despairing din reverberating along the rails and the subterranean live wire, so penetrating to the very soul, and violating every privacy of the cockney universe.

For almost exactly half a century the LCC trams were the dominant feature of mobile London, and especially South London. Every main road was laid with steel rails. In the poorer suburbs, whose local authorities could not afford to maintain the road surface, the rails gradually emerged some inch or more above the broken setts, woodblocks, macadam, their edges sharpened and polished like sword blades by the friction

A splendid view of the Royal Car as it waits to receive its guest, the future King George V. The red carpet is in place and soon the ceremonial handshakes will be over. Then the Prince will proceed to Greenwich to declare the whole enterprise well and truly open. Sadly, the water based connection between Greenwich, Westminster and Chelsea perished through lack of demand. The steamers were decommissioned on 1st November 1907.
B.J.Cross Collection

and grind of the wheels, which at every curve resisted the confinement of the permanent way, thrusting with heated flanges, metal against metal, and raising an outcry of shrieks, scratchings, groans and dull sound blocks as of a community of machines suddenly animated with hatred.

At the big road junctions this metallic hell made night and day hideous and terrifying. The constant movement of the brown monsters, giants with neither head nor tail, eyes nor limbs, nothing but bellies of steel and glass; the interweaving yet blind movement of these trams, impervious to the contest of free traffic that rushed, dodged, avoided and cut in around them, mounted during rush hours to a nightmare fantasy. The roar of it, the clangour of the gongs, the sudden formations in a halted procession, a dozen or more of these expressionless land-arks, the surge forward, the partings, with shrieks of vehicular agony at rail points; and the vision of the half mortals packed on the lower deck, the upper deck, swaying together in one soporific inertia, drugged with tobacco smoke, the night's overhang, the day's labour, and the subconscious certainty of this enduring slavery; the menace of the road surface, with its oiled and tyre polished setts, its armoury of razor edged rails; all these things, a piling up of threats and horrors, came to a sinister perfection at Camberwell Green . . .

This Caliban, the LCC tram, served a good purpose, and was a dutiful slave in spite of its hideous shape and raucous conduct. It carried me and millions like me, at a minimum cost, enabling us

to save a ha'penny or a penny a day, which could be accumulated to buy a book. It was thus a patron of culture, of the arts . . .

Richard Church's true debt to the tram emerges in the last paragraph. He managed to use the time spent in commuting to good purpose – to enhance his knowledge through reading on the daily journey between Camberwell Green and the Elephant and Castle. To him the tram was an instrument of education.

Frank Swinnerton gives a wonderful evocation of South London as he describes a night-time tram ride in his 1917 novel NOCTURNE. The tram to him is an everyday conveyance with just that touch of mystery and romance, which can turn a humdrum ride into something magical. His tram is

Above **The workforce employed on track construction was a hardy bunch as this photo shows. Rails and all the conduit yokes and fittings had to be positioned manually. No hoists or other mechanical devices were on hand to alleviate the backbreaking toil. Just** as the railway navvies before them, the LCC permanent way workers and gangers moved into a location and completed the excavating and track laying in record time. They were the unsung heroes of the urban transport revolution.

certainly not the raucous monster of Richard Church's Camberwell Green. The author paints a picture of his main character Jenny, who is returning on a winter's evening from central London to her home in Kennington.

Less laborious but equally backbreaking was the task of cleaning out point blades. These two men have a single red flag to act as a warning to oncoming traffic. The LCC was nothing if not thorough in its maintenance schedules, so much so that the points being cleaned here are on the very little used curve from Greenwich Church Street into Nelson Street. Added to this was the fact that these were trailing points, which were normally reset by the tram passing over them.
D.Jones Collection

Six o'clock was striking. The darkness by Westminster Bridge was intense; and as the tramcar turned the corner from the Embankment Jenny craned to look at the thickly running water below . . .

As the car proceeded over the bridge, grinding its way through the still rolling echoes of the striking hour, it seemed part of an endless succession of such cars, all alike crowded with homeward bound passengers, and all, to the curious mind, resembling ships that pass very slowly at night from safe harbourage to the unfathomable. It was such a cold still night that the sliding windows of the car were almost closed, and the atmosphere of the covered upper deck was heavy with tobacco smoke. It was so dark that one could not see beyond the fringes of the lamplight upon the bridge . . .

The man sitting beside Jenny continued to puff steadfastly at his pipe, lost in the news, holding mechanically in his further hand the return ticket which would be presently snatched by the hurrying tram conductor . . .

The change pit attendant performed a vital role in the smooth running of the tramways. Delays at changeover points between the conduit and overhead methods of current collection had to be kept to a minimum. Here at Wandsworth a southbound car has a plough forked into its carrier. H.Nicol / National Tramway Museum

As soon as the tramcar had passed the bridge, lighted windows above the shops broke the magic mirror and gave Jenny a new interest, until, as they went onward, a shopping district, ablaze with colour, crowded with loitering people, and alive with din, turned all thoughts from herself into one absorbed contemplation of what was beneath her eyes. So absorbed was she, indeed, that the conductor had to prod her shoulder with his two fingers before he could recover her ticket and exchange it for another " 'Arf asleep, some people!" he grumbled, shoving aside the projecting arms and elbows which prevented his free passage between the seats. 'Feyuss please!' Jenny shrugged her shoulder, which seemed as though it had been irritated at the conductor's touch. It felt quite bruised. "Silly old fool!" she thought, with a brusque glance. Then she went silently back to the contemplation of all the life that had gathered upon the muddy and glistening pavements below.

In a few minutes they were past the shops and once again in darkness, grinding along, pitching from end to end, the driver's bell clanging every minute to warn carts and people off the tramline. Once, with an awful thunderous grating of the brakes, the car was pulled up, and everybody tried to see what had provoked the sense of accident. There was a little shouting, and Jenny, staring hard into the roadway, thought she could see as its cause a small girl pushing a perambulator loaded with bundles of washing. Her first impulse was pity – 'Poor little thing'; but the words were hardly in her mind before they were chased away by a faint indignation at the child for getting in the tram's way. Everybody ought to look where they were going. Ev-ry bo-dy ought to look where they were go-ing, said the pitching tramcar . . .

Tum-ty tum-ty tum-ty, said the tram. There were some more shops. There were straggling shops and full blazing rows of shops. There were stalls along the side of the road, women dancing to an organ outside a public house. Shops, shops, houses, houses, houses . . . light, darkness . . . Jenny gathered her skirt. This was where she got down . . . she was upon the iron shod stairs of the car and into the greasy roadway. Then darkness, as she turned along beside a big building into the side streets among rows and rows of the small houses of Kennington Park.

Jenny's experiences on the tram were not untypical of the life led by many unmarried women who commuted to work in the second decade of the twentieth century. The scenes she witnessed were woven into the fabric of pre First World War London, where brightly lit shops stayed open late, people danced outside their local and poor children scuttled about trying to earn a few extra pennies.

Some youngsters cultivated an interest in the LCC and its entire works. Robert A. Perkins takes up the story:

I was born in South London in 1913, and I remember the LCC trams very well indeed. In fact I was born in St James's Hospital, Balham in May 1913, just 10 years after the first electric tram ran along the High Road, and the year in which trailers appeared on the Tooting – Embankment circular route. I remember the open top trailer cars. They were OK at the London end, but became a bit of a nuisance at Tooting, Longley Road terminus. They had a separate depot at Marius Road, Balham, which was the first depot for the electric cars before the big depot at Clapham Common was brought into use . . .

I have been thinking about those good old far off days and of my parents and grandparents, aunts and uncles. They used to take me on long tram rides out to Abbey Wood, Woolwich Common and even Epping Forest on the LCC North London system – Service 81. In those days we travelled through the Kingsway Subway on single deck cars, either Class F or G. I remember the first double decker Class E/3 number 1931 painted all over white, emerging from the subway in the year 1931 – September I think it was.

The HR/2 Class was already operating on the Dulwich routes replacing the four wheelers. I liked the four wheelers, but they did sway about, particularly at speed. The HR/2 trams made a peculiar noise, a sort of bell like clanging noise, but they could certainly attain a good speed with their four motors (35hp) making each car a 140hp vehicle. They could make short work of Dog Kennel Hill. There were times when I thought the four wheelers wouldn't make it up that hill, particularly when they were full.

When I was about 12 years old, I discovered the first LCC Tramways substation – or rather the first substation that I had seen. It was the 'Gables' at St John's Hill, Battersea. On a hot summer afternoon I heard a high pitched hum, while cycling on my new fairy cycle, coming from a small building with green doors, one of which was open, because of the warm weather. I stood there mesmerised, looking at what I though were 'engines'.

After a long time a friendly voice said, "Are you thinking of buying the plant son?" He went on to explain that the machines were not engines, but synchronous motor generator sets, four of them. It said on a brass plate 'Dick, Kerr & Co., Synchronous Motor'. I was not much wiser, but the man said that the synchronous motor was driven by alternating current supplied from the main generating station at Greenwich, and this was coupled to a 600 volt direct current generator supplying the conductor rail of the tramways with current. I am sure it was that encounter with that very nice substation attendant that made me decide to become an electrical engineer. Which eventually, many years later, I did, ex – Battersea Polytechnic. Such a converting would be frowned upon today, I am thinking.

It is worth remembering that the London County Council had a very real stake in improving the educational standards and aspirations of the capital's population. The acquisition of learning spread from schools, colleges and poly-technics to the tramways department. Employees were encouraged to voice their own opinions in a constructive way through the submission of an essay or a paper, which could be read at a depot meeting. Inevitably, topics centred on tramway matters, staff relations, improvements in services and technical advancements that could aid efficiency. Overtly contentious or political themes were discouraged by the Council. It was felt that a union meeting was the proper forum for this type of debate. Also criticism of individuals, such as unfair inspectors or over-zealous officials was actively discouraged.

A typical LCC publication in this field was entitled PAPERS GIVEN AT DEPOT MEETINGS – JUNE 1928, which won the Institute of Transport Gold Medal for the best paper of the year on Road Transport (Passenger). The first submission – THE COMMERCIAL ASPECT OF LOCAL PASSENGER TRANSPORT. A PAPER READ AT STREATHAM DEPOT – covers service, passenger comfort, fares policy and publicity. These were all vital areas in the scramble to maintain or enhance passenger numbers in the face of bus competition. Another paper, entitled SALESMANSHIP AND GOODWILL, was read at Poplar, New Cross, Hackney and Holloway Depots. This had paragraph headings of *Regular Running, Speed, Courtesy, Comfort and Facilities*. A final section in the 1928 papers is concerned with tramway schedules, and it was delivered to audiences at Wandsworth and Hampstead Depots. Again the topics of speed, car headways, duty cycles and interworking with other services come to the fore.

Excerpts from the SALESMANSHIP AND GOODWILL article give a flavour of the era:

Our tramways undertaking is nothing more or less than a huge store with 1,600 branch shops, whose stock in trade is rides of different lengths.

The tramways have dictated what the price of those rides should be. It is not we who have cut our prices, it is our competitors who have come down to ours. Tramways initiated the first reduction of fares soon after the close of the war and gave London its cheap pennyworth again. Tramways introduced the cheap midday fares, return tickets at reduced rates, a very complete system of transfer facilities for the city bound worker, and the shilling all day ticket. Add to these facilities workman fares and all night

services, and one might expect that the public served by the tramways would be more or less under a debt of gratitude to the tramways, and our goodwill thereby assured at a high level. Especially so when one remembers that in districts not served by tramways, these facilities are conspicuous by their absence.

But our experience is that our goodwill is not by any means assured. It is rather amazing, but it is very true. An unnecessary pirate bus, perhaps making one or two journeys a day and in no way providing a service, can invade a tramway route and apparently make a living out of it, and it is this surprising indifference on the part of a portion of the public to its own interests, both as travellers and ratepayers, which we have to fight . . .

The average speed of the Council's system is now nearly nine and three-quarter miles per hour (15.7km/h), and has been increased since 1921 from nine miles per hour (14.4km/h). This is a matter for congratulation, but don't let us be satisfied with that – put on your thinking caps and let us know where improvements can be made – speed with efficiency means everything . . .

Now, at times, passengers are difficult to handle; at one depot we were informed that some passengers by paying a penny fare think they have not only bought the car, but also the uniform on the conductor's back. We know your difficulties and that the patience of a Job is required, but the soft answer does turn away wrath sometimes.

We have also heard of an official who is the devil incarnate when on early turn, but becomes a cooing dove when on late turn. A conductor deals with about 800 passengers a day, so you can imagine the mess a really grumpy one can leave

behind him . . .

It is a pleasure to see the way some conductors handle a car load of passengers – missed fares a rarity, return tickets punched or cancelled correctly – "fares please" said politely, but as if meant – no argument with passengers, except to courteously indicate what can or cannot be done . . . Conductors must be students of human nature, and it is not very far wide of the mark to say that smart drivers and conductors are the tramways best publicity agents…With these points in mind and such other improvements as occur to you, let us get down to brass tacks and say it all in money.

Last year (i.e.1927) we were short of meeting all our charges by £120,000 i.e. 3 per cent down, or about sevenpence in the pound.

I told you, early on, our undertaking was a big shop with 1,600 branches. Every driver and conductor are joint managers of one of these moving shops, and each of these shops was short at the end of each week by thirty shillings (£1.50), that is two shillings (10p) a shift . . . During the past four years, against an avalanche of omnibus competition, a great deal has been achieved. Are we too optimistic in thinking that an extra passenger per car mile is within our capacity for improvement?

Above **Craftsmen employed by the LCC were skilled and reliable. They had to have some stamina in order to cope with the never ending procession of tramcars needing repair and renovation. An E Class car is probably having upper deck bulkhead doors fitted. The dash is metal sheet, but a large proportion of the rest of** the bodywork is hardwood and plywood panelling.

Above right **It was regarded as a cardinal sin if a tramcar went out on the road in a dirty or grubby condition. Cleaners were employed at most depots and sometimes mechanical means was used, as here at Holloway Depot.**

The mention of the shilling all day ticket in these paragraphs introduces us to one of the icons of the LCC Tramways. This ticket was the key to knowledge for many thousands of Londoners. There has never been a transport facility so fondly remembered as the humble all day ticket, which gave its user the freedom to roam the metropolis. Long after the trams had ceased to be a presence on the London scene, the shilling all day was regarded as one of the bargains of the century. It was introduced on 3rd January 1925 and was originally intended only for weekend use, on Saturdays or Sundays. From 21st July 1925 it was issued for travel on a daily basis all over the County of London, in the Leyton area and between Merton and Wimbledon. By the time the LCC was absorbed by the LPTB one could travel over most East

London municipal lines, on LUT cars within the boundaries of the County of London and on Croydon Corporation services. In the September of 1930, Mr W. Westley of Highgate set a record for the shilling all day ticket by travelling 207 miles (333km) in just less than twenty-two hours.

Cheap fares for workmen have already figured in this account, however, from 19th April 1920, the Council introduced the 2d Cheap Midday Fare, which was applicable to a through journey on all cars arriving at central London termini in a time slot from 10.30am to 4.30pm. On outbound cars the ticket was valid from 10am to 4pm. These lower fares helped win back customers.

The LCC mantra of *Speed – Courtesy – Comfort – Facilities* was invoked throughout the rest of the decade and into the early 1930s. There was a ready willingness on behalf of the management and staff of the tramways to counter the criticisms uttered by the general public. Frequent complaints were made about trams arriving in bunches – commonly known as a banana service. Ventilation of tramcars in the summer and lack of heating in the winter came in for some stick from the passengers. Then there were the safety factors of people having to cross streams of traffic to board or alight from a Council tramcar. All these points were the subject of lively debate. Some

aspects surfaced in the edition of PLATFORM, the review of the essay competition and efficiency meetings session of 1903–31. By this time, matters were looking up for the beleaguered LCC, but the General Manager still saw fit to encourage the crews for one last effort to win the battle for passengers.

For the second year in succession we face the Londoner without fear of being told that 'we are on the rates'. But owing to greater unemployment, trade depression and, to some extent, greater and more effective competition the profit this year is very substantially less – £30,000 instead of over £120,000.

A Royal Commission (qv), whilst setting out advantages attaching to tramways that indicate it is a clean, speedy and well controlled form of transport . . . spoils the picture for us by asserting that tramways are obstructive and a cause of congestion and accidents.

We have been attacked in a newspaper for taking such steps as the law allows to protect passengers boarding or alighting. 'Bullying the motorist', says the newspaper. The authorities are much concerned to see that a pedestrian can cross the road in safety . . . Conductors, and motormen too, have done much to assist passengers to and from the kerb. Experience shows that a boldly extended

The LCC telephone network contributed to the successful operation of the system. A traffic regulator at Stamford Hill uses the phone atop section box 344 to contact Control Headquarters at Hackney (LCC Tramways, Northern Section). On the northern side there were 36 'selective' telephones at major traffic intersections. A further 17 of these instruments were installed in car sheds. The control room in Hackney could call up these 53 locations. A further 111 non selective phones were installed on section boxes at half mile intervals. Tram crews could open these with a key and summon assistance from Hackney.

Our last tramway stalwart is the chap who stood out in all weathers at the southern portal to the Kingsway Subway. His job was to extend a red flag to alert passing traffic to the presence of a tramcar crossing over the Victoria Embankment. He shared with his colleagues the pointsmen a lonely existence, but an important one, which demanded vigilance at all times. Often former drivers and conductors ended their days doing the job of flagman or pointsman.

arm is sufficient for any considerate motorist and that he welcomes such guidance . . .

Is our financial position today a very happy one? It is and it isn't. Owing mainly to our own efforts we are paying our way; on the other hand, we are still very vulnerable to competition – 1,300 pneumatic tyred buses of 50 and 60 seats are being placed up against us and we have to fight for our traffic as hard as ever we did. When you compare the old 34-seater B-type bus with the LT 60-seater bus, no words of mine are necessary to describe the keener weapon of competition. The extra passenger a mile is all essential. Self improvement has cost us extra rates. Trade depression has cost us a loss of passengers. These two items alone – apart from the sharpened edge of railway and omnibus competition – will eat seriously into our small margin of profit.

The article ended by a rallying cry from T. E. Thomas, the General Manager – Let your motto, then, be this: ANOTHER PASSENGER A MILE.

CHAPTER FOURTEEN
Design and Publicity

THE ELECTED members were aware that the London County Council needed to present itself as modern but not extravagant – solid and trustworthy but not unimaginative. In modern parlance the Council was very image conscious. The trams were of course highly visible to the ratepayers, which made the task of keeping them clean, mechanically sound and presentable a top priority. Depot buildings, passenger shelters, publicity materials, maps and guides also came within the ambit of good taste and style. Not that everyone agreed on the Council's artistic leanings. The architectural style of LCC depot buildings has been variously described as '*grimly utilitarian*', '*municipally inspired*' or an '*extravagant waste of money*'

depending on the aesthetic viewpoint of the beholder or the political leanings of the observer. The Chief Architect to the Council, W. E. Riley, was instrumental in formulating a distinctive car shed design, which took inspiration from the Roman Doric form. This was regarded by many as a sensible middle way between the overblown fussiness of late Victorian ornamental style and the stark, slab like warehouse design of some company owned tram depots – in short, the LCC wanted to attract kudos.

Yellow bricks served as the main building material for the depot walls. On the interior these walls were covered to a height of 5ft 6in (1.68m) from the ground by a relief of white bricks. Roofs were slate covered and Helliwell skylights were installed for

increased daytime illumination. Brick walls were often abutted to stone facings, and on the main entrance to many depots, archways and keystones were constructed in Portland Stone. The whole façade presented an appearance of understated importance – a feeling of solid municipal achievement, which would impress an observer on a first visit to an LCC tram depot. The sightseer looking up at all this had to remember that, in pre-Health & Safety days, maintenance pits and machinery were unguarded, and that at some very busy depots, the poorly paid staff had precious little time to stand back and admire the classical perspectives revealed by their architectural surroundings.

Somewhat less grand were the solid urban structures that characterised the various headquarters of the Tramways Department. The offices were at 303 Camberwell New Road from 1899 to 1906; they then moved to 62 Finsbury Pavement, on the boundary of the City of London. From 1918 to the end of tramcar operation by the LCC, they were situated at or near 23 Belvedere Road, Lambeth. The extension of County Hall in the mid 'twenties resulted in the Tramways Department seeking temporary accommodation in offices on the Victoria Embankment. County Hall itself was designed by Ralph Knott and construction started in 1921. The southern wing was completed the following year, but the northern wing was opened in stages from 1931–33.

1084 LCC TRAM DEPOT STREATHAM HILL SW JOHNS

Above 'Solid but not unattractive' is how one commentator described the general style of LCC car sheds. The retention of trees round the site at Streatham has enhanced the location of the depot. However, there is evidence from this photo that some weathering of the stone facades has taken place. Given the atmospheric pollution in Edwardian London this is not surprising. The low wall on the left of the view has been strategically placed for the crews to sit on whilst waiting to start their shifts.

Right The LCC Tramways HQ at 301-303 Camberwell New Road certainly does not stand out as a structure of architectural merit. These buildings were used from 1899 to June 1906, when operations were transferred to 62 Finsbury Pavement in the heart of the capital.
J.B.Gent Collection

L.C.C. TRAMS OFFICE, CAMBERWELL, S.E.

LONDON'S TRAMWAYS

OUR WAY TO THE PARTY

The Council's design brief included passenger shelters and tram stops. It had become obvious that, just as customers preferred top covered cars, they also did not relish the prospect of waiting in the rain for their next tram. Clearly, some form of shelter had to be erected at important tram stops. Finances did not permit the construction of a passenger shelter at every tram stop, but at major junctions the Council would erect a small wooden building whose style can only be described as rural vernacular. Space would usually be found for a range of LCC posters advertising tramway facilities, and the standard LCC tram map would be positioned as a reference feature for all potential travellers.

A larger, and it has to be said, less attractive form of shelter appeared at the Blackfriars end of the Victoria Embankment. The original terminus at this location had also boasted a shelter. Taking the form more of a roofed queuing enclosure, it was constructed facing the end of the track. Unfortunately, this farsighted move by the Council proved rather less practical in reality after several careless motormen overran the end of the track and damaged the structure!

Passenger demand had shot up due to the new wartime employment conditions, and the Council found that an extra shelter was needed. The TRAMWAY & RAILWAY WORLD for 9th September 1915 takes up the story:

A very short time after the opening of the first sheltered queues for tramway passengers at the Blackfriars Bridge end of the Victoria Embankment in London at Easter 1911, the need was felt for additional accommodation. The six lines of passengers that converge from the entrances at each end of the structure to the central openings, from which they pass to the cars, at times extended from 20 to 50 yards (18 to 45 metres) or more beyond the roof.

The shelter is the arrival and departure point of a large proportion of the many thousands of workers engaged in the City of London. The businessman and the factory girl are prominent among them, and before the structure was erected they had to take their chance in undignified and dangerous rushes to the cars. To a lesser extent the scramble still prevails at other points along the Victoria Embankment, notably at Waterloo Bridge, Charing Cross, and Westminster Bridge. Waterloo Bridge and the SECR Bridge over the Thames at Charing Cross provide protection from the rain at those places, and at Westminster there is a small shelter far back on the foot pavement. Further west at the Victoria Street end of Vauxhall Bridge Road there is at present neither regulation of passengers nor a shelter for them. At these points the traffic may not be heavy enough to require the same arrangements as at Blackfriars, but at Victoria a shelter at least is necessary. Failing that course, the barrier system might be adopted, as is the case at Southwark Bridge, as soon as the reduction of the staff entailed by the war can be made good.

We are also told in the article that the welfare of the public was paramount in the granting of part of the roadway by the Corporation of the City of London – a pity that this magnanimous gesture did not extend to other tramway plans for the City, but no doubt the establishment felt they had done their bit for the country in its time of need. The new structure sanctioned by the City was built in steel and cast iron and measured 97ft 6ins (29.7m) in length, 7 feet (2.1m) in width and 8ft 6ins in height (2.6m). The original 1911 shelter was constructed of oak and was 180 feet (54.8m) long. Again, the redoubtable W. E. Riley had a hand in the design of the new shelter.

Posters affixed to tram shelters played an important role in a very effective publicity campaign. They formed part of an organised strategy to increase public awareness of the services offered by the Council. Newspaper advertisements and leaflets were also essential to encourage passengers on to the trams. However newspaper advertising was expensive. In 1928, the Council was charged £132 for one

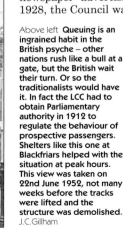

Above left **Queuing is an ingrained habit in the British psyche – other nations rush like a bull at a gate, but the British wait their turn. Or so the traditionalists would have it. In fact the LCC had to obtain Parliamentary authority in 1912 to regulate the behaviour of prospective passengers. Shelters like this one at Blackfriars helped with the situation at peak hours. This view was taken on 22nd June 1952, not many weeks before the tracks were lifted and the structure was demolished.** J.C.Gillham

Left **John Gillham's camera also focused on a smaller, but better designed shelter on Southwark Bridge Road, just south of the railway bridge at the junction with Union Street.** J.C.Gillham

Nearly all British tramways, both privately owned and municipal, derived much needed revenue from advertisements affixed to tramcars. The LCC was no exception, and as this photo shows, an active campaign was underway to promote the virtues of a travelling hoarding, which could be seen by many Londoners. Advertisers could apply to head office at Finsbury Pavement to claim their space on the side of Car 700 and its sisters.

Below **Full page advertisements were used by the LCC to drum up support for the selling of car space for commercial revenue.**
Below centre and right **Front covers of staff magazines.**

insertion in the DAILY MAIL – ironically the same newspaper, which had campaigned so vociferously against the Progressives in the 1907 Election.

In a discussion document, which did the depot rounds in 1928–1929, the ways and means of advertising the tramways were tackled. What is noteworthy in the following article is the Council's philosophy of educating and informing the public through good art and design:

Posters in shelters add splashes of bright colour and catch a traveller in a mood when he is very ready to be interested. We like to believe that five minutes spent in Stamford Hill Shelter waiting for a car seems like five seconds to anyone

examining the posters and maps there. For larger positions we use the walls of schools, offices and works of the LCC and other public bodies . . .

Every month the department issues a pictorial poster. Over 70 have been printed. The first one in colours epitomised Caledonian Market. Those in preparation include the Zoo and Putney. Sometimes a poster illustrates a travel feature, such as Comfort and Speed. At Christmas passengers were asked to shop early – and they did . . .

Some of the most valuable positions are in the cars themselves. Let to traders these spaces would produce hard cash. Used for advertising the Tramways they yield quite as much in increasing receipts from passengers and by building up prestige. Our posters are eagerly sought by schoolmasters and mistresses. For one picture there were 500 applications. They hang in classrooms, and are used for encouraging sightseeing and for teaching history and geography . . .

It is not enough to advertise, say, Waterlow Park outside the Archway only. To do that would be to preach to the converted. Waterlow Park must be displayed here, there and everywhere. From Camden Town to Catford, at any point where there is a tramcar within half a mile or so.

Maps are displayed in business houses,

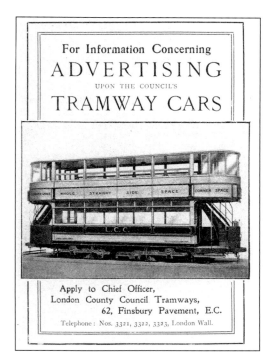

For Information Concerning
ADVERTISING
UPON THE COUNCIL'S
TRAMWAY CARS

Apply to Chief Officer,
London County Council Tramways,
62, Finsbury Pavement, E.C.
Telephone : Nos. 3321, 3322, 3323, London Wall.

The PLATFORM

A Review of Last Year
and the Outlook To-day

LONDON COUNTY COUNCIL TRAMWAYS

A Record
of selected
Papers read at
DEPOT
MEETINGS
Winter Session
1928-29

PROGRESS

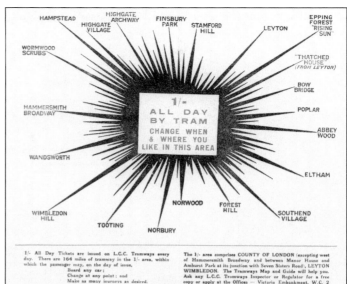

hotels, public resorts and schools. This year the edition increased to 4,200. Nothing is paid for the space occupied, clear evidence that they are welcomed. They were the first maps to be shown in London streets, opposite stopping places, and they hang in classrooms or corridors of 1,600 schools.

The children of today will be your grown up passengers tomorrow. At one school in Greenwich the headmaster asked how many boys aged from 7 to 10 had been to London proper, that is, across the bridges. There were 130 boys. How many do you think had crossed the Thames at Blackfriars, Westminster or Waterloo? Only 50; 50 out of 130 . . . The number of Islington children who had seen the Thames was only one in three. Think of that when you run from The Angel to the Thames Bank in 12 minutes.

When the advertisement has been planned, designed and printed, there remains the all important question of distribution

and display. This is where the staff can be of great help.

A torn poster in the street, an out of date notice in the car, a sign not switched on at night – these things are the bugbears of outdoor advertising . . .

Passengers write to the offices and say they cannot obtain a map. Conductors should politely refer applicants to inspectors and regulators. To the latter we say: Keep a large enough supply. Renew it when it is low. Keep all maps and leaflets clean as they come from the printers. Bins at regulators' points have boxes for holding maps and so on, nice wallets are provided for carrying them. Offer copies to everyone not familiar with tramway facilities . . .

The best publicity agents of the Tramways are the motorman, conductor, the inspector and regulator, men in a

position every minute of the day to advertise the system by word, deed and bearing.

On the other side of the advertising fence, there were plenty of tramcar component suppliers who sought to involve the Council in the endorsement of their products. This was generally handled by means of advertisements placed by different companies in the main trade magazines. LCC tramcars appeared in views promoting trackwork, plywood, traffic control systems, gears and trucks, seats and safety glass – to name but a few.

The contribution of the LCC to the field of cartography also bears some investigation. The first route maps to help passengers find their way around the system appeared in the OFFICIAL TRAMWAYS GUIDE, published 1908 and priced at one penny per copy. This was remarkable value for around 140 pages of text detailing tram

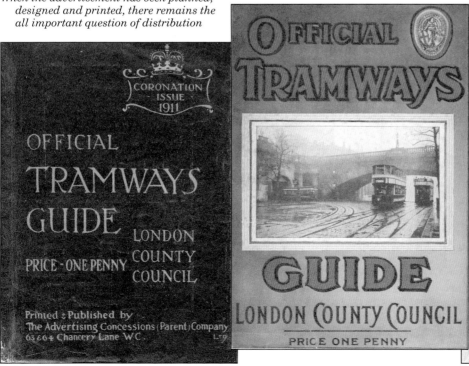

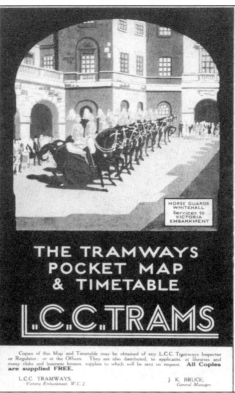

routes, timetables and places of interest *en route*. A revised edition of the guide was published in 1909 and the third edition appeared in 1911. Entitled the CORONATION ISSUE, in honour of King George V's ascent to the throne, it contained 186 pages plus a large fold out route map. The success of this venture probably influenced the Council to produce a series of route maps from 1913 to 1933. Editions appeared at monthly intervals from January 1913 to April 1915, then wartime conditions interrupted the flow and maps were published for July 1915, October 1915, January 1916 and April 1916.

The LCC Map and Guide reappeared in 1919 and then flourished until the transfer to London Transport in 1933. A feature of each map was a cover drawing of a London landmark that could be reached by Council tramcar.

Although the official map also contained details of service frequencies, a more detailed guide was needed especially when the shilling all day ticket gained popularity. Charles G. Harper was commissioned by the Council to write a guidebook called ROUND & ABOUT LONDON BY TRAM. It was published in two volumes, one for the NORTH OF THE THAMES (EXCLUDING VICTORIA EMBANKMENT) and one for SOUTH OF THE THAMES. Line drawings, maps, photographs and clearly explained itineraries completed each work. A healthy proportion of advertisements

helped finance the project. As befits a literary endeavour sponsored by the LCC, the tone is very pro-tram and the reader is left with the distinct impression that this is the only method of surface transport worth considering for an outing. Some of the prose is spiritually uplifting for the tramway enthusiast and a sentence like – *The breezes blow fresh and clean on the rising ground of Southend and Downham, through which tramways have been constructed as far as Grove Park Station* – almost takes the process of tram riding to another ethereal plain altogether!

Of course the opposition Combine was not slow in cashing in on this opportunity and its London guides promoted the tube railways, General motor buses and company operated tramways. Lording it over all, the METRO-LAND guides published from the offices of the Metropolitan Railway at Baker Street Station studiously avoided any mention of alternative transport systems. These books usually ignored the existence of the LCC Tramways, and the compliment was returned by the Council who made no mention of the Combine except where joint services were operated with the MET and LUT. The genuine explorer of London was thus obliged to purchase a range of publications just to find out where all the transport services went. Perhaps this was yet another argument in favour of a unified transport undertaking for London.

Illuminated stop signs and direction boards had their place in the LCC's

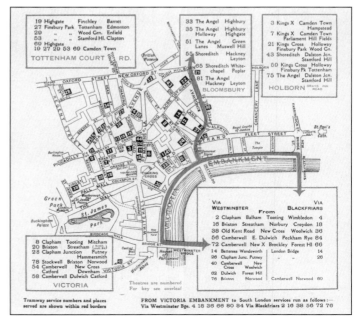

Left Stop signs sometimes served to give service information as here at Kennington. The shelter pictured earlier in the chapter is at the far end of the iron railings. The trees are bare and winter has come for the LCC Tramways – quite literally in this case, as the newly formed LPTB has just abandoned the former LCC service 6 on the Tooting Junction to Mitcham Cricket Green section. *LT Museum*

Below left Simplicity and elegance in design are evident in this lamp-post and car stop. In an era when buses would stop when hailed, the electric trams pioneered fixed stopping places. The idea of compulsory and request stops then became familiar to **Londoners.** *LT Museum*

Below This splendid looking shelter offers a seat for waiting travellers and doubles as a public convenience for those folk who have arrived at the fork of the road by Kennington Park Road and Brixton Road.
At 12 minutes past 11 of a summer's day we can tarry awhile to admire the display of colourful posters or even peer into the regulator's cabin to see if we can acquire the latest LCC timetable and **tram map.** *LT Museum*

Bottom It's all go at Archway Tavern, Highgate – even the wooden cabin has a hurried look about it, as if it had been erected quickly to prevent the GPO putting another telephone box on the road island. The standard LCC tram map – one of the last the Council produced – is pasted up to act as a guide for potential passengers. A spare plough rests against the sand bin behind the tram conductor. *LT Museum*

publicity drive. Their positioning was crucial in catching the passing trade generated by visitors to the centre of London. Signs in the neighbourhood of the Kingsway Subway and Westminster, Parliament Square were deemed particularly effective in reminding potential patrons that they did in fact have an alternative to the tube and the bus. The philosophy behind the signs was dealt with in a discussion paper under the heading *Anticipating the Enquiry*:

At one time it was considered sufficient to say CARS STOP HERE. The present practice is to supplement this information: to name the places served and the car numbers for them. This is the kind of service that the public appreciate. In these days of intense movement the street is more and more a place for advertising travel. The town crier has come back. But his appeal is less strident, more subtle. He employs the skill of the artist and the printer. He puts a sign here, in a strategic position, to catch the eye of the tired pedestrian. At night he lights up the sign . . .

Eye catching posters, and distinctive leaflets were distributed to newspaper editors together with any positive stories about tram services. The Council realised early on the benefit of favourable press coverage, and to an extent, in the last decade of operation the Tramways Department put more effort into contacts with the media. A discussion paper from 1929–30 puts the situation in context:

I am sometimes inclined to doubt whether the publicity work of the trams has reached the peak of development. Much admirable work has been done along the more obvious lines. Posters, newspaper advertisements, notices on trams and in streets seem to be well organised and effectively displayed. Use is made of news

columns and even wireless. But I wonder if more cannot be done to get the trams into the news columns in a favourable light. That is where publicity really tells. If you are to influence the man in the street and make him see the trams as a worthy and desirable feature of London life, you have to enlist the aid of the newspaper sub editor. The journalist works under orders, and often the orders of an employer hostile to London's tramways. But it is nevertheless possible to get the ear of the journalist if you can persuade him that your story is not propaganda, not publicity, but news.

When the tramlines at Aldgate were reconstructed by direct labour it was possible to induce the press to notice the fact at length. This sort of publicity should be developed. It has to be carried on carefully, by discreet men who know

the ways of Fleet Street; but I am convinced that it is essential if the trams are to be made more popular.

There is no doubting the tone of this piece, but the author is somewhat naïve in imagining that there was a level playing field as regards the press perception of tramways. By the end of the twenties the *Scrap the Trams* bandwagon was well and truly rolling. Motoring and other pressure groups were manipulating the media to cast the trams in the worst light possible. They convinced many editors that tram free streets would solve traffic congestion and the parking problem at one fell swoop. The BBC, as always, tried to present a balanced approach, and in March 1926, Motorman Albert Curtis broadcast a talk from the Savoy Hill Studios. His theme was MY DAY'S WORK – THE DUTIES OF A LONDON TRAM DRIVER.

But whatever came over the airwaves, the relentless opposition to fixed track transport in the highway gained ground and influence. So much influence in fact, that the LCC's charm offensive fell on deaf ears. The ordinary folk of London were probably enticed to make a few extra tram rides to parks and historic landmarks, but the manipulators of power in the capital paid no heed to the bright posters – they were certain that the tram's days were numbered.

LONDON'S TRAMWAYS

OLD FURNITURE AT THE GEFFRYE MUSEUM KINGSLAND RD. TRAM SERVICES 43, 45, 47, 49

Right **The backroom boys also got into the act, and humble Stores Van 08 took its turn to promote the Council's tramways. It was hoped that parents and children who caught sight of this car would be persuaded to use the LCC** trams on trips out during the school holidays. Cheap return fares enabled many poorer families to visit the Zoo, Greenwich Park, Lessness Abbey or Hampstead Heath.

Below **Cigarette cards are a useful reference to colour at a time when most images were recorded in monochrome only. This card was issued by Carreras during the First World War and was one of 60 headed TYPES OF LONDON and illustrated by Julius M. Price. The caption on the reverse side reads:** The duties of the County Council Tram Driver are both monotonous and cold. It requires a considerable amount of skill to drive a heavy tramcar through the crowded streets and the driver must undergo a long course of training before he is entrusted with complete control of one.

BLACK CAT
CIGARETTES

1492

COUNTY COUNCIL TRAM DRIVER

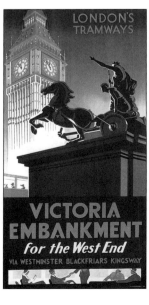

LONDON'S TRAMWAYS

VICTORIA EMBANKMENT
for the West End
VIA WESTMINSTER BLACKFRIARS KINGSWAY

LONDON'S TRAMWAYS

HIGHGATE BY SERVICES 7 11 AND 15

SHOP EARLY

RIDE IN COMFORT BY LONDON'S TRAMWAYS

CHAPTER FIFTEEN
New Trams for Old

GEORGE MORTIMER Pullman was born on 3rd March 1831 in Brocton, New York. He went to Chicago and founded the Pullman Palace Car Company in 1867. He then made his fortune by manufacturing sleeping cars and dining cars for America's expanding railroads. The standard of workmanship became a byword for a luxurious finish and quality materials. Thus the Pullman name went down in history, and the LCC Highways Committee coined the noun pullmanisation for a renovation programme targeted at trams from Classes E, E/1 and M. One wonders whether the elected members actually did their homework on this one, because those Labour and Liberal councillors with a social conscience were probably unaware that

Pullman ended his days embroiled in violent conflict with his workers. At one clash between troops and Pullman employees there were 23 fatalities in the ensuing riot – anyway, pullmanisation it was and the process began during 1925.

The new General Manager, J. K. Bruce, was the guiding light behind the scheme, and W. E. Ireland, the Chief Rolling Stock Engineer, ably assisted him. Mr Ireland was appointed in charge of the workshops and depots of the LUT in 1902, and two years later transferred to the LCC. He was a major influence on the design of Charlton Works, which was geared to production line assembly. Although it might be said that his talents were stifled by the rather conservative approach of A. L. C. Fell, he was always alive to the possibilities of introducing new technology to the Council's tram fleet.

During 1922 the National Physical Laboratory, the Hoffman Manufacturing Company and the LCC got together to test a standard car, which had been fitted with roller bearings. The test car set off from Tierney Road, Streatham through Brixton and Kennington to Westminster Bridge. It

then returned along the Embankment, down Blackfriars Road and Kennington Park Road to Clapham. From here it went via Tooting and Mitcham Road to return to its starting place at Streatham. Certain tractive resistance tests were conducted on Camberwell New Road. The conclusions quoted from Mr Ireland's office were as follows:

The results of the tests indicate that a considerable saving in electrical energy can be effected by the employment of Hoffman roller bearings on the armature spindles and axles of a tramway car, the saving varying from about 30 per cent, when the car is carrying half its full load, and stops at each Board of Trade station (compulsory stop as laid down by the Board of Trade inspector – author), or less frequently, to about 20 per cent, when it is fully loaded and stops at both Board of Trade stations and intermediate stations. The mean saving shown as a result of all the electrical consumption tests made, averaging over a distance of nearly 63 miles (101km), was 23.64 per cent.

Class D Car 392 is facing imminent retirement from the fleet. These vehicles had performed sterling service, but they were deemed unsuitable for pullmanisation. Consequently they remained in the old livery until withdrawal. Car 392 disappeared in October 1930. G.N.Southerden

On Friday, 22nd June 1923, the Chief Rolling Stock Engineer was again active in the technical debate when he gave a keynote speech at the Tramways & Light Railways Congress in Swansea. His chosen topic was *Tramway Rolling Stock*, and he expounded at length on the problems facing the LCC and some possible solutions in the form of lightweight rolling stock. The whole speech was later reprinted with copious diagrams, one of which has been reproduced in this book. The gist of the preamble was that he always approached the subject of electric tramway rolling stock from the engineering point of view. Therefore, he had to evaluate the difference performances of double deck and single deck prototypes.

W. E. Ireland showed that he was not blinkered as to the success of single deck vehicles around the world, nor was he blind to significant rolling stock developments occurring in the United States. He was obviously cautious about recommending wholesale change to the LCC, but his research into lightweight tramcars had been thorough and had involved investigating the trade off between body styles and seating accommodation. Obviously, the Council demanded high capacity vehicles – 78 seats plus standing room – and the design of any new car hinged on the ratio of car weight per seat. This was crucial in determining the optimum cost and current consumption level of each tram.

This 78-seat criterion could be matched by the startlingly modern design of the single deck coupled unit. However, it had an added advantage of increased room for standing passengers. Intriguingly, the new car appeared to have no provision for conduit operation. As far as can be judged, the LCC rolling stock engineers had studied various American ideas and had come up with an original London concept – some seventy-seven years before Croydon Tramlink introduced articulated cars to the streets of London! The general advantages of the proposed single deckers were summarised as:
Greater loading and unloading capacity to serve rush hour traffic, owing to the

Left Class C cars had been traversing Dog Kennel Hill for some years and they too were due for replacement. This particular tram was delicensed in July 1930. *G.N.Southerden*

Below Unlike classes A, C and D, all the standard cars of Classes E and E/1 were given the pullmanisation treatment, as shown here in this view of a newly outshopped car on Service 2. In everyday service two trolley poles were unlikely to be hooked down at one end only except when the car was about to enter the depot. *LCC*

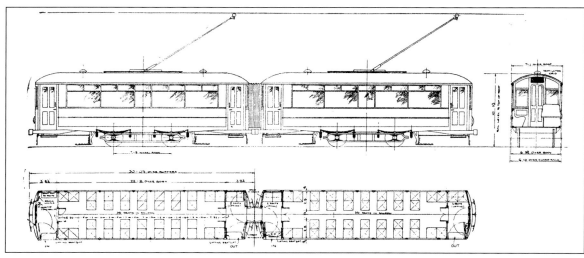

Left What might have been! This futuristic single deck unit was the Chief Rolling Stock Engineer's contribution to the 1923 Congress in Swansea. Questions abound – was this a serious proposal? Were these coupled trams intended as replacements for classes F and G?

number of entrances and exits provided.
Reduction in energy consumption and
maintenance costs.
Lower axle loads, tending to longer life of
tracks, tyres and other mechanical
components.

Whether Messrs Ireland and Fell ever discussed this project in great detail is doubtful, bearing in mind that British tramway managers seemed to be permanently wedded to their double deck tramcars. It is interesting to speculate how these high capacity trams would have been used. Certainly, the heavily trafficked Embankment circles would have benefited from their passenger carrying ability. One could speculate further that loading islands would have become widespread on routes, some of which would have been converted from conduit to overhead trolley. Perhaps the new trams would have led to the devel-

opment of high speed rapid transit lines – who knows. What is likely is that the new design must have stimulated some lively after dinner discussion in the smoke filled rooms of the Congress. There the matter rested and the dream faded. W. E. Ireland's next assignment was the distinctly more pedestrian, but nevertheless vital, task of upgrading the fleet.

The genesis of pullmanisation occurred with the delivery of the 1922 batch of E/1 cars. These trams were fitted with higher powered motors, improved lighting and ventilation. But aside from this, they still owed a lot to traditional design, whereby open platforms and lower deck bench seats were retained. To the average passenger they weren't much of an improvement on the existing rolling stock. Clearly, the introduction of these trams was only the first shot in a long war of attrition with the buses.

Public demand for improved facilities had to be met. High on the agenda was the abandonment of the lower saloon bench seats, which were to be replaced by transverse, upholstered seats. Some thought was also given to the comfort of upper saloon passengers, although it was not until 1927 that spring cushion seats were ordered to replace the traditional upper deck wooden ones.

Car 1235 was given the initial makeover in 1926, and this was followed by Car 1817, which merited the following description:

... Structurally, the new vehicle is of the London County Council's Class E/1 bogie type, with the following modifications in the direction of increased comfort ... In the lower saloon the seating space for each passenger has been considerably increased by a reduction of the total number of seats from 32 to 27. Longitudinal seating for three passengers is fitted in each of the four corners of the saloon, while the remaining space is occupied by five transverse seats for two passengers each at the left hand side, and five similar for one passenger each at the right hand side of the centre aisle. All the seats, and the corresponding backrests are most comfortably upholstered over a special arrangement of spiral springs.
The transverse seats are of a special design so arranged that passengers, if they desire, can always sit facing the direction of travel, and the construction is such that the action of reversing a backrest from one direction to another will automatically traverse the seat forward to such an extent as to ensure that its full width, measured from the face of the backrest, is available for the passenger's comfort. This ingenious mechanism also serves the purpose of depressing the seat cushion on the side nearest the backrest, so that an angle of repose most suited to the passenger's comfort is maintained between the relevant surfaces of the seat and the backrest.
The special attention devoted to the lighting of this experimental car has been well

Above left **In this posed publicity view a number of 'typical passengers' are depicted savouring the delights of the renovated upper saloon. This area was the haunt of smokers, and the fixtures, fittings and ceilings soon became stained with a film of nicotine residue from cigarette and pipe smoke. The ladies at one end of the car have conveniently distanced themselves from the City types occupying the middle seats. The atmosphere on the bench seats by the stairwell partition could be described as 'cosy'; often, regular groups of** passengers would manage to occupy this area to indulge in conversation and banter. LCC

Left **Inside one of the refurbished vehicles the interior was brighter and the traverse seats more comfortable for the lower deck traveller. It was also claimed by the Council that passengers could relax more and thus enjoy reading the newspaper whilst journeying to and from work. At night, enhanced lighting banished the gloom associated with older tramcars.** LCC

repaid, as an increase of over 65 per cent in efficiency has been secured by additional lamps and their rearrangement in conjunction with white enamelled reflectors of a new pattern. A cork carpet is laid on the floor, which is protected at the edges of the doorways and the motor inspection hatchways by hardwood edging strips.

A new arrangement of signal bells, operated by air at atmospheric pressure, has been installed, and for the convenience of the passengers four bell pushes are fixed on the underside of the ceiling, while others are provided outside each doorway, more especially for the conductor's use. The ceiling handrails have been disposed as necessary in the lower saloon to suit the revised plan of seating, and two, running the full length of the upper deck, have also been provided.

The scheme of interior decoration has been planned with the special purpose of securing better diffusion of the light during the period when artificial illumination is necessary, so that passengers in any part of the saloon may be able to read in comfort. The main framing and moulding are of light oak treated in the natural grain and relieved by a few panels finished to a darker shade of antique oak. The ceilings, rails and cornices above the level of the main windows at the sides of the saloon, also the corresponding portions of the end bulkhead frames are finished in pure white enamel.

All the metal furnishings are oxidised to a steel black surface, and the upholstering material for the seat coverings has a velvet surface with a neat diamond pattern arranged in contrasting shades of light blue, brown and black.

The external finish of the tramcar is dealt in quite a fresh style, for while a shade of primrose cream is retained for the lighter parts of the body, vermilion panels etc., relieved by black lines and decorated corners, are introduced in place of the midland red panels etc., relieved by gold lines as was previously used. The coat of arms of the London County Council has been used to decorate the centre waist panel at the side of the lower saloon in place of the initials LCC, which have previously appeared in this position.

All this work was carried out at the Central Repair Depot in Charlton. Car 1817 took its first passengers on 21st June 1926. It worked from Clapham Depot and was an immediate success with the travelling public. The new vermilion livery was applied to all renovated cars in the pullmanisation scheme. Approximately 100 other trams were given the treatment in 1926–1927, and many trams also received red leather upholstered seats on the top deck. Passengers on the Tooting to Embankment services had the benefit of the refurbished cars and traffic receipts improved accordingly.

It sounds rather churlish to be critical of

the LCC at this juncture. After all, this was a genuine attempt to wrest back lost passenger traffic. However, the renovated cars still bore a design, which was rapidly becoming antiquated. They had no driver's windscreens – the Metropolitan Police saw to it that out of date regulations were invoked to give the motorman precious little protection against the elements. Technically, all the electrical equipment could hardly have been referred to as state of the art. Air brakes, which were commonplace in North America, were conspicuous by their absence. Roller bearings, which had proved their worth in the 1923 trials, were not substituted for the original axle boxes.

One wonders why the undoubted talents of Mr Ireland and his team were not put to work on a number of designs for new vehicles, which could have been produced at Charlton Works. The probable answer lies in the lack of finance and the conservative attitude of the decision makers. The same lack of funds probably doomed any large scale track reconstruction programme that would have involved the placing of loading islands at all principal stops. As it was, when the Council did attempt something new in the shape of a projected E/2 car built on the passenger flow principle, the design never left the drawing board. Luckily through the efforts of several dedicated enthusiasts we can now view the plan of what might have been.

However, we are getting ahead of ourselves. The view from the late twenties was that pullmanisation had been a success and that a vital share of the passenger market had been recaptured. During 1927–28 a further 250 trams underwent the process, and experience gained by the staff at the CRD enabled the whole project to be speeded up. Classes E and E/1 were the main targets of the scheme. Another 500 cars were earmarked in 1928–29 and Charlton Works began to turn out two pullmanised trams every working day. The loss of seating capacity on a standard car – down from 78 to 73 – was more than made up by the increased ridership.

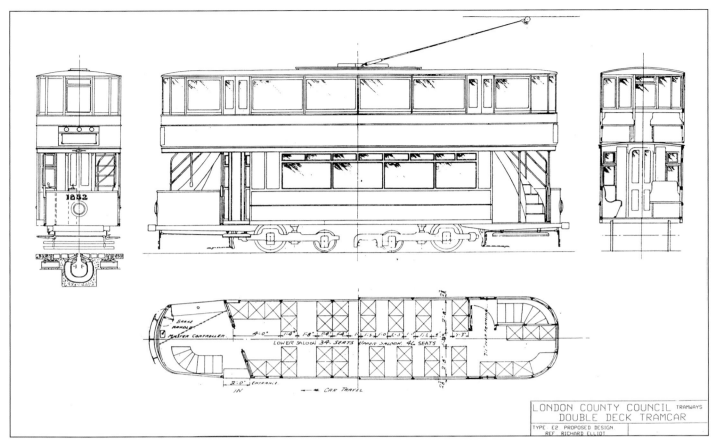

LONDON COUNTY COUNCIL TRAMWAYS
DOUBLE DECK TRAMCAR
TYPE E2 PROPOSED DESIGN
REF RICHARD ELLIOT

Below Car 1539 just looks plain ugly. The designers and fitters at Charlton thought this one up in February 1930. Luckily the platform vestibule was quickly consigned to the recycle bin. LCC

Right Out of all the restyling projects there emerged Car 795 in February 1932. This aluminium and grey painted vehicle certainly drew some complimentary comments from passengers and passers by. Although the experimental livery was not pursued, some general design traits were incorporated into the new E/3 and HR/2 cars. LCC

Above Class E/2 was another LCC pipe dream, although as we can see by this plan, the finished car would have been mostly traditional in design. The front entrance layout would presumably have led to passengers using the motorman's platform staircase to reach the upper saloon.
Terry Russell / Roy Hubble

On 6th March 1929, the first Class M Car 1472 emerged in renovated form. Again, this move might have surprised tramway experts, especially in the light of the LCC's espousal of bogie cars. However, there was a sound logic behind the decision to upgrade these single truck vehicles. They had proved their durability under London conditions; they worked on Service 11 and in South London. They were also considered ideal for routes with lower patronage or for the back street services, which were run from Leyton Depot through other parts of the East End. Finally, being a shorter version of the standard LCC tramcar, spare parts and fittings were easily interchangeable between E/1 and M Class trams.

In the early 'twenties it became obvious that major fleet renewals would have to be undertaken in the near future. Cars from Classes A, C and D were all nearing the end of their active lives. Already the Council had disposed of most of the members of Class B, and it was acknowledged that it was only a matter of time before road failures and increasing maintenance bills doomed the original electric fleet. The pullmanisation

process was deemed unsuitable for the more elderly cars, thus leaving the Council little option but to consider the purchase of new vehicles. The first task to be undertaken was the replacement of Class C cars working the Dulwich routes. These single truck trams had been ably assisted by Class M cars, but the time was now right for newer, higher powered bogie cars to be employed on the hilly routes. Appropriately the prototype car was registered as Class HR/1 Car 1852 – HR standing for hilly route.

The appearance and body style of the latest addition to the fleet revealed no fundamental surprises to traditionalists. On the other hand, bearing in mind that the competing Combine companies had rolled out their first Feltham prototypes from 1929 onwards, the omission of any streamlining or indeed, the lack of a fully enclosed body with platform doors on the new LCC model, must have come as a great disappointment to modernists. It could be argued that the Council had produced a powerful car to a design that passengers immediately recognised. Therefore, there was no need to educate the travelling public to new boarding or alighting arrangements. Whatever its merits or demerits, the beast was functional and sturdy! The distinguishing feature of Car 1852 (the fleet number had been originally allocated to the ill fated E/2 car) was the wide centre window pillar on the lower saloon. This design peculiarity was repeated on the 552–601 batch of E/1 cars, which took the numbers of the old subway single deckers. Further features of note were that Car 1852 rode on equal wheel bogie trucks powered by four motors developing in total 140hp. Roller bearings were fitted to the axle boxes and the plough carrier was attached in the traditional way to the end of one of the trucks. For use on overhead wire sections the tram possessed two trolley poles.

The bodywork of Car 1852 was of composite construction – wood and metal, but the prototype HR/2 Car 1853, which followed later in 1929, was largely built of metal. Car 1853 had flush sides to the lower saloon, rather than the traditional waist and rocker panels that had characterised British tramcar design in the early years. Upholstered seats were to be found on both decks – moquette in the lower saloon and non inflammable (!) red leathercloth for the smokers in the upper saloon. As with its sister car, this vehicle was fitted with a truck mounted plough carrier and two trolley poles.

Both trams were paraded in front of the elected members at Stangate, just opposite County Hall. The reception on 26th February 1929 went off well, and the two vehicles were then dispatched on trials, which of course included the famous Dog Kennel Hill. In point of fact, the LCC also had its eye on Highgate Hill as possible

operating territory for the HR/2s. Both gradients were ones on which the new tramcars could show a clean pair of heels to the competing motor traffic. The use of predominantly metal bodywork meant that these vehicles would also be permitted to carry passengers through the enlarged Kingsway Subway.

Cars 1854–1903 formed the production batch of fifty HR/2 trams built in 1930 by English Electric. An important difference from the prototype HR cars was the fitting, as standard, of centrally mounted plough carriers independent of the trucks. The new design of carrier proved itself successful and on 12th May 1931, the manufacturers, Higgs & Hill, were asked by the LCC to produce 500 units, so that this technology could be applied to older cars as well. This initial run of cars was followed in 1931 by

the 101–160 series, which sported driver's windscreens and were not fitted with trolley poles. The main intention here was to operate this batch on the Highgate Hill to Moorgate service that covered exclusively conduit tracks. As events were to prove, these sixty cars were to spend the rest of their working lives on conduit routes, and the option of adding trolley poles was never exercised by the LCC or by London Transport. Braking arrangements included magnetic track brakes, slipper brakes and provision to prevent the car running back on gradients. The trucks were EMB radial arm, equal wheel bogies, which were considered to be the height of modernity – the equal wheel tucks under 101–159 were a modified version of those under cars 1854–1903.

The odd one out in the 101–160 series

was Car 160. It was soon deprived of its equal wheel trucks, which were purloined to fit under show Car 1, and Car 160 had to put up with maximum traction trucks instead. By 1931 it had been reclassified as the only E/3 with no trolley poles!

Mention has already been made of the enlarged Kingsway Subway, which opened on 15th January 1931. To work the new subway services the council ordered one hundred E/3 Class cars. These vehicles had identical bodywork to the HR/2s, but differed from them in that they ran on maximum traction bogies each powered by one 57hp motor. They were manufactured by Hurst, Nelson and were delivered without driver's windscreens. This unvestibuled design was old fashioned and the LCC quickly pressurised the Metropolitan Police. The Commissioner gave way

Above The 4-motored HR/2 trams created an immediate impression when they were placed in service on the Dog Kennel Hill and Highgate Hill routes. Car 1892 is in pristine condition at Peckham Rye terminus. EMB trucks of type 6 were fitted as standard. R.Elliott

Left In the lower saloon of HR/2 Car 138 the seating layout was quite familiar to Londoners and would remain so until the final demise of trams in July 1952. The sprung moquette covered seats were an improvement on the previous wooden benches of older tram classes, but they were still sufficiently firm to encourage 'correct posture'! LCC

Below A variation of the type 6 truck was produced by EMB for the LCC. Radial arms supported the axleboxes instead of the more traditional hornways. These trucks were fitted to HR/2 cars 101–160. Similar trucks were also supplied to Liverpool and Johannesburg. R.Elliott

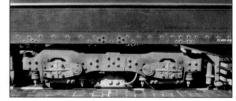

graciously and he granted temporary licences for the cars to receive vestibules. By 1932 all E/3s had been fitted with Alpax metal alloy windscreens equipped with safety glass.

Relations between the LCC and Leyton Council had improved somewhat by the turn of the decade, and the East London municipality must have felt suitably honoured when an agreement was reached to supply Leyton with fifty E/3 cars. They were numbered 161–210 and were allocated from summer 1931 mainly to Service 61, with some trams of this batch being stationed at Bow Depot. Each Leyton E/3 was painted in the standard LCC red and cream, but displayed the Leyton coat of arms instead of the LCC one.

The one escapee from the wholesale destruction of older trams was single-deck Car 600, which lasted into London Transport times. The late Richard Elliott, one time employee at Charlton Works, once suggested to the author that this vehicle, now masquerading as a works car attached to Holloway Depot, had been temporarily equipped with a trolley pole to aid its peregrinations around London.

Whatever the eventual fate of Car 600, the rest of Classes F and G disappeared from the scene when the Kingsway Subway was enlarged. Cars from Classes A, C and D were gradually taken out of service and their bodies were either scrapped or sold on as sheds or temporary accommodation on farms and plots in the Home Counties. Some groups of these former trams lasted, many in rustic isolation, into the 1950s and 1960s. Any salvageable parts did not appear on the open market, but were retained at Charlton for recycling into the production line of wheels, axles, brake gear etc.

The tramway engineers at the LCC must have got the appetite for experimenting and innovation. During the late 'twenties and early 'thirties a number of pet projects surfaced, some more practical than others. There were experiments with different liveries and colour styles – orange, red and unpainted aluminium all made their fleeting appearances. The unpainted aluminium panelling formed part of Car 795, which emerged from the CRD in February 1932. Various new designs were tried for driver's windscreens. As always, the problem where to put the handbrake handle resulted in some weird and wonderful, rather bulbous vestibules, until the inclined handbrake plus standard vestibule was introduced.

The debate as to the best method of overhead current collection – bow collector/pantograph or trolley pole – had rumbled on for several decades. As early as 1903, the British Electric Traction Company had equipped the small Sheerness system with Siemens bow collectors atop traditional British double deck trams. The experiment was only partly successful and the system expired in 1917, due in some measure to the dearth of spare parts from Germany, then an enemy nation. The discussion about current collectors came up regularly in tramway management circles, but nothing was really achieved until the 1930s. Maybe there was a reluctance to abandon the tried and tested trolley boom, and it is also possible that many transport committees regarded the bow and pantograph technology as foreign, or even worse German, and would therefore have no truck with it. The LCC made a half hearted attempt to buck the trend and commissioned trials on the recently constructed Downham to Grove Park section. Here the overhead had been strung to permit the operation of trolleys as well as bows and pantographs. Car 1172 was fitted with a pantograph in May 1933; at the same time Car 1360 emerged with a bow collector. Both vehicles went through the motions, but the coming of the LPTB in July curtailed the experiment, and the results were filed away to be forgotten. In the light of the growing cost of maintaining the conduit, it would seem that the Grove Park trials were merely a sideshow.

The Council also toyed with the idea of improved seating, and set out cars 120, 147, 168 and 1989 with bucket seats on the lower deck. These became the bane of conductors, as they were difficult to turn quickly at termini, when rush hour crowds waited to board. Different types of cushions, upholstery and back rests were also subject to scrutiny, as well as sundry varieties of extractor ventilators, destination boxes, half drop windows, platform mirrors and braking equipment. All told, this mania for improvement was very creditable, but it came too late to save the LCC Tramways from absorption into a public body, which had a distinctly sceptical stance as to the continuation of tramcar services.

However, the last big effort on behalf of the LCC produced a real gem – Bluebird Car 1 of 1932. The technical press was well briefed, and it is worth quoting at length from one of the Council's publicity releases. The author was G. F. Sinclair, who had taken over as Chief Rolling Stock Engineer from W. E. Ireland, who had retired on 31st December 1931. It would seem from this extract that the latter's *revolutionary* articulated car of 1923 had been scuppered by the traditionalists:

What type of car would be most suitable to the metropolitan area will always be a debatable question. The single deck car, either of the 2-unit articulated type, as recently introduced in Calcutta, or the long single deck central entrance American car, have all the advantages of

lightness and economical operation. However, to meet the average loading of 65 seated passengers, the physical dimensions of single deck cars would prohibit their use, owing to the limitation of permissible overall length and width on the permanent way and at depots . . .
The experimental car (LCC Car 1), which is illustrated has been constructed by the London County Council and has the streamline effect (the tram was painted blue and white, thus earning the nickname 'Bluebird' – author), which has come so much to the fore in vehicle design during the last few years. The car has a seating capacity of 66 and a standing area of 56 square feet (5.2m²). The driver's compartment, being separated from the lower saloon, allows standing passengers on what has hitherto been space wasted at one end of the car . . . Spiral staircases in a car enable the maximum seating capacity to be provided, but do not encourage passengers to ride in the upper saloon, so a straight staircase has been designed with the two lowest steps slightly turned towards the platform.

Car 1172 is depicted at Grove Park whilst taking part in pantograph trials. Opinions vary as to whether the search for a replacement of the trolley pole was worthwhile. Many believe the LCC should have been pressing for the replacement of the costly conduit system, rather than tinker at the edges with pantographs and bow collectors. The route from Downham change pit was equipped with overhead fittings that would accommodate the traditional trolley as well as the other forms of overhead current collection. Had the Grove Park link been built, it has been suggested that all trams working in the Eltham and Grove Park areas would have been converted to bow collectors – then gaining popularity on several British city systems. LCC

Ventilation and Lighting have been improved and an electric signal bell system, and warning gong operated from the line supply, electric heating, etc., have been introduced. The driver has been given a seat and the vestibule windows forming his compartment are arranged to open to any desired amount. Air operated windscreen wipers are fitted and through ventilation is provided in the cab. Air operated doors of the folding type are used to enclose the platform. These are only operated at the termini,

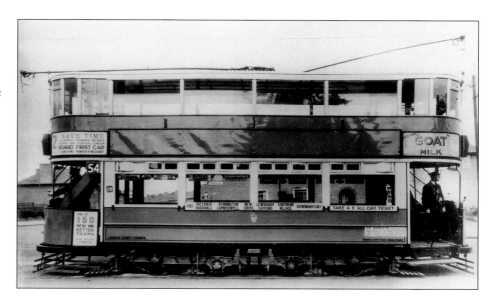

and by their adoption it has been possible to have a straight through lower saloon, avoiding what are known as bulkheads. The body is mounted on equal wheel bogies, with a four motor electrical equipment and air brakes.

The car destination and route number boxes have been built into the canopy dash, and side indication has been arranged on a large illuminated side box, which allows side boards to be dispensed with . . .

The article continued in similar vein to describe the lightweight body materials and the equal wheel trucks. These were chosen over the maximum traction variety because the LCC was eyeing up the prospects of running Car 1 and its successors on Dog Kennel Hill and Highgate Hill. Four 35hp motors powered eight 26½ inch (673mm) wheels. The electrical equipment was fairly straightforward and it was claimed that the car could outperform in acceleration and braking any other tram used in London. It was truly a one off car.

Air brakes were fitted as standard and it might have been thought that this system, so widely used on foreign trams, would be welcomed by rolling stock engineers and motormen alike. However, in practice, drivers assigned to Bluebird preferred to rely on the magnetic brake. An interesting letter, dated 28th December 1932, from D. F. Brown, Brake Engineer to the Westinghouse Brake Company, hints at the problems experienced by novice air brake users:

Release of Air Brake during Magnetic Application . . .

It is necessary to release the air brake when the magnetic brake is applied. A pilot valve fixed to the top of the controller admits air to the piston chamber of a reversing valve when the magnetic brake is applied, the pilot valve being operated by means of a cam on the controller handle . . .

NOTE: The air brake will not reapply in the event of a magnetic brake failure.

It was always claimed by London Transport that even senior motormen disliked driving Car 1 because of their unfamiliarity or distrust of the braking systems. As it was, this tram remained the only one in captivity and from July 1933, was quickly classified non standard by its new owners.

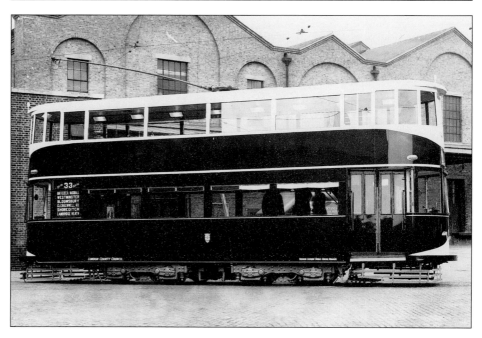

The design of the new tram owed much to the talents of John Harding and H. J. Rivett. These two had worked together on the E/3 project and it was natural that they should continue their work on Car 1. On the retirement of Mr Harding in January 1941, his colleague paid him the following tribute:

By temperament an individualist, he often spent many hours after normal office hours setting out in his own way data for new tram contracts, going into every detail of design, never being satisfied to leave even the smallest detail to the caprice of a contractor.

The LCC was indeed fortunate to have such men in their employ, and this loyalty and attention to detail was to be found amongst most employees from Messrs Harding and Rivett down to the coach-builders, foundrymen, truckmen and electricians at Charlton Works. They all had a hand in the Council's new creation and were justifiably proud of the finished tramcar when it was unveiled to delegates of the 22nd Annual Congress of the Tramways Light Railways & Transport Association. This august body was holding its yearly meeting in London, where the twin spectacles of the UCC Feltham trams and LCC Car 1 held the attention of the members. The group visit to Charlton Works was somewhat overshadowed by an animated debate, which had broken out between S. R. Geary, Operation Superintendent LCC Tramways, and R. S. Pilcher, General Manager Manchester Corporation Transport. Both were airing their opinions on G. F. Sinclair's discussion paper on *Traffic Experiences with Modern Tramcars.* What concerns us here are the references to LCC practice and the inevitable comparisons between Car 1 and the UCC Felthams,

which were being used on the LUT and MET systems – in fact, it all resembled a rerun of the municipal versus company saga, now presented in terms of who could produce the best tramcar for London!

Mr S. R. Geary in reply to Mr W. Vane Morland, General Manager Leeds City Transport: *As an operator who has to operate vehicles belonging to eight undertakings and involving twenty-five different types of car, there are one or two questions I should like to ask* (here the speaker is referring to cars and operators using LCC tracks; the aggregate total is probably a record for through running over a single municipal system – author) . . .

In foggy weather in London all sorts of trouble arise which last for days afterwards owing to the serious overheating of resistances following on driving on the resistance notches. We have always managed to maintain our cars in service during foggy weather, but we suffer for it badly afterwards . . .

Gadgets to the traffic man are anathema. The Feltham type of car introduced a nice controller, and to make it safe they have put a fuse in so that if you go over the notches too fast the fuse blows and you get no power. That is the type of thing you get from a rolling stock man . . .

S. R. Geary then had a tilt at a number of devices such as air bells, trolley heads and trolley reversers, which he said the LCC had rejected because the trolley rope was pushed too far away from the car at termini. He was also adamant that the Council had done all it could to enhance the changeover procedure from conduit to overhead. He cited the latest body mounted carriers as proof positive of the desire to speed up services.

R. S. Pilcher, already well known in transport circles and the author of several books on tramway and bus operation, picked up a thread that the LCC had showed inconsistency in approach to tramcar design.

Some years ago the LCC advocated heavyweight cars, and I remember going to a conference and advocating lightweight equipment. The criticism from London was that they took the opposite policy, and in fact weighted their trucks. Now, however, we have lightweight equipment in London, and I congratulate Mr Sinclair and the London authorities on adopting what I think is generally accepted as the proper equipment. I take it that these new cars have small wheels, and that is another point of controversy. Years ago, when I advocated the small wheel and light weight motor, all kinds of difficulties were pointed out; it was stated there would be difficulty in braking, difficulty in acceleration, and so on; but these are points which Mr Sinclair has demonstrated as non existent. Indeed, he has demonstrated that this type of equipment has many advantages.

R. Stuart Pilcher was credited by his friends as having clarity of vision and a strong self belief. His detractors, of which there were many, tired quickly of his pontificating on just about every subject under the sun. But on one issue, he was spot on – contemporary attempts to modernise trams and tramways in Great Britain would eventually prove useless. Therefore, he doubted whether LCC Car 1 or indeed any other new tram would sway public opinion back to tramways. By the early 1930s, Mr Pilcher definitely counted himself in the bus camp.

Mr C. J. Spencer, General Manager Metropolitan Electric Tramways Company, rounded off the discussion with some pertinent remarks on tramway operation in the metropolis. No doubt he was aware that his Feltham cars would inevitably attract comparison to LCC Car 1.

I am particularly pleased to see the unanimity of view between myself and Mr Sinclair on the design of cars. I am delighted to find that with one or two small alterations it is much the same car that our companies have had for some time (a slight exaggeration, the Felthams or Type UCC cars were delivered to the LUT and MET in 1930–1931 – author). The differences are differences of detail. Mr Sinclair and his colleagues hold a different view from ourselves as to the efficacy of the front exit, but that is a matter worthy of discussion . . .

Mr Spencer then confined himself to specifics, mentioning that Mr Sinclair had presented an interesting chart showing the peaks and valleys of a day's London traffic. This confirmed the belief, prevalent among London tramway managers that the volume of traffic always demanded high capacity vehicles. This was in contrast, so they thought, with the average demands of a provincial city.

The merits of two motor versus four motor equipments were touched upon, as well as the old debate about what sort of braking best suited London conditions and London motorman. This is what Mr Spencer had to say on this point:

With regard to air brakes, when the new Feltham car, with its combined magnetic and air brake, was introduced on the London United Tramways, no instructions were given to the men. They were allowed to use either brake as they pleased, and we found that about 90 per cent of the total stops were made with the air brake as a matter of preference. The driver prefers to use this brake, feeling that he is safe for an emergency stop with the magnetic brake. That was on the Uxbridge route where our cars are not mixed up with those of any other authority, and therefore the drivers did not acquire any good or any bad habits from their confreres. On the Tally Ho Corner route (central London to North Finchley), however, where the cars were mixed with the LCC cars, the experience was not quite the same, and the men seemed to prefer the magnetic brake.

Clearly, he suspected there was some sort of malign influence at work on the part of LCC motormen to corrupt his boys on the MET, when it came to ignoring the air brake. However, this criticism was as nothing when G. F. Sinclair took R. S. Pilcher to task about comments made on the discussion paper. Mr Sinclair was obviously livid – he pitched into his opponent:

I should like to say that he (Pilcher) has been so long out of sympathy with tramcar work that anything he says is out of date. I would point out that Mr Pilcher has the capacity for throwing figures about, and we are unable to contradict him. On one item I would point out that Mr Ireland, my predecessor, wrote what I consider to be one of the most able papers ever written on the tramcar. Mr Ireland laid down principles of which Mr Pilcher apparently has not read. Mr Pilcher states that in London we formerly advocated heavy cars, but he did not take the trouble to read that we had lightweight motors when Edinburgh (where Mr Pilcher was employed) had cable tramways.

Having effectively stunned Mr Pilcher, G. F. Sinclair went on to describe the new LCC car in terms of its carry capacity. He stated that with a full load of standing passengers the new twenty ton vehicle could shift 95 passengers. Furthermore, he believed that it was no use committing precious funds to build bigger depots to suit new trams, which did not fit into the existing arrangements – here he was having a pop at Mr Spencer and his Felthams. Perhaps, he resented all the publicity about alterations at Finchley Depot to take the longer and wider Feltham type cars . . . *In the matter of depots in congested areas it would be nonsense to buy property at high prices to increase the size of depots to enable you to alter the size of the car, and generally to provide more room for the rolling stock. The LCC buys all cars out of capital, but we try to re-equip out of revenue.*

It became apparent that the rivalry between the LCC and the Combine could not be kept under the surface. Mr Sinclair thanked Mr Spencer for 'some very nice remarks' and then went on to say, '*I am sorry that he (Spencer) refers to our new car as only a little improvement on what he has done at Feltham*'. Mr Spencer immediately denied saying this; whereupon G. F. Sinclair described the Feltham type as a *soapbox*, and he hoped when delegates had seen the new LCC Car 1 they would agree with him

that the LCC rolling stock engineers had '*improved things a little*'. The Chairman then closed the discussion.

This bickering amongst transport professionals did little to enhance the tramway cause. Indeed, it could be argued that, in the context of the early 1930s, they were fiddling whilst tramway Rome burned! The bus and trolleybus people were gaining victory after victory as tram systems across the country fell to the rubber tyred invaders.

After its presentation to the Tramways Light Railways & Transport Association, Car 1 slipped away to begin passenger trials. Bluebird was sent to Holloway Depot for proving runs through the Kingsway Subway, and in July 1932 the travelling public could sample the car on services 33 and 35. A special team of drivers and conductors was allocated to the new vehicle. Its eye catching livery soon made an impact and it was assumed that a production batch of similar vehicles plus 150 further cars from Classes E/3 and HR/2 would enable the Council to remove the last of the M Class and to service the proposed extensions in Southeast London. However, political events were moving swiftly. The nation was experiencing a severe trade depression, and the capital's traffic congestion problems were exercising the minds legislators at Westminster. They then agreed a unified public transport structure for London. Needless to say, the projected fleet of new LCC trams never appeared. The only real legacy of the LCC rolling stock regime was the accumulated expertise of designers and engineers at Charlton Works. In a matter of months after the annexation by London Transport, many of this team would turn their talents to developing the engineering base for another sort of electric vehicle – the trolleybus.

As the new fleet headed for the open highway, members of the C Class were towed to Chiswick Depot – there to be sold to anyone with the cash and the means to cart the tram away.

THE YEARS 1930–1933 represent the
concluding chapter of the London
County Council Tramways. The
Indian summer of fleet renewal faded into a
harsh blast of winter when all tramcars and
services were subsumed into the London
Passenger Transport Board. The unified
transport board, touted by the Royal
Commission in 1905, had metamorphosed
into a large scale organisation whose brief
was to co-ordinate, promote and modernise
road and underground railway transport
throughout the LCC area and beyond into
the growing suburbs of Greater London. In
fact the LPTB had almost *carte blanche* to
do what it wanted, and the traditions of the
LCC Tramways had to compete with all the
other factions and operations in the new
conglomerate.

Informed public opinion came down
against the tram as a viable solution to
chronic congestion problems. It was firmly
believed by many that the tram caused
congestion, and private motorists and buses
could use the road space vacated by the
tramcar more efficiently. Trolleybuses
looked a good alternative when the operator
wished to retain the electrical infrastructure of a former tramway. It was considered
in some quarters patriotic to insist on
trolleybuses, because they used home
grown fuel. Whatever the point of view, it
was generally agreed that tramways had
had their day and that removal of a fixed
track in the middle of the highway would
encourage the free flow of rubber tyred
vehicles.

In 1931, the Royal Commission on
Transport effectively sounded the death
knell for the first generation of British
tramways. The learned body of individuals
recommended that no more tramways be
constructed and that the remaining systems
be progressively converted to either buses
or trolleybuses. A grudging admiration for
the crowd shifting potential of the tramcar
was tempered by the suggestion that
increased bus services, wider thoroughfares, smoothly surfaced streets (i.e. no
slippery granite setts edging tramlines),
dual carriageway arterial roads and a
greater number of roundabouts would
provide the magical solution for many years
to come. Trams, modern or otherwise,
simply did not fit into the scheme of things.

The LCC, to its credit, got on with the
job. A change of hand on the tiller came
with the retirement on 30th June 1930 of

General Manager, Joshua Kidd Bruce. He
was replaced by an equally imposing name –
Theodore Eastaway Thomas. As we have
noted, the rolling stock situation was eased
by the acquisition of new vehicles and the
Council still had a firm belief in supplying
quality transport to its burgeoning housing
estates. Powers had been granted for the
Grove Park to Eltham line; Woolwich
Council had been particularly keen to push

The trolleyless HR/2 Class
cars always projected an
image of solidity. They
were bought for their hill
climbing abilities and they
did not disappoint. Here
at the top of Dog Kennel
Hill Car 119 has just
entered the quadruple
track section.

Unfortunately, there seem
to be no passengers on
board to enjoy the ride
down the hill to Dulwich.
G.N.Southerden

forward the construction and opening of the Westhorne Avenue section. In September 1931 tram tracks at Well Hall, Eltham were altered to fit in with the new roundabout. This was necessary for the expected traffic generated by the South Circular Road and the A2 Rochester Way. Westhorne Avenue actually diverged from Rochester Way a short distance west of the roundabout.

In the autumn of 1931 a service from Beresford Square, marked 46EX or 44EX, entered Westhorne Avenue and worked the first hundred yards or so of the new extension to a crossover opposite Elmbrook Gardens. On 1st October, provisional Service 44A was extended to a terminus by Briset Road, just before the railway bridge. Finally, on 30th June 1932 the connection from Briset Road to Service 46 tracks at Eltham Green was opened to the public. Service 72 was diverted from Forest Hill to run from the Victoria Embankment, Savoy Street to Beresford Square, Woolwich via Westhorne Avenue. No doubt, Woolwich Councillor William Barefoot and his colleagues were particularly pleased that they had twisted the LCC's arm and had succeeded in getting construction started before the Grove Park to Eltham Green link. The Ministry of Transport had held up progress to such an extent that the aforementioned connection was never built. The new 72 tram service was vital for the public transport needs of the large LCC housing estates either side of Westhorne Avenue. As it turned out, this extension was the last completely new tramway on London soil for sixty-eight years

Tramway developments had also been taking place in central London. On 2nd February 1930, the Kingsway Subway was shut pending conversion to a larger tunnel, which could take double deck cars. Round the clock work, with the exception of the hours between noon on Saturday and 10pm on Sunday, was necessary to complete the task. At the northern end of the subway the roof was raised to achieve the requisite clearance; for the rest of the subway the track base was lowered and tons of London blue clay was excavated. It was estimated that a minimum height of 16 feet 6 inches (5 metres) was needed for this next stage of development. As the TRAMWAY AND RAILWAY WORLD put it:

Although of late years 200,000 passengers have been carried every week day, single deck cars have not proved profitable; but it is estimated that the reconstruction of the subway and cars will yield a gross profit of £12,600 a year. In addition, direct communication will be given by double deck cars between any districts north and south of the Thames, besides enabling rolling stock from the northern tramways to take a direct route to the repair works at Charlton in the south. At present the only means of access is via Hammersmith and Putney Bridge.

While the subway is closed, Pullman double deck cars operate between Highbury and the Bloomsbury end of the subway, the route having practically a 24 hour service, except on Saturdays. Transfer tickets at the midday fare of 2d are issued for passengers alighting at Farringdon Road, Holborn, or Bloomsbury to complete the journey on an Embankment car to Westminster, the County Hall, and Christ Church.

The LGOC are running a frequent connecting service of omnibuses to

Left **Car 953 is depicted at Brockley Cross around 1930. Service 72 had once worked between Southwark Bridge and New Cross Gate, and it was extended in January 1911 to run as far as Forest Hill.** H.Nicol/National Tramway Museum

Above **The date is 30th December 1930 and work proceeds frantically at the southern portal of the Kingsway Subway. The subway has been enlarged. Now it remains to lay the conduit tracks and to finish off the walls and roof in time for opening day. Note the contractor's narrow gauge railway to the right of the picture.** Hulton Getty

Charing Cross, via the Strand and Northumberland Avenue, returning via the Embankment and Temple Station on the return journey, at 1d fare each way.

It is interesting to note here that the animosity between the London General and the LCC obviously did not extend to purely business transactions in relation to supplying a temporary bus service whilst the subway was out of use. The enlargement of the subway had been planned for some time and a publicity campaign featuring new tram routes was in active preparation. It was intended to run services from Hackney to Wandsworth, Leyton to Westminster, Highbury to Brixton, and from Highgate to New Cross. The planned car frequency was thirty trams an hour in each direction of the Kingsway Subway.

The formal opening took place on 14th January 1931; a contemporary account takes up the story:

At the entrance stood a special car painted in white, black and gold (Car 1931), and the Chairman of the Council, Major R. I. Tasker, started it on a run through the subway, past the Aldwych and Holborn Stations and up the Southampton Row ascent to Theobalds Road. Two other cars followed. From Theobalds Road the cars returned to Holborn Station, where the passengers alighted and inspected the enlarged station.

Mr E. H. Kemp, Vice Chairman of the Highways Committee, in moving a vote of thanks to the Chairman, pointed out that the enlarged subway and the running through it of double-deck cars, provided the most rapid means of access between important areas north and south of the Thames. As the route short circuited the congested areas of the Strand, Charing Cross and Whitehall, it should do much to facilitate travel.

They had been told that tramways were obsolescent. If a transport business that paid its dividend, redeemed its stock, maintained the road which it did not altogether use, and at the same time showed a clear profit, was obsolescent, the meaning of the word was not so obvious as it appeared. In addition the tramways carried over two million passengers each weekday at an average fare of little more than a halfpenny per mile. The public had lately been informed that twenty-five million pounds was lost annually by traffic congestion in

the centre of London. This tram subway under the busiest part of London might, perhaps, point out to traffic experts how other traffic from south to north might proceed with relief to congestion.

The account of the opening goes on to state that the total cost of the work carried out by contractors John Cochrane & Sons Ltd. was in the region of £330,000, but this sum also included a figure of £76,000 for the recycling of electrical equipments and the construction of new tram bodies. The new intermediate stations were described in detail. Mr J. H. Parker designed the Holophone prismatic reflector lighting scheme at Aldwych and Holborn. Around 230 units had been employed to illuminate both stations. The columns and ceilings had been treated so that they reflected the light. A neo-classical style was adopted and this impression was enhanced by the use of

travertine stone at Holborn Station. The LCC publicists were quick to tell the public that this cream coloured marble had also been used by the Emperor Vespasian in the construction of the Coliseum in Rome! Walls were panelled so that advertising and Council posters could be displayed attractively. Finally, the entrance staircases from street level had been renovated with patent non-slip treads. There were no escalators or lifts from platform to street level – a state of affairs that was quite usual in an era when facilities for the disabled were very restricted. As trams arrived at either Aldwych or Holborn, passengers had to board and alight via the motorman's platform.

As has been mentioned, the publicity department went into overdrive promoting the latest transport facility. A special booklet was issued by the Council, which detailed the new services, connections and

With the opening of the Kingsway Subway new E/3 cars appeared on through services across London. Here on the Albert Embankment by the construction works for the new Lambeth Bridge, we observe a tram making its way from Wandsworth to Hackney Station on the recently introduced Service 31.
G.N.Southerden

transfer fares available when travelling through the Kingsway Subway. Service 31 operated from Wandsworth to Hackney on weekdays and from Westminster to Leyton on Sundays. It was promoted as the first permanent tramway link between South London and the boroughs of Metropolitan Essex. The journey time was 73 minutes.

Service 35 went from New Cross Gate to Highgate and was timed at one minute under the hour. A weekday rush hour service, numbered 33, was instituted between Brixton, Water Lane and Highbury Station. Subsequently, on 14th May, the southern terminus of the 33 was removed to West Norwood. A similar route extension happened in North London. On 8th October 1931, the service was prolonged as far as Manor House. Fine tuning of services 31 and 35 also resulted in changes of termini. Cars on service 35 were extended from New Cross to Forest Hill, and for a short spell in 1931–32, the route actually reached Downham on the Grove Park line. In Southwest London the summer Sunday 31 service was extended from Wandsworth to Tooting Junction.

South-west London was again in the news on 30th August 1931, when the last through LCC cars ran to Hampton Court via Wimbledon and Kingston. The LUT had wired the route for trolleybuses, and on 15th December, the Wimbledon tram terminus for services 2 and 4 was cut back from Wimbledon Hill Road to just outside the Town Hall. The significance of all this was that trolleybuses had replaced trams on one of the LUT's trunk services. The anti-tram lobby now had tangible evidence in its fight to win over public opinion.

Politicians and transport professionals were also studying the merits of the trolley-bus as a possible successor to the tramcar in

Centre left **The demise of the 'out county' section from Wimbledon to Hampton Court was inevitable once the LUT started dabbling with trolleybuses. This interesting interlaced curve in Worple Road at the junction of Francis Grove will soon fall derelict under the newly erected trolleybus overhead wires. A standard LCC E/1 is working inbound on Service 4.** H.Nicol / National Tramway Museum

Left **Leyton Council were highly favoured when the batch of E/3 cars 161–210 arrived in LCC livery, but bearing the red and gold Leyton coat of arms on the waist panel of each tram. On the reserved track adjacent to Whipps Cross Road they performed well and top deck passengers would have had a good view of this section of Epping Forest. Car 202 has been delivered with bogie side plates. Many observers thought these enhanced the appearance of the car, but they were soon discarded as being non standard.** LCCTT

London. The respective strengths and weaknesses of all forms of public transport were no doubt on the minds of the legislators, administrators and civil servants struggling to draft the new London Passenger Transport Board Act. We have seen that Herbert Morrison modified the original concept in 1929, but the idea of a unified transport authority was still very much alive.

The Labour Government fell in August 1931 and matters were held up somewhat, however, planning continued in the matter of transferring the London municipal tramways, including the LCC system, to a new public body on a basis of no profit and no loss. Which is to say that the new transport authority would absorb the accumulated deficits. This approach obviously had its appeal, and the Conservative majority on the LCC was persuaded to fall into line. The preamble to the first Bill stated:

The new Authority would have no interest in extending particular forms of transport. It would have no tramway, tube or omnibus bias. Its transport policy would be determined by technical fact and public interest . . .

The Bill received a second reading in the Commons on 23rd March 1931 and went to the Select Committee stage, where the LCC agreed on the amount of compensation for the tramways. The Committee and report stages and the third reading of the Bill were curtailed by the general election. It had been thought that the incoming of the new Coalition/Conservative government would torpedo its chances, but the talking continued. In February 1933 the Bill passed its third reading in the Commons and it received the Royal Assent on 13th April. Just over a month later, on 18th May, the Chairman and board members were appointed. On the night of 30th June 1933, the LCC Tramways effectively passed into history.

The Chairman of the London Passenger Transport Board was Lord Ashfield of Southwell, who had been plucked straight from the Combine. He was quite clear on the task confronting him and he expounded his worldview to a gathering of the Royal Society on 24th March 1933. His speech, which was reported in the TRAMWAY AND RAILWAY WORLD, took as its theme London Passenger Transport and Street Congestion. He was anxious to explain the problems of congestion and to suggest some remedies that would relieve unemployment. On this latter tack, it was clear to the future Chairman that construction of new and wider roads would mop up the unemployed in the civil engineering industry. The building of underground railways would also aid the flow of commuters to and from the great city. Buses were to be used along the improved thoroughfares, which would feature roundabouts at intersections and a coherent system of one way streets in the central area. As for the trams, he wasn't very optimistic:

Above **At Manor House the crew of Car 1922 catch a short break before the return journey to West Norwood. This view was taken a month after the formation of the LPTB, but the tram still retains its LCC crest.**
N.D.W.Elston

Left **Car 1 is seen at the other end of Service 33. There is little doubt that 'Bluebird' was placed on a Kingsway Subway service to maximise publicity for the new tram.**
G.N.Southerden

At many points in London, as for example at the Elephant and Castle, the existence of tramways constitutes a special aspect of the problem, for tramways are undoubtedly a cause of congestion. They occupy the middle of the road, and following traffic has to be held up while passengers are picked up and set down; while those tramway terminals which are located at important junctions, occupy valuable road space just at those points where it is most required. The solution of the tramway problem appears to lie in the direction of producing a trackless trolley vehicle of equal capacity to that of the tramcar, free from the rigidity imposed upon it by the necessity of running upon rails. Where vehicles of this type have been operated in London it is satisfactory to note that there has been a distinct reduction of traffic congestion, and a greater fluidity of traffic movement as a whole has resulted.

The oracle had spoken! Lord Ashfield's remarks would represent the policy of the LPTB. In political and transport circles he was preaching to the converted, and it was generally agreed that the tramcar had had its day. Although the Combine had introduced Feltham cars to win back passengers, the results of the LUT trolleybus conversions in the Kingston area had been impressive. The travelling public stated the obvious. They preferred a vehicle that picked up and set down at the kerb. The new trolleybuses were comfortable and a definite improvement on the old, sometimes open top, tramcars. Politicians of the left

were placated when they learnt that trolley-buses, being classified in Parliamentary terms as a form of trackless tramway, were obliged to offer workmen's fares. Thus the switch from trams to trolleybuses produced very few ripples in the political pond.

Many opinions have been offered as to the nature of the acquisition of the London County Council system, and the subsequent decisions not to proceed with the Grove Park to Eltham Green extension, and not to order any new trams. Much of the political infighting at the time has occupied the attention of historians. Thousands of words have also been written on the tussles between Socialists and Conservatives as to the precise make up of the new board. Speculation has been rife and the '*what if*' propagandists have suggested that a revitalised municipal transport board headed by the LCC would not have been so hasty in throwing away its tramway assets. One fact is certain – the chief architect of the LPTB project, Herbert Morrison, was never more than lukewarm as to the retention of tramways. At a meeting in February 1931,

Herbert Morrison, the then Minister of Transport, had expressed an opinion that he had to *keep his mind free from favouritisms or prejudices in respect of any form of transport, and to be guided by facts* – facts in this case, which would be supplied by the report of the Royal Commission.

The composition and ethos of the LPTB reflected contemporary thinking. There is very little evidence to support the pro-tramway argument. Indeed, the opposite is true. With the honourable exception of Ilford, the tram owning municipalities breathed a collective sigh of relief when they handed their transport systems over to the new operator. The councils concerned could then concentrate on other public services and rehousing projects, which were top of the agenda. Already, in 1929, Barking Council had given up the ghost as regards active tramway operation, and, as we have seen, money was not forthcoming for extensions and replacement tracks at congestion trouble spots. New trams did filter through from Croydon, East Ham, West Ham and Walthamstow, but they were to the

approved LCC standard design – i.e. they looked outdated, when compared to the Felthams.

Just as the Royal Commission had been particularly insular in its analysis of the future of tramways, so the new London Passenger Transport Board followed suit. The opportunity to judge best continental practice or to investigate what was going on in the American street railway industry was not taken. Such progressive developments as loading islands, segregated tracks and the replacement of the conduit did not figure in the Board's thinking. The

motoring lobby was dictating the pace of change.

From an operational point of view it was more efficient to make the LCC Tramways the centre of the new Board's activities. The fleets of the company and municipal systems acquired on 1st July 1933 were renumbered using the LCC car notation as a base. Company and municipal insignia on the side of trams were quickly painted over, and from May 1934 the familiar London Transport fleet name began to appear. Obviously some trams included in the last round up would not pass muster with the

Above left **Class E Car 409** waits at Kew Bridge terminus next to an LUT tram. Only a tram enthusiast would have sat through the whole journey to the other end of the line at Hop Exchange. The route was circuitous to say the least, and it involved crossing the Thames three times.

Above right **A world away from the Thames-side delights of Kew Bridge**

was the back street tramway network of East London. M Class Car 1721 battles its way through Stratford on Service 7 from Chingford Mount to the Victoria & Albert Docks. West Ham Car 33, working Service 6 from Stratford to Canning Town, is about to reverse, and will follow its LCC sister tram along West Ham Lane and Church Street.
G.N.Southerden

In Chapter Eight a picture of the original terminus at Park Road, Forest Hill was featured. We return to the same location in 1932. The driver of HR/2 Car 1867 is no doubt slightly peeved because he is going to have to get down to change the points with his point iron. At busy junctions the LCC employed pointsmen, but here out in the suburbs it all had to be done in the time honoured fashion.

LPTB. With this in mind, Percy Croom Johnson, Permanent Way Engineer of the LCC, was asked to delegate rolling stock and track experts to visit the ailing systems of Bexley / Dartford and Erith. Their report alarmed officials at 55 Broadway, SW1 – the new headquarters of the London Passenger Transport Board. Arrangements were made to transfer a suitable number of Class M cars to replace the antique specimens in North Kent. The permanent way in the area was in such a state that the imported LCC trams were only permitted to be driven at half power.

Other members of the LCC Tramways hierarchy also joined the LPTB. Former General Manager, T. E. Thomas was put in charge of the central, south and east divisions, and from October 1933 he was appointed General Manager – Trams and Trolleybuses. S. R. Geary became Operating Superintendent – South and East, and G. F. Sinclair was given the job of Rolling Stock Engineer to oversee a much enlarged fleet of trams. Other LCC employees, crew members, depot workers and technical staff at Charlton Works were transferred to the new authority with the minimum of fuss.

A last splutter of the LCC Tramways flame occurred on 28th August 1933, when the reconstructed Putney Bridge opened for traffic. Gone were the gutter running tram tracks and in their place was a broad carriageway enlarged from 48ft (14.6m) to 78ft (23.7m). The project had been started in 1930 and the new double track tramway was now placed centrally in the roadway.

The aftermath of the great London Transport upheaval left the LCC Tramways seemingly little changed, but the relentless pressure to co-ordinate services and to introduce new technology was felt at all levels of the tramway industry. The LPTB had powers granted in Section 23 of the Act to abandon part or whole of any tramway, provided they gave three months notice to the local highways authority, to whom the

Top left **Car 1114 retains its LCC style fleet numerals, but it has lost the Council crest on the waist panel. The LCC may have just relinquished control of its tramways, but the advertising contract for LCC evening classes is yet to expire. The evening educational sessions offered by the LCC were part of the grand design to give Londoners enhanced job skills and to provide creative activities for leisure times.** N.D.W.Elston

Centre left **A few days after the LPTB takeover an E Class car scoots across Hammersmith Broadway with General bus ST 109 in hot pursuit. The two rivals now worked for the same organisation.** H.Nicol / National Tramway Museum

Left **We have already mentioned Lessness Abbey Woods, which stretch out behind Car 1402 as it turns into Knee Hill, Abbey Wood. The opposite side of the road is actually in the County of Kent, and the LCC rails on Knee Hill were only laid a couple of feet into London territory. For through travellers, such as there were, a change of tram was necessary to continue one's journey to Belvedere and Erith. The LCC and Erith Council tracks were not connected, and this remained the situation until 18th December 1933, when the LPTB installed a single track connection for ex-Erith cars to be stabled at Abbey Wood Depot.** R.Elliott

rating value of the tracks was paid. This enabling legislation was used in the period up to 1940 to replace a hefty chunk of the erstwhile tram system. The intervention of the Second World War delayed the extermination of London's first generation tramway system until July 1952. Services 36, 38, 40, 44, 46 and 72 lasted to the end and their extinction signified a final tribute to their LCC forebears.

Monuments to the London County Council can still be found in the form of several buildings scattered around London. The generating station on the Thames waterfront at Greenwich is a prominent landmark. Various depots have miraculously survived the ins and outs of the last few decades and a visit to the former car sheds at Stamford Hill and Bow will reveal to the onlooker the grandeur of LCC design. The frontage of Hammersmith Public Library is a smaller version of the façade of the former Streatham, Telford Avenue Depot. Unfortunately, time and the demolition man have done their best to eradicate many former tramway sites, and only the name – Felltram Way, SE7 – gives an acknowledgement to past glories. The Central Repair Depot at one end of this small street was razed some years back.

LCC cars 106, 1622 (now restored as a London Transport rehabilitated tram) and Bluebird Car 1 were saved from the scrappers and are preserved at the National Tramway Museum. E/1 Car 1025, in LT livery, rests at London's Transport Museum, Covent Garden, and can be easily inspected and photographed by visitors. HR/2 1858, for a time displayed outside Chessington Zoo, is today at Carlton Colville. The northern ramp to the

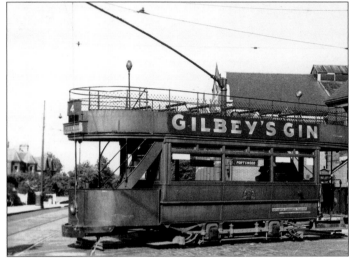

Kingsway Subway, complete with conduit tracks, still marks the passing seasons in dignity, as if waiting for the next generation of tramways to appear on the scene. Maybe the wait will be worth it. If the success of the Croydon Tramlink encourages other schemes, it is entirely possible that several former LCC trunk tramway routes will see the return of electric traction. The wheel will have turned full circle.

Above A former LCC Class B tram is seen nearing the end of its career at Southampton. Note that it has been converted back to open top condition.

Above right Resilient to the end, this former LCC tram stop is pictured in London Road, Elephant and Castle on 22nd June 1952. In its time it had seen open top tramcars, suffragette marches, columns of troops setting out for the trenches in France, General Strike riots, the Blitz and V1 flying bombs. But its days are almost ended, and the London tramcar will shortly be no more.
J.C.Gillham

Every story must end with a happy retirement and our account of the fortunes of the LCC Tramways is no exception. A guard dog, tethered by a chain and living in a barrel, has now replaced the depot inspector in looking after this former A or D Class car. The rolling Downs are a suitably scenic setting for a tranquil rest after a busy career. E.G.P. Masterman

Tram Services and Car Sheds

As one might expect, tram services evolved over the years according to passenger needs, availability of rolling stock, opening of new routes etc. The following information is taken from guides dated 1908, 1911, 1913, 1927, and 1933.

1908 – London Tramways Guide

The London Tramways Guide for 1908 was the first comprehensive listing of tram services and of the places of interest accessible by LCC trams. The guide contained some 152 pages and was sold to the public for the princely sum of one penny. The opening part of this publication contained listings and photographs of places of interest in London. The second section of the guide detailed LCC tram services, which were referred to by route numbers. It must be noted that these numbers did not appear on the Council's tramcars. The through fare for most routes was 2d.

1 HAMMERSMITH to HARLESDEN (electric traction). Journey time 22 minutes.

2 EUSTON ROAD to Hampstead and HIGHGATE (horse traction).
Journey time: Hampstead to Euston Road 23 minutes; Highgate to Euston Road 26 minutes.

3 HOLBORN to Hampstead and HIGHGATE *Swain's Lane* (horse and electric traction). Services from Swains Lane and Hampstead are worked as far as Kings Cross by horse traction, and from that point to Holborn by electric traction. Journey time 33 minutes.

4 EUSTON ROAD to FINSBURY PARK (horse traction).
Journey time 33 minutes.

5 CLERKENWELL to Highgate, Holborn to FINSBURY PARK (horse and electric traction). Journey time 28 minutes. Section of the route from Kings Cross to Holborn, along Grays Inn Road, is worked by electric traction.

6 MOORGATE, Aldersgate and Holborn to Highgate and FINSBURY PARK; and MOORGATE to KINGS CROSS (horse and electric traction). The services contained in this route are all worked by electric traction except that along Liverpool Road. Journey times: Moorgate to Highgate 30 minutes; Aldersgate to Highgate 27 minutes; Holborn to Highgate 27 minutes; Moorgate to Finsbury Park 30 minutes; Aldersgate and Holborn to Finsbury Park 27 minutes; Moorgate to Kings Cross 16 minutes, along Liverpool Road 12 minutes.

7 Moorgate to Highbury Station (via New North Road) and the Manor House (horse traction). Journey times: Moorgate to Manor House 37 minutes; Moorgate to Highbury 18 minutes.

8 Holborn, Moorgate, Dock Street, Norton Folgate to Stamford Hill, and Bloomsbury to Cambridge Heath (electric traction).
From Stamford Hill terminus there are four distinct services of cars to Holborn, Moorgate, Dock Street and Norton Folgate respectively. The time occupied on the journey varies from 30 minutes in the case of the Stamford Hill to Moorgate and Norton Folgate routes to 37 or 39 minutes in the case of the Stamford Hill to Holborn and London Docks routes. From Cambridge Heath a service is run to Bloomsbury in connection with a service of horse cars from Lea Bridge Road to Cambridge Heath, but through tickets are issued.

9 ALDGATE to STAMFORD HILL (horse traction). Journey time 48 minutes.

10 SMITHFIELD MARKET *St John Street* to HACKNEY *Mare Street* (horse traction). Journey time 35 minutes.

11 CASSLAND ROAD to WEST INDIA DOCKS (horse traction). Journey time 29 minutes.

12 ALDGATE to BOW BRIDGE (electric traction). Journey time 26 minutes.

13 BLOOMSBURY and Aldgate to POPLAR (electric traction). From Poplar there are two distinct services, one to Aldgate and the other to Bloomsbury. The time occupied on the journey to Aldgate varies from 18 minutes in the morning and evening to 22 minutes during the rest of the day, and on the Bloomsbury route from 38 minutes to 47 minutes.

14 HIGHBURY STATION (*via* Kingsway Subway) to Kennington Gate and TOWER BRIDGE (electric traction). The time occupied on the journey between Highbury Station and Kennington Gate varies from 41 to 44 minutes, and that between Highbury Station and Tower Bridge from 47 to 50 minutes.

15 WATERLOO BRIDGE to WOOLWICH ROAD (electric traction). Journey time one hour.

16 BLACKFRIARS to Woolwich Road and New Cross, and Waterloo Station to NEW CROSS (electric traction). Journey times: Woolwich Road to Blackfriars Bridge 52 minutes; New Cross Gate to Waterloo Station 26 minutes.

17 WATERLOO BRIDGE to BLACKWALL TUNNEL (electric traction). Journey time one hour.

18 WATERLOO STATION to Lee Green, and St George's Church to CAMBERWELL (electric traction).
Journey times: Lee Green to Waterloo Station 50 minutes; St George's Church, Borough to Camberwell Green 17 minutes.

19 SOUTHWARK BRIDGE to Catford, and Greenwich to CATFORD (electric traction). Journey times: Southwark Bridge to Catford 46 minutes; Greenwich South Street to Catford 18 minutes.

20 VICTORIA to CATFORD (electric traction). Journey time 55 minutes.

21 CHARING CROSS to Rye Lane, and Blackfriars to NEW CROSS GATE (electric traction). Journey times: Charing Cross to Rye Lane 30 minutes; Blackfriars to New Cross Gate 32 minutes.

22 VICTORIA EMBANKMENT and Southwark Bridge (St George's Church on Sundays) to Dulwich and PECKHAM RYE (electric traction).
Journey times: Embankment to Dulwich or Peckham Rye 45 minutes; Southwark Bridge to Dulwich 36 minutes.

23 VICTORIA to Dulwich and PECKHAM RYE (electric traction).
Journey time 36 minutes.

24 VICTORIA EMBANKMENT, Blackfriars, Southwark Bridge and St George's Church to STREATHAM (electric traction).

Journey times: Victoria Embankment *John Carpenter Street* to Streatham 46 minutes; Telford Avenue to Charing Cross 36 minutes; Blackfriars Bridge to Streatham 40 minutes; Southwark Bridge to Streatham 39 minutes; St George's Church to Streatham 37 minutes.

25 VICTORIA STATION to STREATHAM (electric traction). Journey time 36 minutes.

26 VICTORIA EMBANKMENT, Waterloo Station, Blackfriars Bridge and Southwark Bridge to Tooting and MERTON (electric traction).
Journey times: Victoria Embankment to Tooting Broadway 52 minutes; Waterloo Station to Tooting Broadway 43 minutes; Blackfriars Bridge to Merton 49 minutes; Southwark Bridge to Tooting Broadway 45 minutes.

27 THE HOP EXCHANGE to TOOTING JUNCTION (electric traction). Journey time 66 minutes.

28 VICTORIA EMBANKMENT to CLAPHAM JUNCTION (electric traction). Journey time 40 minutes.

29 VAUXHALL to East Hill, and Chelsea Bridge to LAVENDER HILL (horse traction). Journey times: Vauxhall to Wandsworth East Hill 36 minutes; Lavender Hill to Chelsea Bridge 12 minutes.

30 CAMBERWELL to NORWOOD (horse traction). Journey time 33 minutes. Owing to reconstruction of portions of this route for electrical traction, the service will vary from time to time.

31 TOOLEY STREET and Old Kent Road to DEPTFORD (horse traction).

Journey times: Tooley Street to Deptford 35 minutes; St James's Church to Tower Bridge Road; Bricklayers Arms 12 minutes; Tower Bridge Road to Rotherhithe Red Lion 20 minutes; Raymouth Road to Canal Bridge 8 minutes.

32 GREENWICH TUNNEL AVENUE to PLUMSTEAD (horse and electric traction). Journey times: Tunnel Avenue to Beresford Square (horse traction) 25 minutes; Beresford Square to Plumstead (electric traction) 10 minutes. The route will, it is hoped, by the end of the summer of 1908, be extended from Plumstead to the county boundary at Abbey Wood.

1911 – Official Tramways Guide

The Coronation Issue 1911 of the Official Tramways Guide was similar in format to its 1909 predecessor. During the intervening three years the system had gained more electrified routes. These services are still numbered in the 1909 format. It was not until 1912 that the familiar route notation of even numbered services south of the Thames and odd numbered ones north of the River came into use. Route maps are as they appeared in the guide.

An interesting feature of both the original guides is that they did not give information as to the three light colour codes used to denote separate services at night. The coloured lenses were positioned just above the destination box of each tramcar. Coloured reflectors appeared in ruby, amber, green and blue, as well as a white or clear lamp. The different coloured lenses served their purpose at night, but for those Londoners who had problems with reading,

the daytime destination displays must have been difficult to cope with. The Council ruled out the adoption of symbols and shapes to denote services; this practice had been used in Dublin and other cities to help those who were illiterate. The light codes were given up after the adoption of service numbers.

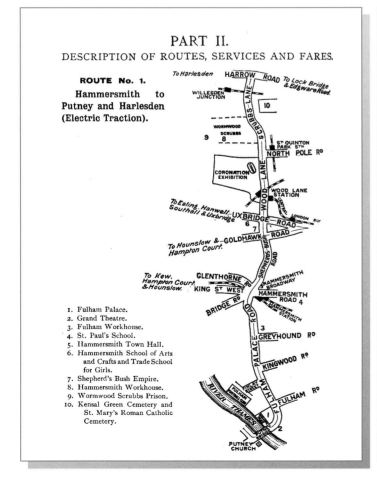

PART II.
DESCRIPTION OF ROUTES, SERVICES AND FARES.

ROUTE No. 1.

Hammersmith to Putney and Harlesden (Electric Traction).

1. Fulham Palace.
2. Grand Theatre.
3. Fulham Workhouse.
4. St. Paul's School.
5. Hammersmith Town Hall.
6. Hammersmith School of Arts and Crafts and Trade School for Girls.
7. Shepherd's Bush Empire.
8. Hammersmith Workhouse.
9. Wormwood Scrubbs Prison.
10. Kensal Green Cemetery and St. Mary's Roman Catholic Cemetery.

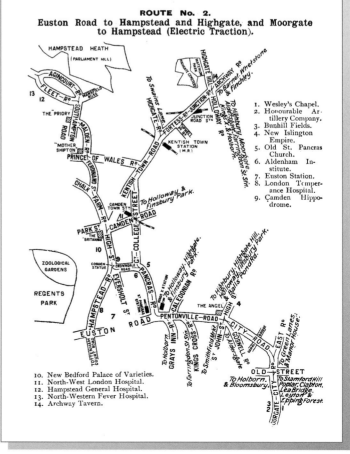

ROUTE No. 2.
Euston Road to Hampstead and Highgate, and Moorgate to Hampstead (Electric Traction).

1. Wesley's Chapel.
2. Honourable Artillery Company.
3. Bunhill Fields.
4. New Islington Empire.
5. Old St. Pancras Church.
6. Aldenham Institute.
7. Euston Station.
8. London Temperance Hospital.
9. Camden Hippodrome.
10. New Bedford Palace of Varieties.
11. North-West London Hospital.
12. Hampstead General Hospital.
13. North-Western Fever Hospital.
14. Archway Tavern.

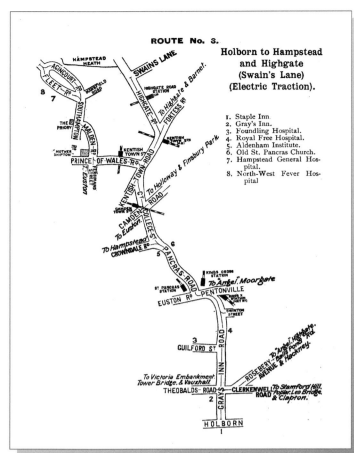

ROUTE No. 3.

Holborn to Hampstead and Highgate (Swain's Lane) (Electric Traction).

1. Staple Inn.
2. Gray's Inn.
3. Foundling Hospital.
4. Royal Free Hospital.
5. Aldenham Institute.
6. Old St. Pancras Church.
7. Hampstead General Hospital.
8. North-West Fever Hospital

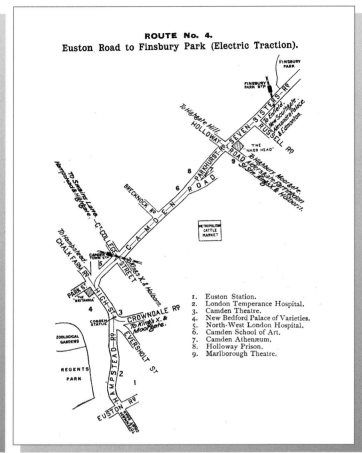

ROUTE No. 4.

Euston Road to Finsbury Park (Electric Traction).

1. Euston Station.
2. London Temperance Hospital.
3. Camden Theatre.
4. New Bedford Palace of Varieties.
5. North-West London Hospital.
6. Camden School of Art.
7. Camden Athenæum.
8. Holloway Prison.
9. Marlborough Theatre.

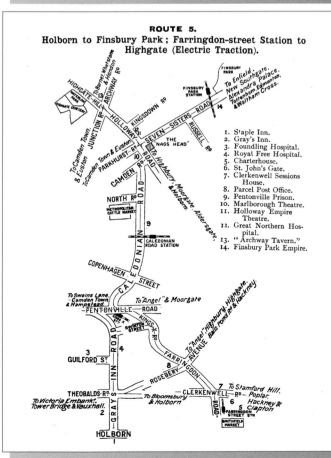

ROUTE No. 5.

Holborn to Finsbury Park; Farringdon-street Station to Highgate (Electric Traction).

1. Staple Inn.
2. Gray's Inn.
3. Foundling Hospital.
4. Royal Free Hospital.
5. Charterhouse.
6. St. John's Gate.
7. Clerkenwell Sessions House.
8. Parcel Post Office.
9. Pentonville Prison.
10. Marlborough Theatre.
11. Holloway Empire Theatre.
12. Great Northern Hospital.
13. "Archway Tavern."
14. Finsbury Park Empire.

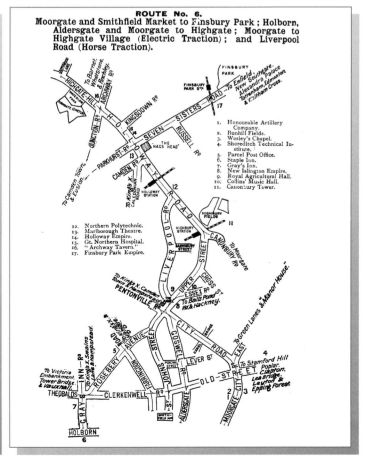

ROUTE No. 6.

Moorgate and Smithfield Market to Finsbury Park; Holborn, Aldersgate and Moorgate to Highgate; Moorgate to Highgate Village (Electric Traction); and Liverpool Road (Horse Traction).

1. Honourable Artillery Company.
2. Bunhill Fields.
3. Wesley's Chapel.
4. Shoreditch Technical Institute.
5. Parcel Post Office.
6. Staple Inn.
7. Gray's Inn.
8. New Islington Empire.
9. Royal Agricultural Hall.
10. Collins' Music Hall.
11. Canonbury Tower.
12. Northern Polytechnic.
13. Marlborough Theatre.
14. Holloway Empire.
15. Gt. Northern Hospital.
16. "Archway Tavern."
17. Finsbury Park Empire.

ROUTE No. 7.
Moorgate to Highbury Station (via New North Road) and the Manor House, Finsbury Park
(Horse Traction).

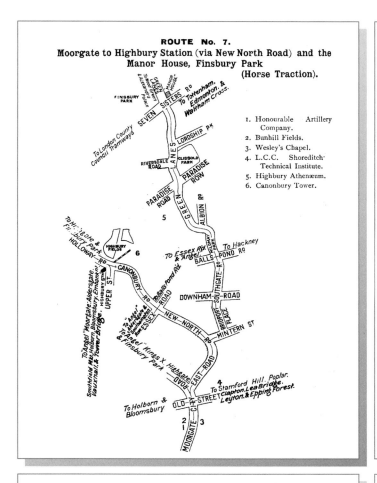

1. Honourable Artillery Company.
2. Bunhill Fields.
3. Wesley's Chapel.
4. L.C.C. Shoreditch Technical Institute.
5. Highbury Athenæum.
6. Canonbury Tower.

ROUTE No. 8.
Holborn, Moorgate, Dock Street, and Norton Folgate to Stamford Hill (Electric Traction).

1. Staple Inn.
2. Gray's Inn.
3. Central Markets.
4. St. John's Gate.
5. Clerkenwell Sessions House.
6. Charterhouse.
7. St. Luke's Hospital.
8. Bunhill Fields Burial Ground.
9. Artillery Ground.
10. Wesley's Chapel and Museum.
11. Shoreditch Technical Institute.
12. London Docks.
13. St. Katharine's Docks.
14. Royal Mint.
15. Toynbee Hall.
16. Spitalfields Market.
17. Royal Cambridge Music Hall.
18. Boundary-street Housing Area.
19. London Music Hall.
20. Shoreditch Olympia.
21. Shoreditch Town Hall.
22. North Eastern Hospital for Children.
23. Britannia Theatre.
24. Metropolitan Hospital.

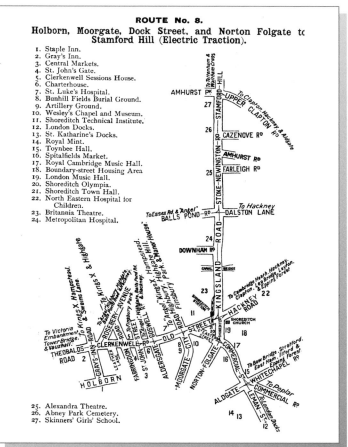

25. Alexandra Theatre.
26. Abney Park Cemetery.
27. Skinners' Girls' School.

ROUTE No. 9.
Bloomsbury and Aldgate to Stamford Hill (Clapton Common).
(Electric Traction).

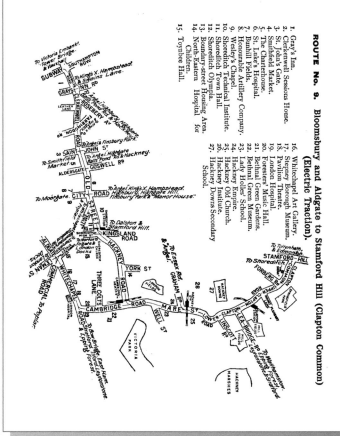

1. Gray's Inn.
2. Clerkenwell Sessions House.
3. St. John's Gate.
4. Smithfield Market.
5. The Charterhouse.
6. St. Luke's Hospital.
7. Bunhill Fields.
8. Honourable Artillery Company.
9. Wesley's Chapel.
10. Shoreditch Technical Institute.
11. Shoreditch Town Hall.
12. Shoreditch Olympia.
13. Boundary-street Housing Area.
14. North-Eastern Hospital for Children.
15. Toynbee Hall.
16. Whitechapel Art Gallery.
17. Stepney Borough Museum.
18. Pavilion Theatre.
19. London Hospital.
20. Foresters' Music Hall.
21. Bethnal Green Gardens.
22. Bethnal Green Museum.
23. Lady Holles' School.
24. Hackney Empire.
25. Hackney Old Church.
26. Hackney Institute.
27. Hackney Downs Secondary School.

ROUTE No. 10.
Aldersgate to Mare Street, Hackney (Horse and Electric Traction).

1. Charterhouse.
2. New Islington Empire.
3. Royal Agricultural Hall.

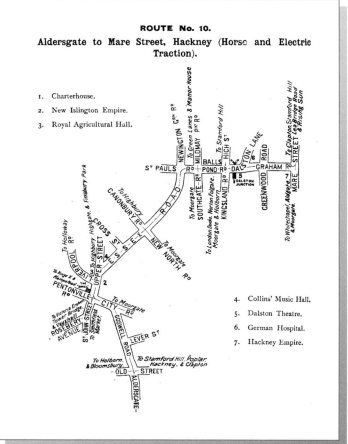

4. Collins' Music Hall.
5. Dalston Theatre.
6. German Hospital.
7. Hackney Empire.

ROUTE No. 11.

Moorgate and Aldgate to Epping Forest (Electric Traction).

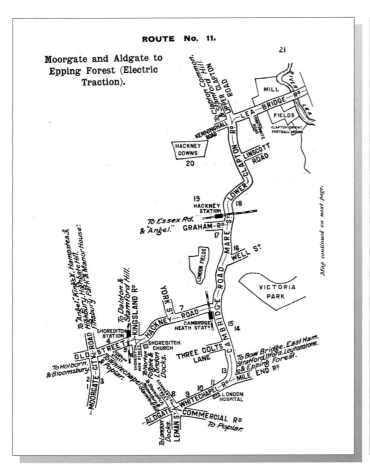

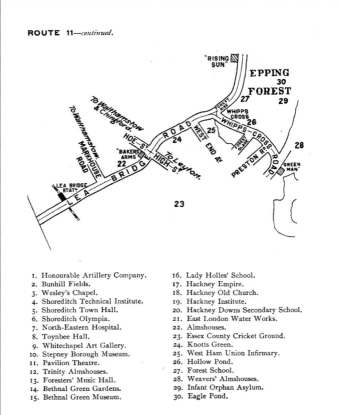

Map continued on next page.

1. Honourable Artillery Company.	16. Lady Holles' School.
2. Bunhill Fields.	17. Hackney Empire.
3. Wesley's Chapel.	18. Hackney Old Church.
4. Shoreditch Technical Institute.	19. Hackney Institute.
5. Shoreditch Town Hall.	20. Hackney Downs Secondary School.
6. Shoreditch Olympia.	21. East London Water Works.
7. North-Eastern Hospital.	22. Almshouses.
8. Toynbee Hall.	23. Essex County Cricket Ground.
9. Whitechapel Art Gallery.	24. Knotts Green.
10. Stepney Borough Museum.	25. West Ham Union Infirmary.
11. Pavilion Theatre.	26. Hollow Pond.
12. Trinity Almshouses.	27. Forest School.
13. Foresters' Music Hall.	28. Weavers' Almshouses.
14. Bethnal Green Gardens.	29. Infant Orphan Asylum.
15. Bethnal Green Museum.	30. Eagle Pond.

ROUTE No. 13.

Aldgate to Epping Forest and Ilford (viâ Stratford) (Electric Traction).

1. Whitechapel Art Gallery.	12. St. John's Church.
2. Stepney Borough Museum.	13. Old West Ham Parish Church.
3. Pavilion Theatre.	14. Woodgrange Cemetery.
4. Foresters' Music Hall.	15. Manor Park Cemetery.
5. Trinity Almshouses.	16. City of London Cemetery.
6. Paragon Theatre of Varieties.	17. East Ham Library.
7. East London College.	18. Ilford Town Hall.
8. City of London and Tower Hamlets Cemetery.	19. West Ham Workhouse.
9. Palace Theatre of Varieties.	20. Weavers' Almshouses.
10. Borough Theatre.	21. West Ham Union Infirmary.
11. Stratford Empire.	22. Hollow Pond.
	23. Forest School.
	24. Infant Orphan Asylum.
	25. Eagle Pond.

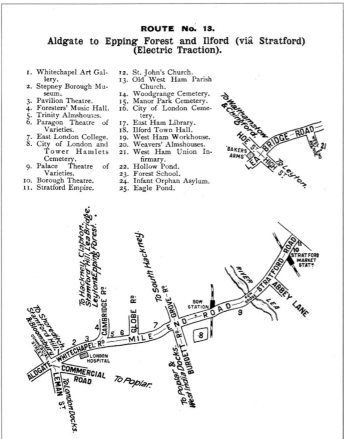

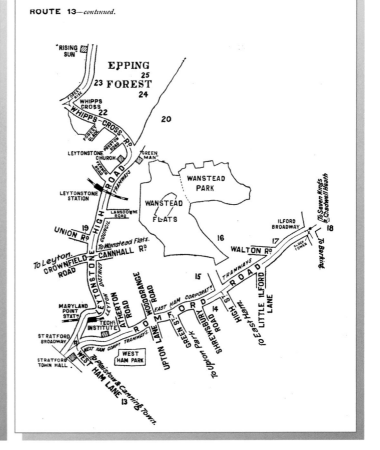

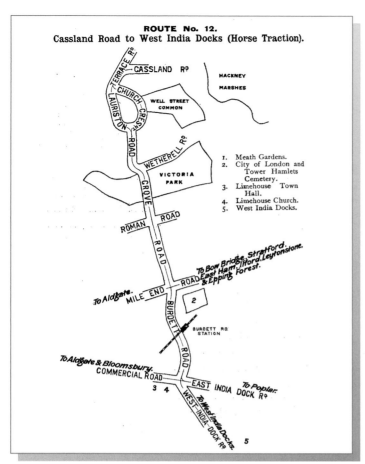

ROUTE No. 12.
Cassland Road to West India Docks (Horse Traction).

HACKNEY MARSHES

1. Meath Gardens.
2. City of London and Tower Hamlets Cemetery.
3. Limehouse Town Hall.
4. Limehouse Church.
5. West India Docks.

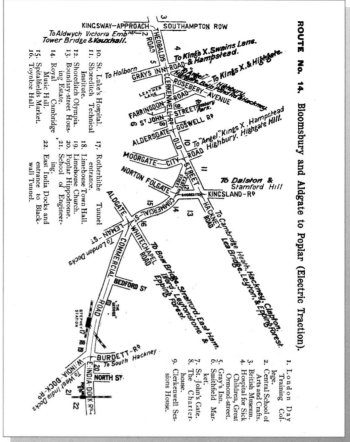

ROUTE No. 14. Bloomsbury and Aldgate to Poplar (Electric Traction).

1. London Day Training College.
2. Central School of Arts and Crafts.
3. British Museum.
4. Hospital for Sick Children, Great Ormond-street.
5. Gray's Inn.
6. Smithfield Market.
7. St. John's Gate.
8. The Charterhouse.
9. Clerkenwell Sessions House.
10. St. Luke's Hospital.
11. Shoreditch Technical Institute.
12. Shoreditch Technical Institute entrance.
13. Boundary-street Housing Estate.
14. Royal Cambridge Music Hall.
15. Spitalfields Market.
16. Toynbee Hall.
17. Rotherhithe Tunnel.
18. Limehouse Town Hall.
19. Limehouse Church.
20. Poplar Hippodrome.
21. School of Engineering.
22. East India Docks and entrance to Blackwall Tunnel.

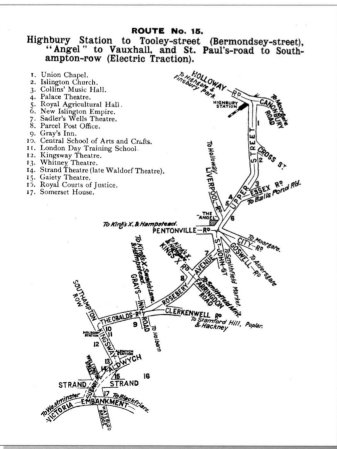

ROUTE No. 15.
Highbury Station to Tooley-street (Bermondsey-street), "Angel" to Vauxhall, and St. Paul's-road to Southampton-row (Electric Traction).

1. Union Chapel.
2. Islington Church.
3. Collins' Music Hall.
4. Palace Theatre.
5. Royal Agricultural Hall.
6. New Islington Empire.
7. Sadler's Wells Theatre.
8. Parcel Post Office.
9. Gray's Inn.
10. Central School of Arts and Crafts.
11. London Day Training School.
12. Kingsway Theatre.
13. Whitney Theatre.
14. Strand Theatre (late Waldorf Theatre).
15. Gaiety Theatre.
15. Royal Courts of Justice.
17. Somerset House.

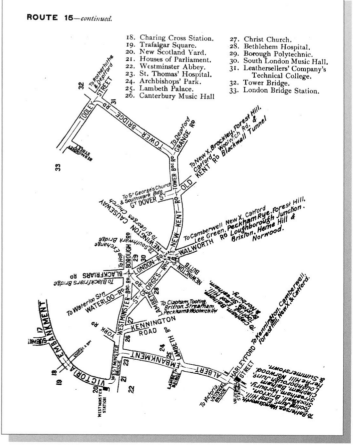

ROUTE 15—continued.

18. Charing Cross Station.
19. Trafalgar Square.
20. New Scotland Yard.
21. Houses of Parliament.
22. Westminster Abbey.
23. St. Thomas' Hospital.
24. Archbishops' Park.
25. Lambeth Palace.
26. Canterbury Music Hall
27. Christ Church.
28. Bethlehem Hospital.
29. Borough Polytechnic.
30. South London Music Hall.
31. Leathersellers' Company's Technical College.
32. Tower Bridge.
33. London Bridge Station.

ROUTE No. 16.

Victoria Embankment to Woolwich-road, viâ Peckham (circular route), Waterloo Bridge to Rye-lane (circular route), and Victoria Embankment to Camberwell Green (Electric Traction).

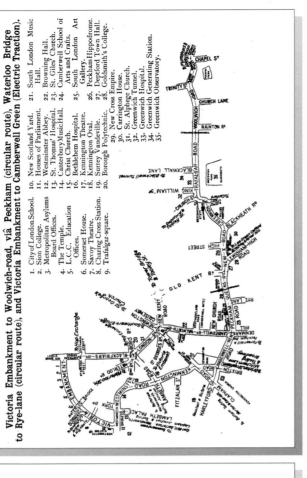

1. City of London School.
2. Sion College.
3. Metropolitan Asylums Board Offices.
4. The Temple.
5. L.C.C. Education Offices.
6. Somerset House.
7. Savoy Theatre.
8. Charing Cross Station.
9. Trafalgar-square.
10. New Scotland Yard.
11. Houses of Parliament.
12. Westminster Abbey.
13. St. Thomas' Hospital.
14. Canterbury Music Hall.
15. Christ Church.
16. Bethlehem Hospital.
17. Kennington Theatre.
18. Kennington Oval.
19. Surrey Vaudeville.
20. Borough Polytechnic.
21. South London Music Hall.
22. Browning Hall.
23. St. Giles' Church.
24. Camberwell School of Arts and Crafts.
25. South London Art Gallery.
26. Peckham Hippodrome.
27. Deptford Town Hall.
28. Goldsmith's College.
29. New Cross Empire.
30. Carrington House.
31. St. Alphege Church.
32. Greenwich Tunnel.
33. Greenwich Hospital.
34. Greenwich Generating Station.
35. Greenwich Observatory.

ROUTE No. 17.

Waterloo Bridge to Blackwall Tunnel and Woolwich-road (circular route) and Waterloo Station to New Cross (Electric Traction).

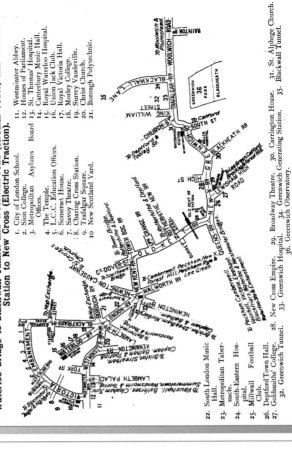

1. City of London School.
2. Sion College.
3. Metropolitan Asylums Offices.
4. The Temple.
5. L.C.C. Education Offices.
6. Somerset House.
7. Savoy Theatre.
8. Charing Cross Station.
9. Trafalgar Square.
10 New Scotland Yard.
11. Westminster Abbey.
12. Houses of Parliament.
13. St. Thomas' Hospital.
14. Canterbury Music Hall.
15. Royal Waterloo Hospital.
16. Union Jack Club.
17. Royal Victoria Hall.
18. Morley College.
19. Surrey Vaudeville.
20. Christ Church.
21. Borough Polytechnic.
22. South London Music Hall.
23. Metropolitan Tabernacle.
24. South-Eastern Hospital.
25. Millwall Football Club.
26. Deptford Town Hall.
27. Goldsmiths' College.
28. New Cross Empire.
29. Broadway Theatre.
30. Carrington House.
31. St. Alphege Church.
32. Greenwich Tunnel.
33. Greenwich Hospital.
34. Greenwich Generating Station.
35. Greenwich Observatory.
36. Blackwall Tunnel.

ROUTE No. 19. Southwark Bridge to Forest Hill (Waldram-Road) and Catford, and Greenwich to Catford (Electric Traction).

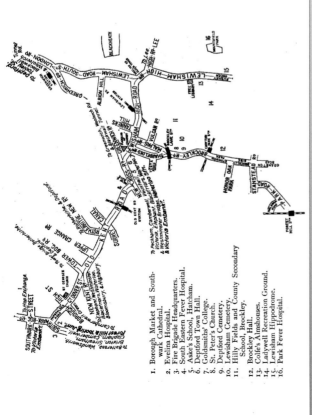

1. Borough Market and Southwark Cathedral.
2. Evelina Hospital.
3. Fire Brigade Headquarters.
4. South Eastern Fever Hospital.
5. Aske's School, Hatcham.
6. Deptford Town Hall.
7. Goldsmiths' College.
8. St. Peter's Church.
9. Deptford Cemetery.
10. Lewisham Cemetery.
11. Hilly Fields and County Secondary School, Brockley.
12. Brockley Hall.
13. Colfe's Almshouses.
14. Ladywell Recreation Ground.
15. Lewisham Hippodrome.
16. Park Fever Hospital.

ROUTE No. 20. Victoria Station to Rye Lane and Catford (Electric Traction).

1. Millbank Housing Estate.
2. National Gallery of British Art (Tate Gallery).
3. St. Giles', Camberwell.
4. Camberwell School of Arts and Crafts.
5. South London Art Gallery.
6. Peckham Hippodrome.
7. Deptford Town Hall.
8. Goldsmiths' College.
9. Blackheath.
10. Hilly Fields and County Secondary Schools, Brockley.
11. Colfe's Almshouses.
12. Ladywell Recreation Ground.
13. Lewisham Hippodrome.
14. Park Fever Hospital.

ROUTE No. 21. Victoria Embankment and Southwark Bridge to Dulwich and Peckham Rye, and Southwark Bridge to Camberwell Green (Electric Traction).

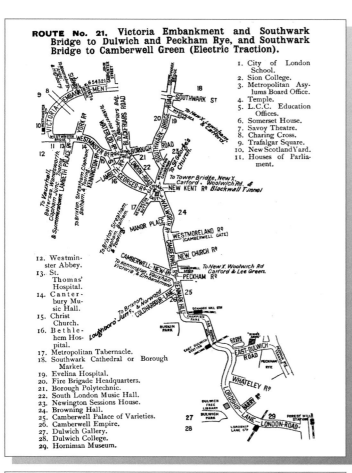

1. City of London School.
2. Sion College.
3. Metropolitan Asylums Board Office.
4. Temple.
5. L.C.C. Education Offices.
6. Somerset House.
7. Savoy Theatre.
8. Charing Cross.
9. Trafalgar Square.
10. New Scotland Yard.
11. Houses of Parliament.
12. Westminster Abbey.
13. St. Thomas' Hospital.
14. Canterbury Music Hall.
15. Christ Church.
16. Bethlehem Hospital.
17. Metropolitan Tabernacle.
18. Southwark Cathedral or Borough Market.
19. Evelina Hospital.
20. Fire Brigade Headquarters.
21. Borough Polytechnic.
22. South London Music Hall.
23. Newington Sessions House.
24. Browning Hall.
25. Camberwell Palace of Varieties.
26. Camberwell Empire.
27. Dulwich Gallery.
28. Dulwich College.
29. Horniman Museum.

ROUTE No. 22.
Victoria Station to Forest Hill and Peckham Rye (Electric Traction).

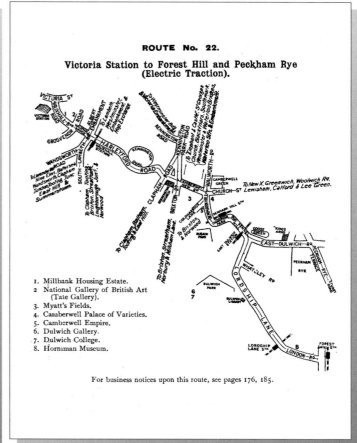

1. Millbank Housing Estate.
2. National Gallery of British Art (Tate Gallery).
3. Myatt's Fields.
4. Camberwell Palace of Varieties.
5. Camberwell Empire.
6. Dulwich Gallery.
7. Dulwich College.
8. Horniman Museum.

For business notices upon this route, see pages 176, 185.

ROUTE No. 23. Norwood to Victoria and Victoria Embankment (Waterloo Bridge), and Brixton Road to St. George's Church (Electric Traction).

1. Somerset House.
2. Savoy Theatre.
3. Charing Cross Stn.
4. Trafalgar Square.
5. New Scotland Yard.
6. Houses of Parliament.

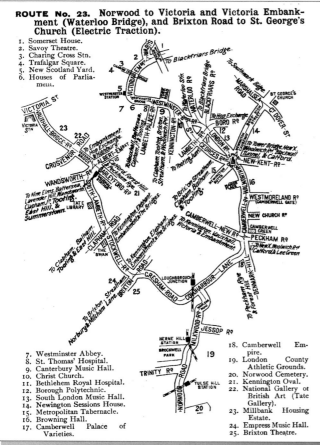

7. Westminster Abbey.
8. St. Thomas' Hospital.
9. Canterbury Music Hall.
10. Christ Church.
11. Bethlehem Royal Hospital.
12. Borough Polytechnic.
13. South London Music Hall.
14. Newington Sessions House.
15. Metropolitan Tabernacle.
16. Browning Hall.
17. Camberwell Palace of Varieties.
18. Camberwell Empire.
19. London County Athletic Grounds.
20. Norwood Cemetery.
21. Kennington Oval.
22. National Gallery of British Art (Tate Gallery).
23. Millbank Housing Estate.
24. Empress Music Hall.
25. Brixton Theatre.

ROUTE No. 24. Waterloo Bridge to Norbury (Circular Route), Water Lane and Southcroft Road (Mitcham Lane).

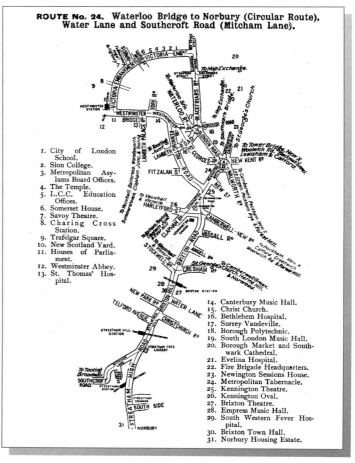

1. City of London School.
2. Sion College.
3. Metropolitan Asylums Board Offices.
4. The Temple.
5. L.C.C. Education Offices.
6. Somerset House.
7. Savoy Theatre.
8. Charing Cross Station.
9. Trafalgar Square.
10. New Scotland Yard.
11. Houses of Parliament.
12. Westminster Abbey.
13. St. Thomas' Hospital.
14. Canterbury Music Hall.
15. Christ Church.
16. Bethlehem Hospital.
17. Surrey Vaudeville.
18. Borough Polytechnic.
19. South London Music Hall.
20. Borough Market and Southwark Cathedral.
21. Evelina Hospital.
22. Fire Brigade Headquarters.
23. Newington Sessions House.
24. Metropolitan Tabernacle.
25. Kennington Theatre.
26. Kennington Oval.
27. Brixton Theatre.
28. Empress Music Hall.
29. South Western Fever Hospital.
30. Brixton Town Hall.
31. Norbury Housing Estate.

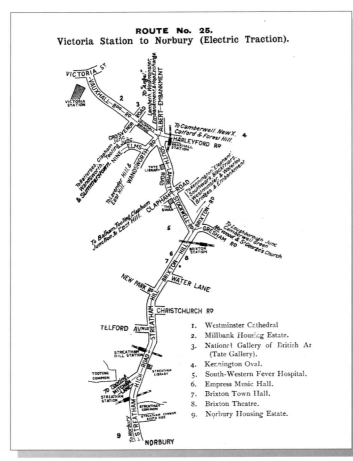

ROUTE No. 25.
Victoria Station to Norbury (Electric Traction).

1. Westminster Cathedral
2. Millbank Housing Estate.
3. National Gallery of British Art (Tate Gallery).
4. Kennington Oval.
5. South-Western Fever Hospital.
6. Empress Music Hall.
7. Brixton Town Hall.
8. Brixton Theatre.
9. Norbury Housing Estate.

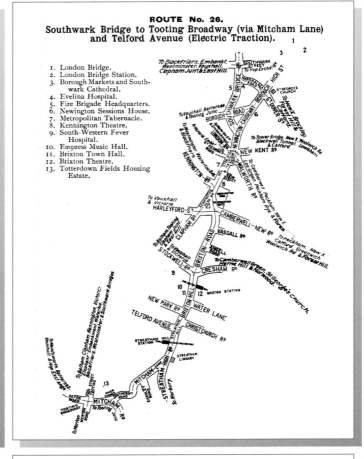

ROUTE No. 26.
Southwark Bridge to Tooting Broadway (via Mitcham Lane) and Telford Avenue (Electric Traction).

1. London Bridge.
2. London Bridge Station.
3. Borough Markets and Southwark Cathedral.
4. Evelina Hospital.
5. Fire Brigade Headquarters.
6. Newington Sessions House.
7. Metropolitan Tabernacle.
8. Kennington Theatre.
9. South-Western Fever Hospital.
10. Empress Music Hall.
11. Brixton Town Hall.
12. Brixton Theatre.
13. Totterdown Fields Housing Estate.

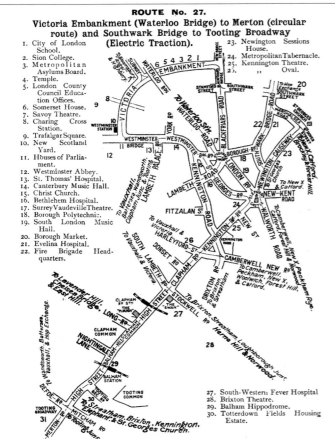

ROUTE No. 27.
Victoria Embankment (Waterloo Bridge) to Merton (circular route) and Southwark Bridge to Tooting Broadway (Electric Traction).

1. City of London School.
2. Sion College.
3. Metropolitan Asylums Board.
4. Temple.
5. London County Council Education Offices.
6. Somerset House.
7. Savoy Theatre.
8. Charing Cross Station.
9. Trafalgar Square.
10. New Scotland Yard.
11. Houses of Parliament.
12. Westminster Abbey.
13. St. Thomas' Hospital.
14. Canterbury Music Hall.
15. Christ Church.
16. Bethlehem Hospital.
17. Surrey Vaudeville Theatre.
18. Borough Polytechnic.
19. South London Music Hall.
20. Borough Market.
21. Evelina Hospital.
22. Fire Brigade Headquarters.
23. Newington Sessions House.
24. Metropolitan Tabernacle.
25. Kennington Theatre.
26. „ Oval.
27. South-Western Fever Hospital
28. Brixton Theatre.
29. Balham Hippodrome.
30. Totterdown Fields Housing Estate.

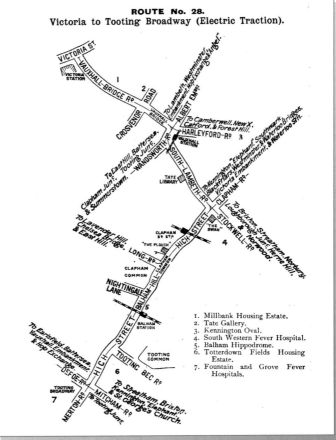

ROUTE No. 28.
Victoria to Tooting Broadway (Electric Traction).

1. Millbank Housing Estate.
2. Tate Gallery.
3. Kennington Oval.
4. South Western Fever Hospital.
5. Balham Hippodrome.
6. Totterdown Fields Housing Estate.
7. Fountain and Grove Fever Hospitals.

ROUTE No. 29.

Hop Exchange to Tooting Junction and Victoria Embankment (John Carpenter-street) to Summerstown (Electric Traction).

1. City of London School.
2. Sion College.
3. Metropolitan Asylums Board Offices.
4. The Temple.
5. L. C. C. Education Offices.
6. Somerset House.
7. Savoy Theatre.
8. Charing Cross Station.
9. Trafalgar Square.
10. New Scotland Yard.
11. Westminster Abbey.
12. Houses of Parliament.
13. St. Thomas's Hospital.
14. London Bridge Station.

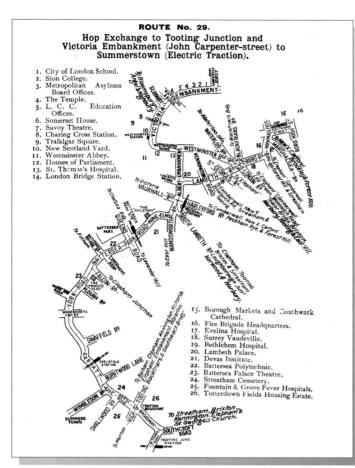

15. Borough Markets and Southwark Cathedral.
16. Fire Brigade Headquarters.
17. Evelina Hospital.
18. Surrey Vaudeville.
19. Bethlehem Hospital.
20. Lambeth Palace.
21. Devas Institute.
22. Battersea Polytechnic.
23. Battersea Palace Theatre.
24. Streatham Cemetery.
25. Fountain & Grove Fever Hospitals.
26. Totterdown Fields Housing Estate.

ROUTE No. 30.

Waterloo Station to East Hill (Electric Traction).

1. Royal Waterloo Hospital.
2. Union Jack Club.
3. Royal Victoria Hall.
4. Morley College.
5. Surrey Vaudeville.
6. Borough Polytechnic.
7. South London Music Hall.
8. Metropolitan Tabernacle.
9. Kennington Theatre.
10. Kennington Oval.
11. South Western Fever Hospital.
12. Clapham Church.
13. Shakespeare Theatre.
14. New Grand Theatre of Varieties.
15. Freemasons' Orphan School.
16. Royal Victoria Patriotic School.

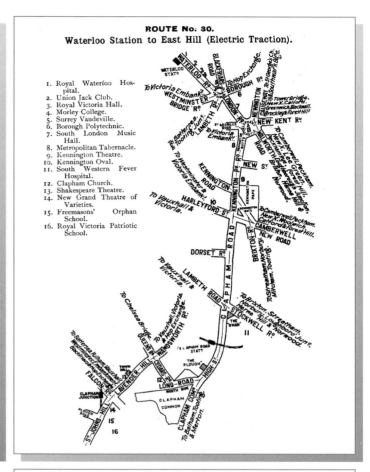

ROUTE No. 31.

Hop Exchange and Victoria to East Hill, and Lavender Hill to Chelsea Bridge (Electric Traction).

1. City of London School.
2. Sion College.
3. Metropolitan Asylums Board Offices.
4. The Temple.
5. L. C. C. Education Offices.
6. Somerset House.
7. Savoy Theatre.
8. Charing Cross Station.

9. Trafalgar Square.
10. New Scotland Yard.
11. Houses of Parliament.
12. Westminster Abbey.
13. St. Thomas's Hospital.
14. Archbishop's Park.
15. Lambeth Palace.
16. London Bridge.
17. London Bridge Station.
18. Borough Markets and Southwark Cathedral.
19. Millbank Housing Estate.
20. Tate Gallery.
21. Vauxhall Station.
22. Kennington Oval.
23. Devas Institute.
24. Ascension Church.
25. Shakespeare Theatre.
26. New Grand Theatre of Varieties.
27. Freemasons' Orphan School.
28. Royal Victoria Patriotic School.

ROUTE No. 32.

Victoria Embankment (John Carpenter Street) and King's Road, Chelsea, to Clapham Junction (Electric Traction).

1. City of London School.
2. Sion College.
3. Metropolitan Asylums Board Offices.
4. The Temple.
5. L.C.C. Education Offices.
6. Somerset House.
7. Savoy Theatre.
8. Charing Cross Station.
9. Trafalgar Square.
10. New Scotland Yard.
11. Houses of Parliament.
12. Westminster Abbey.
13. St. Thomas' Hospital.
14. Archbishop's Park.
15. Lambeth Palace.
16. Kennington Oval.
17. Devas Institute.
18. Battersea Polytechnic.
19. Battersea Parish Church.
20. Crosby Hall.
21. Chelsea Old Church.
22. Carlyle Museum.
23. Chelsea Embankment Gardens.

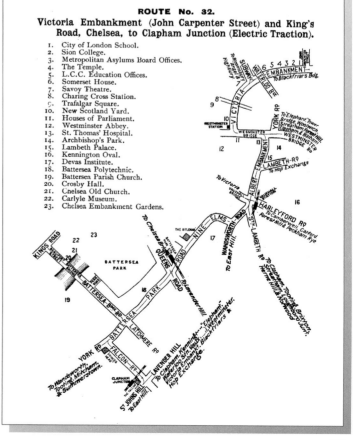

ROUTE No. 33
Tooley Street and Old Kent Road to Deptford (Electric and Horse Traction).

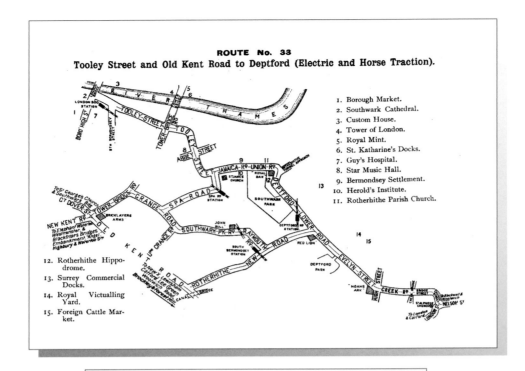

1. Borough Market.
2. Southwark Cathedral.
3. Custom House.
4. Tower of London.
5. Royal Mint.
6. St. Katharine's Docks.
7. Guy's Hospital.
8. Star Music Hall.
9. Bermondsey Settlement.
10. Herold's Institute.
11. Rotherhithe Parish Church.

12. Rotherhithe Hippodrome.
13. Surrey Commercial Docks.
14. Royal Victualling Yard.
15. Foreign Cattle Market.

ROUTE No. 34.

Woolwich Free Ferry to Abbey Wood, and Beresford Square to Eltham (Electric Traction), and Chapel Street to Woolwich Free Ferry (Horse Traction).

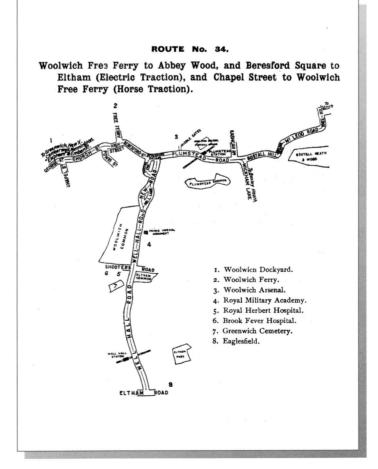

1. Woolwich Dockyard.
2. Woolwich Ferry.
3. Woolwich Arsenal.
4. Royal Military Academy.
5. Royal Herbert Hospital.
6. Brook Fever Hospital.
7. Greenwich Cemetery.
8. Eaglesfield.

1913 – TRAMWAYS GUIDE & MAP

The LCC TRAMWAYS GUIDE & MAP for November 1913 is typical of a series of handy maps, which were distributed in large numbers by the Council. The standard format of a route map on one side of the paper with service and fare details on the other was to be repeated and updated until the end of tramway operation by the Council.

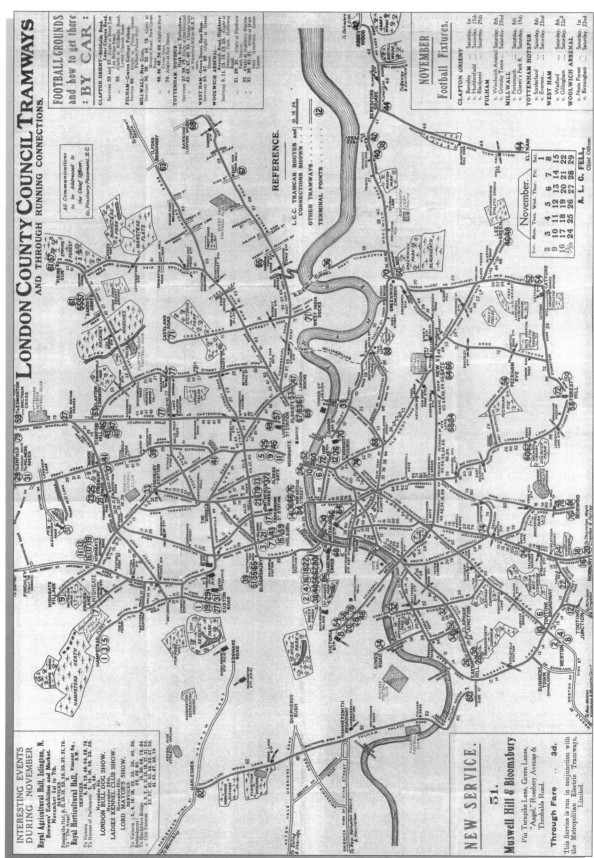

1927 – TRAMWAYS MAP & TIMETABLE

The TRAMWAYS POCKET MAP & TIMETABLE for November 1927 is a sophisticated guide packed with route details, service frequencies, first and last car times and information on all night routes. The map is true to scale and does show connections to neighbouring systems as well as through services. Note that the Grove Park extension has not yet been fully opened for traffic.

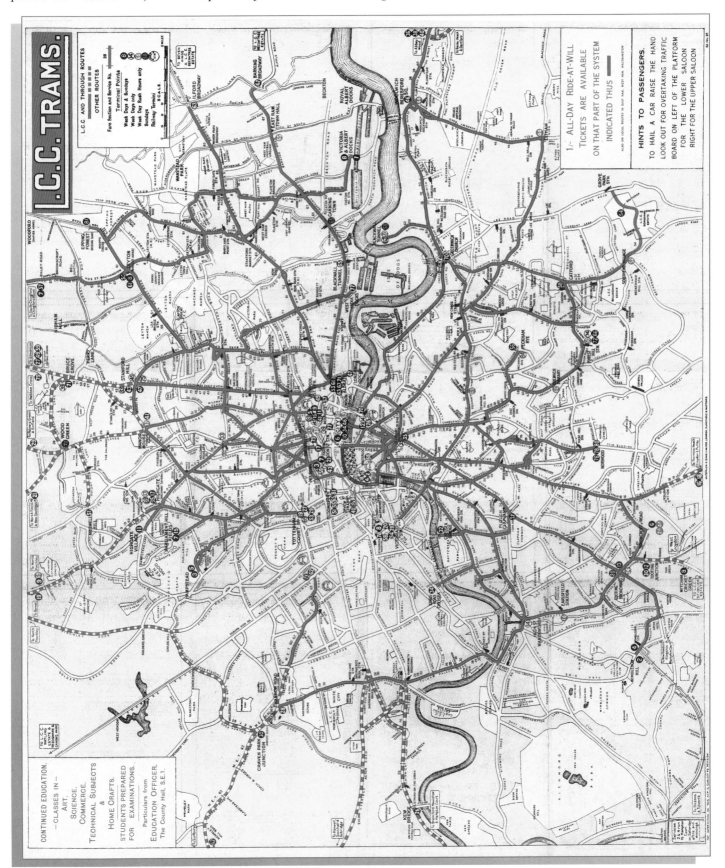

1933 – TRAMWAYS MAP & TIMETABLE

The TRAMWAYS MAP AND TIMETABLE for May 1933 is the LCC's swansong. The map has been updated and now contains inserts for Croydon and the Kingsway Subway. Authorised extensions are clearly shown; closed routes in Barking and Kingston have been omitted, whilst the new LUT trolleybus services have been included. Finally, it will be noted that the purchase of a shilling all day ticket really did give the traveller the freedom of London.

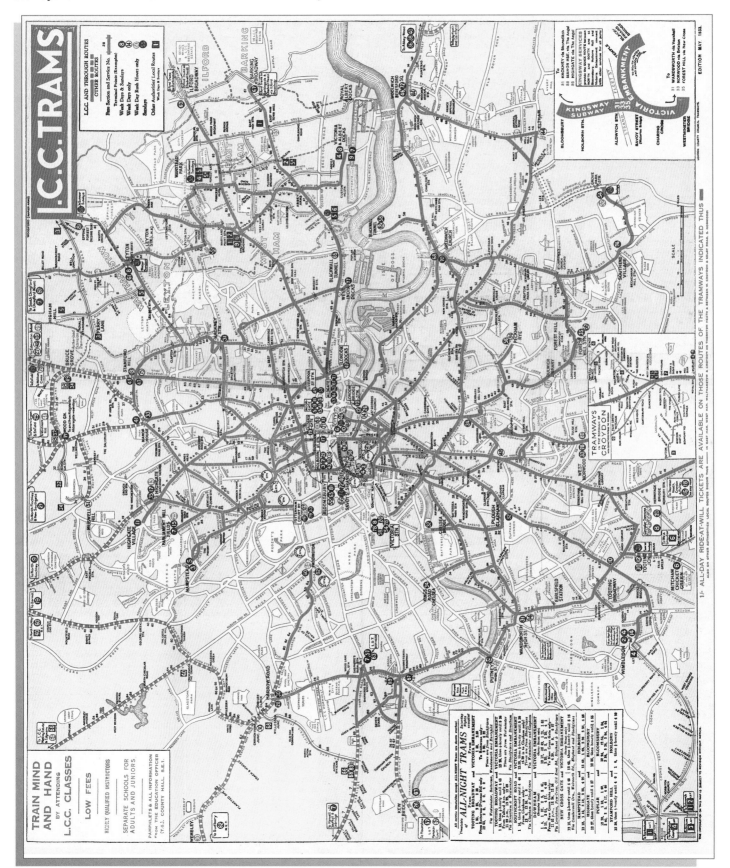

Depots / Car Sheds

Buildings have been divided according to their location in either the LCC's southern or northern divisions. The LCC referred to these premises originally as *car sheds* rather than *depots*, although the latter term gained in currency in official minutes from the mid twenties onwards – tram crews would often just simply refer to *the yard*. Many horse tramway depots, stables, works, grain stores etc. were inherited by the Council and most were deemed unfit for conversion to electric traction. Unless stated otherwise, all depots were equipped with conduit and all tramway property owned by the LCC passed in July 1933 to the London Passenger Transport Board. Some buildings still survive, but the march of time and conversion for use as bus garages has obliterated much of the LCC architectural heritage. The appropriate postal district has been added after each depot.

Southern Section

Abbey Wood – Abbey Wood Road S.E.2
This car shed on the southeastern extremity of the system was opened in 1910 and originally serviced routes 42 and 44. It had a capacity of 25 cars. Enlargement work commenced in 1912 and was finished by 1914. Always an overhead wire equipped depot, Abbey Wood had a traverser giving access to 20 roads with a theoretical capacity of 86 trams, although in practice this total was never achieved. A triangular shaped track layout provided a trailer shunt between the depot and Abbey Wood Road.

Bowles Road – Old Kent Road S.E.1
This site and the one nearby at Leo Street were former horsecar depots pressed into emergency service by the LCC until the opening of New Cross car shed. Access tracks were converted to conduit, but trams were shunted around these two depots by means of an electric cable plugged into a four wheel insulated trolley which ran on two wires. The temporary occupation by electric trams ended in 1906. Bowles Road Depot was sold to the LGOC for use as a motor bus garage.

Brixton Hill – S.W.2
This building had a capacity of 50 cars and was constructed in 1922 with a view to house the fleet of LCC trailer cars. Official policy then changed and the whole edifice became something of a white elephant. Two plough shifts were installed on the entrance track, which led to a fan of seven roads. At first, track was unbonded in the depot and twin overhead wires had to be installed; this situation was later remedied and the normal single wire overhead and bonded track was substituted. The depot was always regarded officially as an outstation of the larger Telford Avenue premises in Streatham.

Car 77 stands on the entrance tracks to one of the world's largest tram depots – New Cross Car Shed. The architectural style could be termed Municipal Doric; it was constructed from Portland stone. Mercifully, this splendid arch was flattened by the Luftwaffe in the Second World War before the demolition men arrived from London Transport on the early 1950s' tram to bus conversion programme!

Camberwell – S.E.5
In effect, two separate depots were built at Camberwell. They were connected by a single track and it was possible to drive a tram from Camberwell Green through the eastern shed, over the traverser and then along the connection to the western shed, over another traverser and out into Camberwell New Road. The initial part of the depot opened in 1905 and an extension was completed in 1914. Capacity was set at around 130 cars.

Chiswick – Chiswick High Road W.4
Converted by the London United Tramways from a former horsecar depot, this facility and the adjacent electricity generating station were opened for electric traction on 4th April 1901. A total of 75 trams could be accommodated on eleven roads diverging from a track fan. Ownership passed to the LCC in 1917, and it has to be said that the Council was reluctant to add Chiswick to its list of car sheds, bearing in mind that Hammersmith Depot was just up the road.
The building was finally occupied by the new tenants on 2nd May 1922. Some trams that had been withdrawn from service were stored here, but apart from this the building was never used by the LCC as a running depot.

Clapham – Clapham High Street S.W.4
This was a conversion from a horse tram depot and the new building was completely opened in March 1905. It contained two traversers leading to 25 storage roads; depot capacity was around 160 cars. There were two entrances, one in Clapham Park Road, and the other in Clapham High Street.

Evelyn Street – S.E.8
This former horse tramway site was connected with trailer operation on services 68 and 70. It reopened in August 1916 and was effectively made redundant by the cessation of trailer operation on 17th April 1924. The yard lingered on for a few months as a convenient site for dismantling the trailers.

Hammersmith – Great Church Lane W.6
Although geographically north of the Thames, this depot and services 26, 28 and 30 were always regarded as part of the southern section. The car shed was constructed in stages and its eventual capacity was 59 cars stabled on eight roads. Access to the depot was by means of a traverser placed (unusually) in front of the main building.

Marius Road – Balham High Road S.W.17
Another horse tramway conversion, this temporary depot was in service from 1903. An outside traverser led to six roads with a capacity of 36 trams. When Clapham opened, it ceased to be a running shed. In September 1915 it was reopened for trailers. This continued until November 1922. The building survived until the late 1970s, then in use with a film company. Some conduit track components were removed by members of the LCCTT for possible future use on a conduit line at Crich. This was done just ahead of the building's demolition.

New Cross – New Cross Road S.E.14
One of the jewels in the LCC crown, this was the largest depot. It had a capacity of 314 cars on 34 storage roads, reached by two traversers. It opened in stages from 15th May 1905. A repair works was included in the layout, but its functions were taken over by the Central Repair Depot, Charlton, which opened in March 1909.

Norwood – Norwood Road S.E.27
This car shed was equipped for overhead trolley operation. It was opened in October 1909 and had a capacity for 61 trams. In practice, since proposed routes south of West Norwood were never built, the depot was never full. Fifteen roads were connected by a traverser.

Plumstead – Lakedale Road S.E.18
The former horse car depot with narrow gauge tracks was temporarily converted in 1908 for use by Class B and D cars on the Abbey Wood service. On the opening of Abbey Wood car shed, Lakedale Road reverted to supplying the few remaining horsecars to work the gap between the electric lines at Woolwich. Each horsecar was transported from the depot (now converted to standard gauge) on a transporter – a flat truck equipped with narrow gauge rails. This arrangement came to an end in November 1913.

Rye Lane – Bellenden Road S.E.15
This was a temporary depot that had its life extended by the LCC. It was used as a holding area for electric trams from 1903 onwards. An outside traverser led to eleven stabling roads. The whole building had a capacity of 40 trams. Outbuildings provided storage space for permanent way materials, timber and rolling stock parts. The area was also used as a depot for the Council's motor vehicles, and in 1922 it was the site chosen to assemble cars 1727-1776.

Streatham – Telford Avenue S.W.2
This former cable car shed was extended in two sections, either side of an important water main. The building opened in stages from 1906 and it eventually contained 28 roads with a capacity of around 140 cars.

Wandsworth – Jews Row S.W.18
This former horsecar shed was reopened in 1906 for electric traction. A traverser gave access to sixteen stabling roads with a capacity of 95 cars.

Northern Section

Bow – Fairfield Road E.3
The depot was equipped with overhead wires and opened in stages from 1908 to 1910. It had a maximum capacity of around 80 cars, but space was never fully utilised. It was used in conjunction with the GB surface contact trials.

Hackney – Bohemia Place E.8
Accommodation was provided for 120 trams on fifteen stabling roads. The depot was opened in 1909 and possessed one traverser pit fitted with two traversers.

Hampstead – Cressy Road N.W.3
This building was another underutilised car shed. It opened in January 1914 and consisted of sixteen roads connected to a traverser. In everyday service the building held around 60 trams, far short of the 157 car capacity.

Highbury – St Paul's Road N.1
A temporary electric car shed was constructed here on the site of a former horsecar depot. It served from 1906 as a storage facility for the first Kingsway Subway trams until Holloway opened in November 1907.

Holloway – Pemberton Gardens N.19
This was the largest depot on the northern section. It could hold around 305 trams on twenty-six stabling roads. An overhaul works and a paint shop completed the facilities on offer.

Leyton – Lea Bridge Road E.10
The original Leyton Urban District Council Tramways depot was inaugurated for electric traction on 1st December 1906. It passed to the LCC in 1921. The building was equipped with overhead wires and was maintained substantially intact until 1931 when a traverser was installed to facilitate movement of the new Class E/3 cars allocated to service 61.

Poplar – Leven Road E.14
A large stores and permanent way supplies yard was attached to this car shed, which opened in 1906. Materials were transhipped from barges at a wharf on the River Lea just behind the depot. A traverser pit connected twenty roads to give a capacity of 96 cars.

Stamford Hill – Rookwood Road N.16
Opened in 1907, this building could house around 140 trams. There were twenty-eight stabling roads connected to a traverser. Unlike some other LCC depots, Stamford Hill was always used to capacity.

There were two permanent way yards with rail connections to the system at Deptford, Greenwich High Road S.E.10, and at Battersea Bridge Road S.W.11. The former site had a wharf access to Deptford Creek, and the latter was situated on the Thames. Union Road Works, Leytonstone E.11 had a horse tramway connection to High Road, Leytonstone, but this was disused by 1912. The works closed in 1911 and car building and maintenance activities were transferred to Charlton.

APPENDIX 2
Track Maps

KEY TO MAIN MAP

Electric tramways within the L.C.C. area

Double track with conduit. . . .

Single track with conduit* . . .

Double track with overhead wire .

Single track with overhead wire* .

Authorised extension . . . . .

Horse tramways – not electrified .

Electric tramways outside the L.C.C. area

Double track overhead wire . . .

Single track overhead wire* . . .

Change pit . . . .

Car depot / Car shed . . . . . .

• Some single track sections shown on this map contained passing loops.

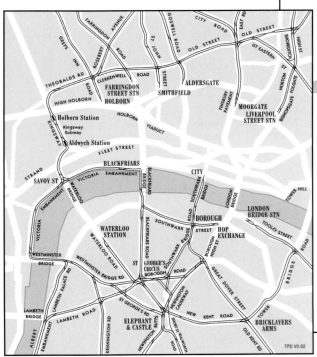

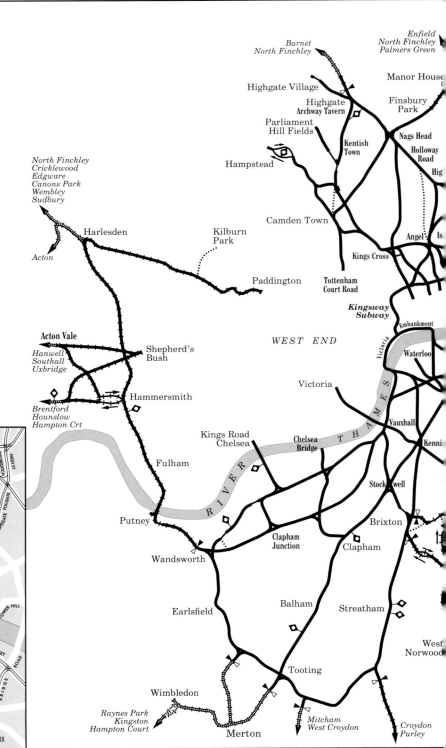

TPD VII.02

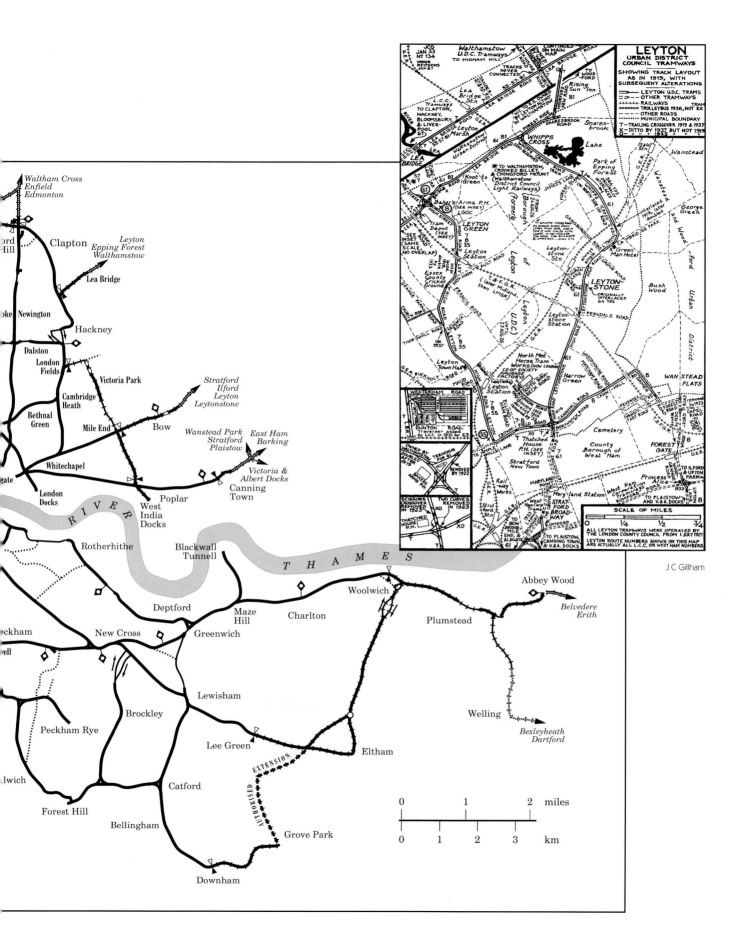

LEYTON
URBAN DISTRICT
COUNCIL TRAMWAYS

SHOWING TRACK LAYOUT
AS IN 1919, WITH
SUBSEQUENT ALTERATIONS

J C Gillham

APPENDIX 3
The Conduit System

Ordinary Londoners referred to this method of current collection as *the third rail*, and many citizens praised its virtues in keeping the blue vault of heaven (when not obscured by atmospheric pollution) free of overhead wires. The fact that it continued in operation from 1903 to 1952 is a tribute to its designers and maintainers. But in real terms, the whole installation quickly became a major financial liability. Driving a tramcar through a complicated tramway junction became an art form. It only need another road vehicle to brake suddenly in front of the tram and the great brown and cream leviathan might be 'stuck on a dead'

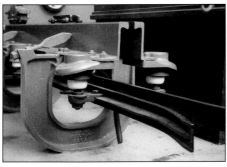

with no power to extricate itself. The two T-shaped electric current rails within the conduit were divided into sections, which a skilled driver could coast across, unless of course he was forced by other traffic to come to a premature halt. A stranded tram normally had to wait a short time until the next car came up behind to give it a nudge back on to a live section of the conduit.

Conduit ploughs sometimes broke, jammed in their carriers or got stuck in the conduit slot. Often crews would be seen removing smouldering ploughs where the insulating material had failed thus causing some short circuit pyrotechnics! The offending plough was then laid on its side and the fire put out by sand or by the crew and bystanders stamping on the flames. The conduit also amplified the noise of the plough passing through, and the gap between the slot rails on the road surface seemed to attract all manner of metal objects – from children's iron hoops to kitchen cutlery – all of which had the potential to short circuit the T-rails.

The British Electric Traction Company was not generally sympathetic to the trials and tribulations of municipal operators. It published the B.E.T. MONTHLY GAZETTE,

which detailed some of the early conduit contretemps. The June 1903 edition has this to say:

A peculiar accident happened a few days previous to the opening of the new LCC conduit system. The chain trace of a brewer's dray became unhooked at the splinter bar. The loose end trailing on the road caught in the slot of the conduit at the junction of two lines. Before the dray could be brought to a standstill, about five links of the chain slid some feet up the slot without breaking and then jammed. Readers may draw their own conclusions as to what might have happened if the line had been working.

The August 1903 edition published a further warning on the dangers of the conduit:

The Highways Committee reported to the London County Council recently that there had been several cases lately of persons maliciously inserting pieces of metal and wire in the conduits on the Westminster to Tooting tramways, the result of which had been to create short circuits, the tramway traffic being in consequence seriously interfered with. 'This malicious interference with the

Above **A section of conduit was kept at the Clapham Depot Driver Training School to help illustrate technical points to potential motormen. Note the short yoke supporting the two conduit slot rails at the top of the picture. A white porcelain insulator is attached on either side of the slot. Each insulator is clamped to one of the two T rails, which supply electric current to the plough.** G.E.Baddeley

Right **By the time the construction crews had got to Lee Green, they had pretty much perfected the art of conduit track laying. To the right, pits have been dug to receive the long and short conduit yokes. The workmen in front of the camera are busily bolting the slot rails and the running rails to the whole assembly. Everything had to be done by hand!** B.J.Cross Collection

Left The location is Gardiner's Corner, Aldgate and the date is August 1929. This major junction has arrived from the manufacturers in numbered pieces, which in theory rendered the installation a straightforward process. Therefore, in the true spirit of Meccano, theory and practice should come together to produce a conduit junction worthy of the designers and durable enough to withstand the incessant pounding of East End tramcars. Supervisory staff adopted different headgear to the flat hats of the permanent way workers. LCC

Below left Double conduit on short single track sections was installed here at York Road, Wandsworth by the Alma Public House, and at several other locations, notably London Street, Greenwich. The only drawback with this arrangement of two conduit slots, one for each direction of travel, was the impracticality of reversing a conduit equipped tram on the single track section. LCCTT

Below The side slot conduit along Kingsland Road was an experiment which was not repeated. The theory was fine, but in practice the use of the conduit slot as one of the running rails caused difficulties, and the stresses and strains thus engendered exacerbated weaknesses in the conduit. LCC

Above left Unfortunately during the LCC era there were not many meticulous observers on hand, like John Gillham, to record the various tramway installations. However the change pit at Lee Green had not altered much since the LCC relinquished control of its tramways. It can be clearly seen where the conduit slot leaves the centre of the track. Here Woolwich bound trams would "shoot" their ploughs, which then stacked up on the central island. Trams going the other way would wait for the plough to be forked underneath into the carrier. J.C.Gillham

Above right The tines of the attendant's fork engage the plough carrier and the tram moves forward drawing power from the overhead wire. Once the plough slides into position on the carrier, the conductor will lower the trolley pole, the motorman will throw an electrical switch, and progress will be resumed on the conduit. J.C.Gillham

conduit, in addition to hindering the smooth working of the tramways and causing numberless delays, is likely to endanger the safety of the passengers on the tramcars, and we have therefore arranged for the issue of a notice offering a reward of £25 to any person who may supply such information as will lead to the conviction of the offenders, and we hope that this course will effectively stop so dangerous a practice.'

Clearly the members of the Highways Committee had the bit between their teeth and they were determined to stamp out the causes of the conduit embarrassment. The narrow gap in the slot rails did not help the situation and it took months of trial and error to convince the conduit designers that the whole structure needed to be improved. The slot was widened slightly to facilitate easier passage for the ploughs, and the whole conduit permanent way was rendered more rigid and robust by using a combination of short and long yokes, instead of just the short yokes employed on the Tooting to central London lines.

The accompanying diagrams give a good idea of the original conduit construction and the modified one, which was adopted as standard over the system.

Left Outside the Duke of Cambridge at Lewisham one of the sturdy LCC breakdown tenders has delivered a crew for track maintenance. Gradually, throughout the latter years of the LCC system, mechanical aids alleviated some of the more laborious and backbreaking trackwork chores. B.J.Cross Collection

Left Every half mile alongside the tramway there would be a section box such as this one. These boxes contained the switching apparatus to isolate the power supply. The small structure on top of the main box contains the departmental telephone. Many of these green painted section boxes survived the tramways, and the LCC planted some of them well off the beaten track. The author remembers one that was situated until the 1960s at the junction of Westcombe Hill and Charlton Road, Blackheath.

CONDUIT PLOUGH

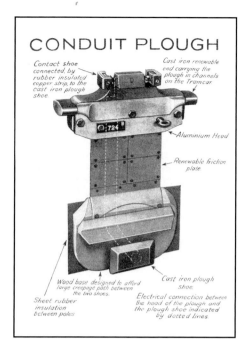

Contact shoe connected by rubber insulated copper strip to the cast iron plough shoe.

Cast iron renewable end carrying the plough in channels on the Tramcar.

Aluminium Head

Renewable friction plate.

Wood base designed to afford large creepage path between the two shoes.

Cast iron plough shoe.

Sheet rubber insulation between poles.

Electrical connection between the head of the plough and the plough shoe indicated by dotted lines.

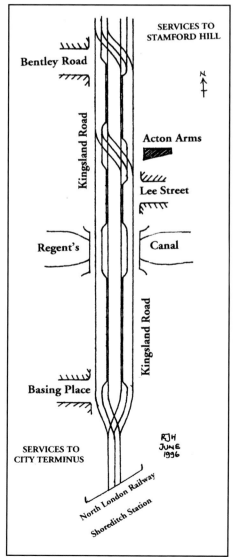

SERVICES TO STAMFORD HILL

Bentley Road

Kingsland Road

Acton Arms

Lee Street

Regent's   Canal

Basing Place

Kingsland Road

SERVICES TO CITY TERMINUS

North London Railway
Shoreditch Station

RJH
JUNE
1996

N

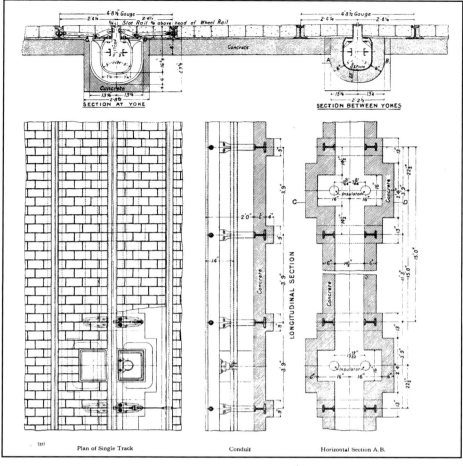

4·8½ Gauge   Slot Rail ¾ above head of Wheel Rail   4·8½ Gauge

Concrete

SECTION AT YOKE   SECTION BETWEEN YOKES

Concrete   Concrete   Insulator   Concrete

LONGITUDINAL SECTION

Insulator

(37)   Plan of Single Track   Conduit   Horizontal Section A.B.

Above left This explanatory diagram was used in several LCC publications to acquaint the general public with some of the salient technical areas of the final design of conduit plough

Above These are the track specifications for the original Tooting conduit line. They include

the use of short yokes and the narrow conduit slot. Much of this work was based on original designs by A.N.Connett, a consulting engineer to the Washington and New York undertakings.

Left Diagram of the unique Kingsland Road side conduit installation. Note that the conduit slot

resumed its normal, centrally aligned location at the bridge over the Regent's Canal. To avoid pointwork complications the central slot was also employed for the crossover by the Acton Arms. This arrangement caused problems with ploughs getting jammed at these locations. A 1908

report lists sixteen delays in as many months; each delay averaged 84 minutes.

Below The combination of short and long yokes plus the use of old rail sections to act as anchors under the roadway show to advantage in this diagram.

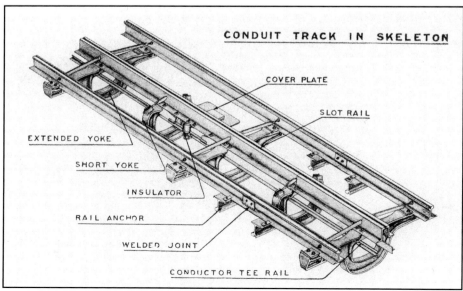

CONDUIT TRACK IN SKELETON

COVER PLATE

SLOT RAIL

EXTENDED YOKE

SHORT YOKE

INSULATOR

RAIL ANCHOR

WELDED JOINT

CONDUCTOR TEE RAIL

Selected Bibliography

Serious students of the London County Council Tramways should on no account overlook the scholarly two volume work by *E. R. Oakley*. The books cover all aspects of tramway operation. THE WHEELS USED TO TALK TO US by *Stan Collins* and edited by *Terence Cooper*, is a splendid evocation of working conditions from an ex-LCC motorman. On the same topic, the LCC MOTORMAN'S HANDBOOK and several other official publications have been reprinted by *Adam Gordon*. Histories of the tramways on the edge of the LCC area should also be consulted: LONDON UNITED TRAMWAYS (two volumes) by *C. S. Smeeton*, METROPOLITAN ELECTRIC TRAMWAYS (two volumes) by *C. S. Smeeton*, TRAMWAYS OF EAST LONDON by *Rodinglea*, TRAMWAYS IN METROPOLITAN ESSEX (two volumes) by *V. E. Burrows*, TRAMWAYS OF CROYDON by *G. E. Baddeley* and TRAMWAYS OF WOOLWICH AND SOUTH EAST LONDON by *Southeastern*.

Recommended technical works containing chapters on the LCC conduit system are ELECTRIC TRACTION by *A. T. Dover* and ELECTRIC TRACTION by *R. H. Smith*. Various open conduit installations that influenced the LCC are described in ELECTRIC RAILWAYS AND TRAMWAYS by *Philip Dawson*. Other technical articles are to be found in back numbers of the TRAMWAY AND RAILWAY WORLD.

The American influence on the early LCC deliberations can by charted in THE CABLE CAR IN AMERICA by *George W. Hilton*, PIONEERS OF ELECTRIC RAILROADING edited by *John R. Stevens* and 100 YEARS OF CAPITAL TRACTION by *LeRoy O. King Jr*.

Many books have been written on the whole saga of London's public transport. Perhaps the best overview is to be found in the two volumes entitled A HISTORY OF LONDON TRANSPORT by *T. C. Barker* and *Michael Robbins*. The formation of the London Passenger Transport Board in 1933 has also occupied many lines of text. SOCIALISATION & TRANSPORT by *Herbert Morrison*, and LONDON'S PASSENGER TRANSPORT PROBLEM by *Gilbert J. Ponsonby* will be of interest in this area. LABOUR RELATIONS IN LONDON TRANSPORT by *H. A. Clegg* gives a clear account of the history of work related issues faced by LCC tram crews. TRAMWAY LONDON edited by *Martin Higginson* covers the financial background to the abandonment of London's trams. An excellent introduction to the pre-electric era is supplied by LOCOMOTION IN VICTORIAN LONDON by *G. A. Sekon*, whilst an eminently readable account of London's road transport is FARES PLEASE edited by *O. J. Morris*.

The London County Council produced books and leaflets on the housing situation in the capital. Many of these have a direct relevance to tramway provision. HOUSING OF THE WORKING CLASSES IN LONDON 1855–1912 and HOUSING 1928–1930 are particularly interesting. A complete record of the LCC's contribution to the First World War effort is contained in LONDON COUNTY COUNCIL: RECORD OF WAR SERVICE 1914–1918 – the book also lists all those employees who gave their lives for their country.

Good photographic albums covering aspects of the LCC trams include ROADS AND RAILS OF LONDON by *Charles F. Klapper*, LONDON'S TRAMS – A VIEW FROM THE PAST by *Paul Collins*, LONDON'S TRAMS by *J. Joyce*, THE LONDON TRAMCAR 1861–1952 by *R. W. Kidner*, and the metropolitan volumes of TRAMWAY CLASSICS edited by the present author. The large scale map series produced by *Frank Merton Atkins* is particularly useful in determining the state of the LCC system in 1914; each map sheet includes notes for subsequent changes in track layout.

A special, honourable mention should be made of TRAMS OF BYGONE LONDON by *Michael Dryhurst*, which was the first tramway publication the author ever owned – it has a lot to answer for!

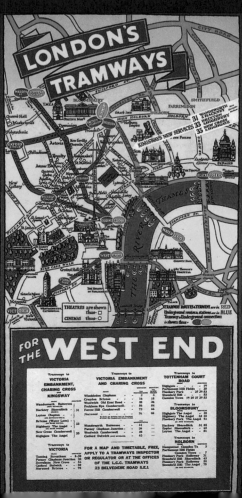